We the People

THE CITIZEN & THE CONSTITUTION

TEACHER'S EDITION

LEVEL 1

CENTER FOR CIVIC EDUCATION
5145 Douglas Fir Road, Calabasas, CA 91302-1440
818.591.9321   www.civiced.org

Directed by the
CENTER FOR CIVIC EDUCATION

and funded by the
U.S. DEPARTMENT OF EDUCATION

under the Education for Democracy Act approved by the
UNITED STATES CONGRESS

Cover:

"Washington Crossing the Delaware," Eastman Johnson (1824-1906) Private Collection
(study after "Washington Crossing the Delaware," by Emmanuel Leutze, the Metropolitan Museum, NY)
© Art Resource, New York. Cover + book design: Mark Stritzel

ISBN 0-89818-170-4

We the People:
The Citizen and
the Constitution

Dear Teacher:

We appreciate your participation in **We the People: The Citizen and the Constitution**. It is our hope that you and your students will find this program an effective means of developing a more profound understanding of and appreciation for the fundamental principles and values of our free society.

The enclosed materials have been carefully designed to help you conduct a successful educational program on the Constitution and Bill of Rights. Several thousand teachers throughout the nation have helped us develop and refine the program. Together, we have attempted to write the text and accompanying materials at a level useful for a wide range of student abilities while providing content challenging to the most academically able. Your experience in using the program with your students will undoubtedly result in the identification of ways it can be improved. We welcome your comments and suggestions regarding the strengths and weaknesses of the program so we can improve it for further use. We are particularly interested in receiving anecdotal information on the effects of the program on student's understanding, skills, attitudes, and behaviors.

We have provided you the best materials we have been able to develop. We realize, however, that ultimately the success of the program depends on you, the classroom teacher. We appreciate your interest in the program and your willingness to use it in your classroom. We want to provide whatever additional help you might need in its implementation.

Additional information, materials, or assistance may be obtained locally by contacting your congressional district coordinator. If you do not know how to reach that person, contact your state coordinator at the location noted in the enclosed brochure or contact our California office at the address and phone number listed on the title page.

Sincerely,

Charles N. Quigley
EXECUTIVE DIRECTOR

Robert S. Leming
WE THE PEOPLE NATIONAL DIRECTOR

We the People: The Citizen and the Constitution

Teacher's Edition

WARREN E. BURGER, CHAIRMAN

COMMISSION ON THE BICENTENNIAL OF THE UNITED STATES CONSTITUTION

CHIEF JUSTICE OF THE UNITED STATES 1969-1986

FOREWORD

Our Constitution has stood the tests and stresses of time, wars, and change. Although it was not perfect, as Benjamin Franklin and many others recognized, it has lasted because it was carefully crafted by men who understood the importance of a system of government sufficiently strong to meet the challenges of the day, yet sufficiently flexible to accommodate and adapt to new political, economic, and social conditions.

Many Americans have but a slight understanding of the Constitution, the Bill of Rights, and the later amendments to which we pledge our allegiance. The lessons in this book are designed to give you, the next generation of American citizens, an understanding of the background, creation, and subsequent history of the unique system of government brought into being by our Constitution. At the same time, it will help you understand the principles and ideals that underlie and give meaning to the Constitution, a system of government by those governed.

TABLE OF CONTENTS

TABLE OF CONTENTS

TABLE OF CONTENTS

UNIT LIST

OVERVIEW OF WE THE PEOPLE PROGRAM

INTRODUCTION

We the People: The Citizen and the Constitution introduces elementary students to the study of constitutional government in the United States. It is not a conventional history text focusing on people and events. This book is a history of ideas. It is designed to help elementary students understand the most important ideas of our constitutional system and how they were developed. Its intent is to provide students with knowledge about how the Constitution came into existence, why it took the form it did, and how it has functioned for the past two hundred years. By gaining such an understanding, students will be preparing themselves for the responsibilities of citizenship.

An effective class project for the program might be a bulletin board display, including a timeline and an illustrated map of the original thirteen colonies. The display can include articles, pictures, stories, poems, artwork, and newspaper headlines that illustrate the key ideas and events in each lesson. In Units Three, Four, and Five, the display could demonstrate the relevance of the lessons to current political activities.

The display can include a timeline to show events that are being studied. Students may wish to add dates and events not mentioned in the text. Another method of displaying a timeline would be to "hang" the dates on a rope or clothesline.

The class may also illustrate an outline map of the original thirteen states. One method to do such a map would be to divide the class into 13 groups. Each group would be responsible for one of the 13 states. Each group would then explain to the class their reasons for selecting the facts, persons, or events they chose to illustrate.

TEACHING METHODS

The *We the People: The Citizen and the Constitution* text for upper elementary grades employs a conceptually oriented approach that stresses the development of analytic and evaluative skills. Because many of the concepts introduced in the program may be unfamiliar to students, methodology draws heavily on strategies that research and field-testing have shown to be successful in developing conceptual understanding. Students will learn how to apply their understanding and knowledge to a wide variety of political questions and issues. They will develop the skills to relate their everyday experiences to basic issues of constitutional government and civic responsibility.

Teaching strategies are varied, including directed discussions, simulations, debates, role-playing, timeline construction, and small-group problem solving. The program allows for and depends upon a wide use of interdisciplinary skills. Art, spelling, vocabulary, mathematics, writing, research, and social studies skills are incorporated in the structure of these lessons.

ASSESSMENT AND CULMINATING ACTIVITY

After students complete the lessons in the text, they take a 30-question multiple-choice test. If they receive an acceptable score (usually 70% or above), they receive a Certificate of Achievement. Teachers may have Certificates signed by their member of Congress or another prominent public official.

As a culminating activity of the program, teachers are encouraged to involve their classes in a simulated congressional hearing. The hearing provides an opportunity for students to demonstrate their knowledge and understanding of constitutional principles. The entire class, working in cooperative groups, prepares and presents statements and answers questions before a panel of community representatives who act as congressional committee members. Teachers and their students may select an in-school simulated congressional hearing or contact other teachers through their district coordinator for an extramural hearing.

Both of the program's major assessment components may be modified as needed to fit the chosen instructional plan. For more information about all aspects of participating in the **We the People** program, please see Appendix C at the back of this book.

CURRICULUM GOALS

The *We the People: The Citizen and the Constitution* curriculum is designed to promote an increased understanding of the institutions of our constitutional democracy and the fundamental principles and values upon which they were founded; develop the skills needed to become effective and responsible citizens; increase understanding and willingness to use democratic processes when making decisions; and managing conflict, both in public and private life.

In studying *We the People: The Citizen and the Constitution*, students develop the ability to identify issues that require political action. They are encouraged through informed inquiry to make a personal commitment to accept the responsibilities associated with the rights we enjoy as citizens— responsibilities essential to the continued existence of a society based on the ideals of freedom, justice, equality, and human rights.

CURRICULUM ORGANIZATION

We the People: The Citizen and the Constitution is about ideas, values, and principles fundamental to understanding our constitutional democracy. The curriculum is organized around ideas that form part of the common core of civic values and concepts that are fundamental to the theory and practice of democratic citizenship in the United States.

We the People: The Citizen and the Constitution may be taught in its entirety, or the teacher may select specific lessons as they relate to general curriculum goals and learning outcomes in a school or district. The lessons need not be taught in any particular order. If you select a single lesson, however, you are only addressing the objectives of that specific lesson and not the goals of a unit.

CURRICULUM RATIONALE

A fundamental hypothesis of the *We the People: The Citizen and the Constitution* curriculum is that education can increase a person's capacity and inclination to act knowledgeably, effectively, and responsibly. It follows that the role of educational institutions must be to help students increase their capacity to make intelligent choices for themselves— to learn how to think, rather than what to think. The alternative, indoctrination, is improper for educational institutions in a free society.

The Center for Civic Education was founded on the belief that the learning experiences provided by a curriculum based on this philosophy result in significant progress towards students' development of a reasoned commitment to those principles, processes, and values that are essential to the preservation and improvement of our free society.

INTRODUCING THE TEACHER'S EDITION

UNIT FORMAT

In the Teacher's Edition, the "Unit Overview" provides a brief introduction to the forthcoming group of lessons and their objectives. In some units, an optional unit project is also suggested. These special projects are varied; some are individual activities and some meant for small-group work. They are designed to complement the class projects that students will be working on throughout their course of study.

LESSON FORMAT

This teacher's edition is designed to complement and extend the student text. Each student lesson begins with the "Purpose of the lesson." This is a brief narrative passage designed to stimulate student interest and guide their reading.

The narrative for each lesson is divided into small segments to make it manageable for students. Strategies for presenting and discussing these materials are given in the "Teaching Procedures" segment of the lesson plans. Skill-building activities are presented within the student text. In some lessons, the key concepts are introduced and are then reinforced through an activity. In other lessons, the activity introduces the concepts and is followed by an explanation and discussion of the concepts.

The lessons include illustrations designed to complement and enhance comprehension of the narrative material. Most of the illustrations are accompanied by a question and require students to interpret information, apply facts, theorize, think creatively, use reasoning, and employ decision-making skills. The illustrations lend themselves to small group or interactive teaching strategies.

Vocabulary terms are highlighted in the student text and defined within the narrative. Definitions explain the usage of the word in its specific textual context. All terms are also defined in the glossary. A variety of vocabulary-building activities can be employed to reinforce understanding of new terms. Students can create their own dictionaries, which they might illustrate. They might write sentences that use each of the terms. A vocabulary test or a writing assignment might be used at the end of the unit as a check for understanding.

Another option would be a class spelling bee that requires students to use the term correctly in a sentence as well as spell it.

Each lesson in the student text ends with a list of questions entitled "Review the lesson" that can conclude the class discussions. Questions might also be assigned for individual or small-group homework assignments. Additional and alternative activities to reinforce, extend, and enrich the concepts of the lesson are included in the "Activities to do" section.

CHARACTERISTICS OF EFFECTIVE CIVIC EDUCATION PROGRAMS

CURRICULUM CHARACTERISTICS

Effective civic education programs are distinguished by at least four characteristics:

Extensive interaction among students.

Teaching strategies that foster interactive and cooperative learning among students are keys to development of civic participation skills and responsible citizenship. Examples of these teaching strategies are small group work, simulations, role-play activities, and moot courts.

Realistic content that includes balanced treatment of issues.

Realistic and fair treatment of issues is an essential component of effective civic education. So is critical thinking about all sides to controversies. If our legal and political systems are presented as flawless or infallible, students will doubt the credibility of the teacher and the practicality of the content. By contrast, if only cases in which the system has failed are presented, students will be less likely to view the system as a positive means for maintaining social order, liberty, and justice. A balance should be sought between respect for the legal and political system and constructive criticism about its application in specific cases.

Use of community resource persons in the classroom.

Interaction with a variety of adult role models who work within our political and legal systems adds credibility and reality to the curriculum and is a powerful influence on development of positive attitudes toward the political and legal systems. Appropriate use of resource persons in the classroom (e.g., government officials from the legislative, executive, and judicial branches, community leaders, and representatives of various international groups, etc.) is strongly associated with increased student interest in issues related to effective citizenship and with positive responses to teachers and the school.

Strong support for civic education by the principal and other important school administrators.

A key to successful implementation of civic education in the schools is strong support by administrators, especially the school principal. Supportive administrators can aid civic education by organizing opportunities for peer support, rewarding teachers for outstanding work, helping teachers explain and justify the program to people in the community outside the school, and providing opportunities for staff development in the knowledge and skills needed to carry out civic education programs. In addition, positive attitudes about civic education on the part of teachers and their colleagues are very important to successful implementation.

Successful citizenship programs actively involve students in the learning process in ways that reflect a high regard for each person. Reflection, deliberation, and discourse are valued and practiced systematically. The development of knowledge and character are pursued in concert as equally important elements of responsible citizenship in our constitutional democracy. Every attempt has been made to incorporate these essential characteristics in the **We the People: The Citizen and the Constitution** curriculum.

INSTRUCTIONAL METHODOLOGY

CONDUCTING CLASS DISCUSSIONS

The study of the history of ideas includes controversy, debate, evaluation, and reflection. So, too, does the study of **We the People: The Citizen and the Constitution**. Effective civic education presents and discusses controversial subject matter. This approach is what makes the curriculum exciting for both students and teachers. Through the discussion process, students develop knowledge, decision-making skills, conflict management experience, and a commitment to citizenship participation.

To ensure that the experience with this curriculum is stimulating and rewarding for both you and your students, consider the following suggestions for successful classroom discussion of controversial issues and contemporary topics.

Emphasize the legitimacy of controversy, compromise, and consensus. They are the lifeblood of a democratic society.

Try to present the central issues of controversy in tangible form. Make allusions to similar problems and dilemmas students face in their own lives.

Stress historical antecedents so students can see how similar conflicts have been managed in the past. Acknowledge those times when we have not lived up to the ideals and principles upon which our nation was founded. Examining the interpretation and application of these concepts over time will help students appreciate the flexibility of our constitutional system and the role individual citizens play in helping our nation better realize its goals.

Emphasize the legitimacy of various viewpoints by encouraging students to examine and present conflicting views in an unbiased fashion. It is incumbent on the teacher to raise any opposing views students may have missed.

Keep students focused on discussing or dealing with ideas or positions, rather than people. Stress that in controversial issues, reasonable people might very well differ.

Encourage students to offer dissenting opinions when they do not agree with the majority—even if they are alone in their dissent.

Help students identify specific points of agreement or disagreement, places where compromise might be possible, and places where it is unlikely to occur. Emphasize that the outcome or the decision that they reach on an issue may not be as important as improving their ability to develop a reasoned decision and to express it in a civil manner, respecting the views of others.

Conclude, or debrief, a lesson or discussion by evaluating the arguments presented and exploring the likely consequences of the various alternatives suggested. An effective debriefing also involves both the teacher and the students in evaluating the process used for conducting a discussion, preparing group work, or presenting a class activity.

Class discussion and sharing of opinions are critical components to this program, therefore, you may wish to establish a few basic ground rules. For example:

- When expressing an opinion, always be prepared to justify it.
- Listen to the opinions of others politely and respectfully. You may be called on to say which opinion (other than your own) you liked best.
- Everyone will get a chance to speak, but only one person will speak at a time.
- Argue with reasons and ideas; do not argue against people.
- You may change your opinion at any time. Be prepared to share your reasons for doing so.

EFFECTIVE QUESTIONING STRATEGIES

Question and response sequences are an important feature of the curriculum. The effective use of questions is critical to the learning process and requires careful planning. While some questions may be useful to establish how much knowledge students have gained, the primary goal of your questioning strategies should be to help students increase their knowledge, understanding, and ability to reach effective, responsible decisions. Therefore, you will want to choose questioning strategies that help students develop the skills of analysis, synthesis, and evaluation.

There are generally six categories of questions you should consider when planning class discussions. Following is a brief description and example of each:

Knowledge. These questions involve recall of specific facts or information.

Example: What are the powers of the legislative branch of government?

Comprehension. This involves the ability to understand the meaning of the material. This may be shown by translating material from one form to another, and by interpreting material.

Example: Create a drawing illustrating a person fulfilling a responsibility of citizenship. What is the central idea of this lesson?

Application. This involves the ability to use learned material in new situations.

Example: What examples can you cite from your own experience where these ideas apply? How might you use this process to resolve a conflict in the future?

Analysis. This involves the ability to break down material into its component parts. This includes identifying the parts and establishing the relationship among the parts.

Example: What are the consequences of the government's invasion of privacy in this situation? Which consequences are advantages and which are disadvantages?

Synthesis. This is the ability to put parts together to form a new whole. The emphasis is on creating new patterns of thought.

Example: What argument can you make to support the idea of increasing the authority of the U. S. Supreme Court?

Evaluation. This is the ability to judge the value of the material for a given purpose. This may be a process for choosing among competing values or deciding whether a principle still meets the criteria of effectiveness for the common good.

Example: How useful are the critical thinking strategies in helping you make a decision about who is responsible for a particular event? What are the likely consequences of the alternatives you have suggested?

It is possible to structure questions so that students listen to and respond to each other and not just to their teacher.

Encourage students' active participation in the following ways:

* Pose a question and ask students to discuss the answer with a partner.

* Ask students to clarify their responses. This will benefit themselves as well as others.

* Ask students to extend their own or other students' responses by providing additional facts, information, viewpoints, etc.

* Ask students to generate questions of their own on material just presented in class.

* Pause at least seven seconds after asking a question to allow students time to think.

* Ask students to expand on their responses if they provide short or fragmentary answers.

* Call on more than one student per question.

* Encourage students to react to other students' responses.

* Call on nonvolunteers as well as volunteers.

ENCOURAGING SMALL GROUP LEARNING

The critical thinking exercises in the student text are generally designed as cooperative learning activities with a study partner or in small group environments. Each individual's participation is essential for the successful completion of an exercise. Students are encouraged not only to contribute academically, but to develop and use appropriate interpersonal skills.

Important issues arise for the teacher in planning and implementing cooperative group learning. One such issue concerns the size of groups. Consideration of the research can help you determine the optimum number of students per group within your classroom.

David A. Welton and John T. Mallan, in their book *Children and Their World: Teaching Elementary Social Studies,* Fourth Edition, Houghton-Mifflin, 1991, have identified some general behavioral characteristics of differently sized groups:

Groups of two. High exchange of information and a tendency to avoid disagreement are two features of pairs. In case of disagreement, however, deadlock occurs because there is no support within the group for either participant.

Groups of three. Triads tend to be characterized by the power of the majority over the minority of one. However, triads are the most stable group structure with some occasional shifting of coalitions.

Groups of even numbers. More disagreement is prevalent in groups with even numbers of members. This is due to the formation of subgroups of equal size resulting in deadlock.

ENCOURAGING SMALL GROUP LEARNING (CONT'D)

Groups of five. The most satisfying learning group size seems to be five. There is ease of movement within the group. The 2:3 division provides minority members with support. The group is large enough for stimulation, yet small enough for participation and personal recognition.

Groups larger than five. As group size increases, so does the range of ability, expertise, and skill. However, so do the difficulties in keeping all members on task, ensuring everyone the opportunity to speak, and coordinating group actions.

Another issue teachers face in planning and implementing cooperative group learning is whether to allow groups to self-select or to establish the groups by assignment. David W. Johnson, et al., in *Circles of Learning: Cooperation in the Classroom*, published by the Association for Supervision and Curriculum Development, 1984, describes the following characteristics of groups:

Student-selected groups are frequently homogeneous with high-achieving students selecting other high achievers, males selecting males, and members of different cultural groups selecting those from similar backgrounds.

There is often less on-task behavior in student-selected than in teacher-selected groups.

More creative thinking, more frequent giving and receiving of explanations, and greater perspective-taking in discussion seems to occur in heterogeneous groups.

A useful modification of the select-your-own-groups method is to have students list three peers with whom they would like to work. Place the students with one person they chose and other students selected by the teacher. Careful consideration should be given to building a supportive environment for students no one selects.

You also may want to consider randomly assigning students to groups by having them count off. For example, to establish six groups of five students each in a class of thirty, have the students count off from one to six, repeating the sequence at the end of six. Then, place the "ones" together, the "twos" together and so forth. Once groups have been assembled, you may want to have them work together over a period of time rather than forming new groups for each activity in the student text.

Below are some general recommendations you may want to consider in implementing small group work in your classroom:

- Make sure the students have the skills necessary to do the work. If they do not, you will quickly know because they will not remain long on task.
- Give clear instructions for completing work and check for understanding of the process or procedures to be followed during an activity.
- Allow adequate time to complete the assigned task. Think creatively about ways to constructively occupy groups that finish ahead of the others.
- Be explicit in dealing with management issues. If someone must report to the class on the group's work, be sure there is a process for selecting a reporter.
- Think about how your evaluation strategies are affected by the use of small groups. Develop methods to reward group efforts.
- Monitor group work and act as a resource to guide your students' development.

COMMUNITY RESOURCE PEOPLE

Involvement of people from the community who possess appropriate experience or expertise can greatly enhance and extend student understanding of the concepts presented in *We the People: The Citizen and the Constitution*. Community resource people can contribute in the following ways:

- make the lessons come alive by sharing real-life experiences and applications of the ideas under consideration
- help implement activities in the classroom such as role plays, moot courts, and simulated legislative hearings and debates
- enrich field experiences by serving as a guide and by responding to questions during visits to places such as courtrooms and legislative chambers
- establish an on-going relationship with a class in which the resource person is available regularly by phone to respond to questions or issues that may arise during a particular lesson

The range of individuals who can serve as resource people is as varied as the community itself. Commonly this includes government officials from the legislative, executive, and judicial branches, community leaders, and representatives of various international groups.

Making the involvement of a community resource person as meaningful as possible requires careful planning. Attention should be given to the following considerations:

A resource person's involvement should be relevant to the lesson or concept under consideration.

The principal mode of involvement should be interaction and participation with students. A resource person should be asked to assist students in preparing a role-play or moot court arguments. The resource person can act as a judge, serve on a panel with students, or respond to questions about specific details of a lesson. Also, a resource person should participate in the concluding discussion of a lesson or activity.

A resource person should offer a balanced picture of the topic, including a variety of perspectives. When objectivity is not possible, you might consider inviting a second resource person to ensure a balanced experience. The guest also should avoid professional jargon and speak as simply as possible.

Before a visit by a resource person, students should be well prepared to maximize their thoughtful participation when the visitor is present.

Most resource persons are not trained teachers and should not be responsible for classroom management. The teacher should be in attendance during the entire visit. Sometimes it might be necessary for the teacher to give direction to the guest by asking appropriate questions or offering clues that can help the resource person communicate effectively with students.

For a successful visit, the resource person should receive a copy of the lesson in advance. Usually, a pre-visit meeting or phone call is useful to help clarify what is expected of the guest.

Owing to busy schedules and the limited length of this program, it is advisable to extend invitations as soon as possible. A committee of students should be responsible for hosting the guests on the day of their visit and for the follow-up thank you letter.

INTERACTIVE TEACHING STRATEGIES

An essential feature of *We the People: The Citizen and the Constitution* is the use of instructional methods that actively involve students in developing and presenting positions on related issues. Students learn to apply their knowledge to contemporary issues as well as to a variety of socio-political questions. In addition, these learning strategies promote certain dispositions and participatory skills that increase students' capacity to act effectively as citizens in a constitutional democracy. For example, students learn to work cooperatively to reach common goals, to evaluate, take, and defend positions on controversial issues, and to deal with conflicting opinions and positions in a constructive manner. These learning strategies also teach students how government works.

The key learning strategies in this curriculum include, among others, legislative hearings, moot courts, and town meetings. The following material describes these instructional methods and offers specific suggestions for implementation in the classroom.

LEGISLATIVE HEARINGS

Legislative hearings are held by committees of the United States Congress and other legislative bodies to gather information on matters of public concern. These hearings are a basic function of legislative branches of government.

Role-playing a legislative hearing provides participants with an opportunity to gain increased understanding of the purpose and procedures of such hearings as well as the roles and responsibilities of committee members. Participants also gain experience in identifying and clarifying the information, interests, and values associated with the subject being discussed.

HOW TO PROCEED

1. Clarify topics. Help students understand the topic of the legislative hearing. The topics are clearly identified in the lessons in the student text and in this edition. You also will want to ensure that students understand the role of committees in the legislative process.

2. Contact resource persons. Invite a local legislator, representatives of local groups or chapters of a national organization to serve as resource people on the topic of the hearing.

3. Assign roles. Explain to participants the purpose of a legislative hearing and assign the appropriate roles:

a. **Legislators.** Six legislators is a practical number for a committee, but the number

LEGISLATIVE HEARINGS (CONT'D)

may vary according to class needs. Designate one legislator as the chairperson to preside over the hearing.

b. **Witnesses.** The number and nature of the witnesses depend on the topic being discussed. The specific roles described in the lessons and in this edition are designed to present differing points of view on the topic.

c. **Recorder.** This role is optional. This person will keep a record of the proceedings and present a review or summary of any recommendations that may emerge during the discussions.

d. **Newspaper reporters.** This role is optional, but is useful in helping students gain insights on the function of the press in the democratic process. Select students to represent newspapers with varying perspectives. Ask them to interview legislators and witnesses, to observe the proceedings, and to write brief articles or editorials about the topic. They should share and discuss their work with the class.

4. Prepare presentations. Allow time for participants to prepare for the legislative hearing in accordance with their assigned roles.

a. Legislators should identify the key issue(s) and prepare questions to ask each witness.

b. Witnesses should define their position on the issue(s), prepare an opening statement, anticipate questions from the legislators, and formulate possible responses.

c. Witnesses may wish to discuss similarities in positions with other witnesses.

d. When appropriate, have a resource person work with the students or allow students to contact outside resources for assistance in preparing their position on an issue.

5. Arrange the classroom. Set up the classroom to resemble a legislative chamber. Include a table for the legislators, a desk for the recorder, and a desk or table for the witnesses. Provide a gavel and nameplates with the students' names and their roles. You may want to arrange the use of a hearing or committee room of a local legislative body.

6. Conduct the hearing. The following procedures should be used to conduct this activity:

a. The committee chairperson calls the hearing to order, announces the purpose of the hearing and the order in which the witnesses will be called to testify.

b. The chairperson calls each witness. The witness makes an opening statement, followed by questions from members of the committee. You may want to establish time

limits, usually three to four minutes for openings and five to six minutes for questions from the legislators. Appoint a timekeeper to enforce time limitations.

c. The chairperson is the first to question the witness, followed by the other members of the committee. A committee member may interrupt to ask a question or make a comment any time during the proceedings.

d. After the witnesses have been heard, the legislators review the testimony, discuss the issue(s) and make recommendations on what their next step(s) will be.

7. Debrief the activity. Debriefing questions vary according to the topic. Begin by having the legislators announce their decision. Discuss the facts and arguments presented on the topic and evaluate the strengths and weaknesses of the positions taken. Ask students to evaluate their experience with the hearing process itself. Conclude the debriefing by having students discuss the effectiveness of this activity as a tool for learning, including how well they performed their role in it. If a resource person assisted with the activity, that person should be included in the concluding discussion.

LEGISLATIVE DEBATE

Legislative debate is often used productively in the formulation and development of laws. Role-playing a legislative debate provides participants with an opportunity to increase their understanding of the purpose and value of the power of legislatures to make laws and to debate matters of public policy.

HOW TO PROCEED

1. Clarify topics. Help students understand the topic of the legislative debate. The topics are clearly identified in the lessons in the student text and in this edition. You also will want to ensure that students understand the process whereby bills are enacted into law.

2. Contact resource persons. Contact state and national legislators or their staff assistants to help serve as resource persons.

3. Assign roles. Consider the entire class as the legislative body with a student or the teacher assuming the role of the presiding officer. Legislators may then be assigned to groups representing various positions on the issue. Groups are clearly identified in the student text and in this edition. You also may want to assign a recorder responsible for tracking key points of discussion during the debate.

4. Prepare presentations. Allow time for participants to prepare for the legislative hearing in accordance with their assigned roles.

Each group should select a spokesperson and a recorder and then proceed to follow the directions given in the lesson. Students should analyze and evaluate the issue before developing their positions. In some cases, they will be asked to offer amendments to the bills already given in the lesson. In others, they may write a proposed bill designed to alleviate problems raised by the issue.

As each group completes its amendment or proposed bill, the spokesperson reports to the presiding officer asking that the bill be placed on the agenda. Bills should be placed on the agenda in the order in which they are received. Students may wish to discuss any similarities in their proposed amendments or bills with other groups to predetermine whether they can unite behind a common proposal.

5. Arrange the classroom. Set up the classroom to resemble a legislative chamber. Include a table for the presiding officer, a desk for the recorder, and a podium if you want to have presentations made more formally. Provide a gavel and nameplates with the students' names and their roles. You may want to arrange for the use of a legislative chamber in your community.

6. Conduct the legislative debate. Time limits for the various steps in legislative debates should be decided ahead of time. The presiding officer should be empowered to cut off speakers

when the time limit has been reached. Conduct the legislative debate using the following procedures:

a. The presiding officer calls the legislature to order, indicates that all votes will be decided by a simple majority, announces the issue, and opens the debate.

b. The first bill on the agenda is introduced by the group's spokesperson. The spokesperson stands, addresses the presiding officer, and describes the bill the group has written. After presenting the bill, the spokesperson may recognize two other members of the group who may make additional comments on the bill.

c. The bill is discussed and debated by the legislature. Representatives from other groups may ask questions, offer criticisms, or suggest modifications.

d. The steps above are repeated for any additional bills that might be introduced during the session.

e. When the discussion and debate on all proposed bills is completed, legislators may move that one of the bills be voted on or that the session be recessed to enable the groups to consider the bills that have been presented. If the session is recessed, each group meets to decide upon a course of

LEGISLATIVE DEBATE (CONT'D)

action. A group may decide to support one of the bills as presented, suggest amendments to one of the bills presented, or develop a compromise bill.

f. When the session is reconvened, the presiding officer asks for a motion to vote on one of the bills as presented, for a motion to amend one of the bills, or for the introduction of a compromise bill. If amendments or compromise bills are proposed, they are individually debated and voted upon.

g. This process is repeated until a bill is passed or the time allotted for the session is up and the legislature is adjourned.

7. Debrief the activity. Debriefing questions vary according to the topic. Discuss the facts and arguments presented on the topic and evaluate the strengths and weaknesses of the positions taken. Also ask students to evaluate their experience with the legislative process itself. Conclude the debriefing by having students discuss the effectiveness of this activity as a tool for learning, including how well they performed their role in it. If a resource person assisted with the activity, that person should be included in the concluding discussion.

PRO SE COURT

A pro se (do it yourself) court allows students to role-play a court case with a minimum of participants and simple rules of evidence. The court is organized as a triad consisting of a judge, who will hear the two sides and make the final decision; a plaintiff, who is the person bringing the action before the judge; and the defendant, who is accused of wrongdoing or causing injury.

Pro se courts provide students with a simplified look at judicial decision-making. Pro se courts provide an opportunity for all students in a class to be involved in the activity.

HOW TO PROCEED

1. Clarify topic. Help students understand the facts and issues in the case. The cases are clearly identified in the lessons.

2. Contact resource person. Invite an attorney or judge to act as a resource person.

3. Assign roles. Divide the class into three equal groups—judges, plaintiffs, and defendants.

4. Prepare presentations. Have the students meet in their respective groups to help each other prepare their presentations. Each student will be actively involved in the role play, so preparation at this stage is vital to effective participation in the activity.

Instruct the judges to review the case and the issues raised. Ask them to prepare questions that they would like to ask of the plaintiffs and defendants during the presentation phase of the activity. The questions should be designed to clarify positions on the issues that the judges will be called upon to decide. Do take some time to review with the judge's group some simple rules of procedure, such as the following:

a. The plaintiff should present first, without interruptions from the defense. The defense presents their case second.

b. Allow brief rebuttals from each side in the case.

c. The judge may interrupt the presentations at any time to pose questions designed to clarify the arguments being made. Instruct the plaintiff and defendant groups to prepare an opening statement and arguments supporting their positions on the issues raised in the case.

5. Arrange the classroom. You will have multiple courts in session simultaneously; therefore, arrange the desks in the classroom into groups of three, one for each of the roles in the activity.

6. Conduct the court hearing. Before beginning the activity, match one student from the judge's group with one student from the plaintiff and one from the defendant groups. You may want to have the judges first take a desk in each of the groupings arranged around the room. Then ask one plaintiff and one defendant to join the group. Matching role-players may be more easily accomplished by providing role "tags" so students can quickly identify who is a judge, plaintiff, and defendant. Conduct the activity using the following procedures:

a. Instruct the judges that when each has a plaintiff and a defendant, he or she may begin the court session.

b. The judge should first hear opening statements by the participants—first the plaintiff and then the defendant. An appropriate time limit should be imposed on these statements.

c. The plaintiff makes arguments and is questioned by the judge.

d. The defendant presents his or her defense and is questioned by the judge.

e. The judge asks each side for brief rebuttal statements.

f. The judge makes his or her decision and explains the reasoning which supports it.

7. Debrief the activity. Debriefing questions vary according to the topic. Begin by asking individual judges to share with the class their decision and the reasoning supporting it. Discuss the facts and arguments presented in the case and evaluate the strengths and weaknesses of the positions taken. Also ask students to evaluate the court process itself. Conclude the debriefing by having students discuss the effectiveness of this activity as a tool for learning, including how well they performed their role in it. If a resource person assisted with the activity, that person should be included in the concluding discussion.

MOOT COURT

A moot court is patterned on an appeals court or Supreme Court hearing. The court, composed of a panel of judges or justices, is asked to rule on a lower court's decision. No witnesses are called, nor are the basic facts in a case disputed. Arguments are prepared and presented on the application of a law, the constitutionality of a law, or the fairness of previous court procedures. In many ways the moot court is like a debate, for each side presents arguments for the consideration of the justices.

Since moot courts are not concerned with the credibility of witness testimony, they are an effective strategy for focusing student attention on the underlying principles and concepts of due process.

HOW TO PROCEED

1. Clarify topic. Help students understand the facts and the legal or constitutional issues in the case. The cases are clearly identified in the lessons in the student text and in this edition. You may also want to ensure that students understand the purpose and procedures observed in appellate court proceedings.

2. Contact resource persons. Invite an attorney or judge to act as a resource person.

3. Assign roles. Assign students to play the roles of justices of the court (in intermediate appellate courts, members of the panel are called judges; in the federal or state supreme

MOOT COURT (CONT'D)

courts they are called justices). You may establish a court of five, seven, or nine justices. Divide the remaining students into two groups representing the litigants in the case. One group will represent the person or group bringing the challenge before the court, or the plaintiff. The other group will represent the person or group defending against the challenge, or the defendant. Sometimes, terms like petitioner or respondent, or appellant and appellee, are used to identify the litigants in an appellate case. For pedagogical purposes, it is best to keep it simple by using the terms plaintiff and defendant.

4. Prepare presentations. Each group should meet to prepare arguments for its side of the case. The group should select one or two students to present the arguments.

The justices should meet to discuss the issues involved and any questions they feel need to be addressed for them to reach a decision. The justices should select one student to serve as chief justice. The chief justice will preside over the hearing. He or she will call on each side to present its case or (more realistically) justices (judges) should ask questions without needing to be recognized. The judges should feel free to interrupt lawyers' presentations whenever they want.

Participants should understand that the factual details presented in the summary of the case were established by a trial and are not subject to further dispute.

Arguments should not concentrate on legal technicalities. Any argument that is persuasive from a philosophical, theoretical, conceptual, or practical standpoint can be made. Groups should rely on principles found or implied in the United States Constitution.

5. Arrange the classroom. Set up the classroom to resemble an appellate court. The justices should be seated at a table at the front of the room. The attorneys for each side should sit on opposite sides of the room facing the justices. Other group members should sit behind their respective attorneys. You may want to take the class to an appellate court-room or to a mock trial room at a law school.

6. Conduct the moot court. The chief justice should preside over the proceedings and begin by calling the court to order. The chief justice should observe the following procedures:

    a. Each side should be allotted five to ten minutes for the initial presentation and five minutes for rebuttal. The chief justice should call for presentations in the following order:

Plaintiff   Initial presentation

Defendant   Initial presentation

Plaintiff   Rebuttal presentation

Defendant   Rebuttal presentation

b. During and/or after each presentation, the justices can and should actively question the attorneys in an effort to clarify the arguments. Attorneys may request time to consult with other group members before answering questions. For clarity and continuity, it is suggested that during the initial presentations lawyers be given three minutes to present their cases before being interrupted with questions.

c. After arguments have been presented, the justices should organize themselves in a circle. They should consider the arguments and make a decision by a majority vote. Each justice should give reasons for his or her position. The rest of the class may sit outside of the circle and listen, but they may not talk or interrupt the deliberations.

7. Debrief the activity. Debriefing questions vary according to the case. Begin by asking the justices to share with the class their decision and the reasoning supporting it. Justices should present dissenting opinions. Discuss the arguments presented in the case and evaluate the strengths and weaknesses of the positions taken. Also ask students to evaluate their experience with the appellate process itself. Conclude the debriefing by having students discuss the effectiveness of this activity as a tool for learning, including how well they performed their role in it. If a resource person assisted with the activity, that person should be included in the concluding discussion.

In an actual case, you should share the Court's decision with the class during the debriefing. To dispel the notion that there is one "right" answer, also share relevant parts of the dissenting opinion. Help students understand the reasoning which supports both the majority and dissenting opinions.

TOWN MEETING

A town meeting provides members of a community with an opportunity to participate in the decision-making process. A community forum usually considers matters of public policy. A town meeting can serve as a local governing and decision-making body by performing functions similar to those of a representative town or city council. It also can be advisory in nature, providing elected representatives with the views of citizens.

HOW TO PROCEED

1. Clarify topic. Help students understand the topic of the town meeting. The topics are clearly identified in the lessons in the student text and in this edition. You also will want to ensure that students understand the nature and purpose of a town meeting.

2. Contact resource person. Invite a member of the city council or a local interest group to serve as a resource person on the topic of the meeting.

3. Assign roles. Organize the town meeting by assigning individuals the following roles:

a. chairperson

b. elected officials who represent the entire community in the town or city council

c. representative groups in favor of the proposition

d. representative groups in opposition to the proposition

e. community members at large

f. recorder

4. Prepare presentations. Allow time for students to prepare for the town meeting in accordance with their assigned roles.

5. Arrange the classroom. Include a table for the chairperson and for the elected officials, a desk for the recorder, and a podium from which members of interest groups and the community can speak. Provide a gavel and nameplates with the students' names and their roles. You may want to arrange for the use of a hearing or committee room of a local legislative body.

6. Conduct the town meeting. The following procedures should be used to conduct this activity:

a. The chairperson calls the meeting to order, announces the purpose of the meeting, and introduces the elected officials in attendance. Elected officials may make a brief opening statement about the importance of the issue

TOWN MEETING (CONT'D)

being considered (not his or her personal views on the topic). The chairperson also establishes any rules that are to be followed during the meeting, such as time limits for presentations.

b. The chairperson has the authority to cut off debate when time limits have been reached. A person may not speak unless recognized by the chair, and no one may interrupt while another person is speaking. If a speaker wanders from the point, abuses other people, or in any way defeats the purpose of the meeting, the chairperson may declare him or her out of order.

c. The chairperson calls upon a representative of the group favoring the proposition to describe that group's position. After the representative has finished speaking, he or she may ask people brought as witnesses to stand and speak. The chairperson announces that any person in favor of the proposition may stand and speak. They will be recognized in the order in which they stand. Alternatively, you may want to have students sign in and ask the chairperson to recognize speakers by the order in which they signed in.

d. The chairperson calls upon a representative of the group opposed to the proposition to speak. After the representative has finished speaking, he or she may ask people brought as witnesses to stand and speak. The chair-

person announces that those people opposed to the proposition will be recognized in the order in which they stand.

e. After all people on both sides of the proposition have had an opportunity to speak, the chairperson opens the question for additional discussion or debate. During this time any person may stand, be recognized, and present his or her point of view or argue against the point of view of someone else.

f. At the end of the discussion or debate the chairperson calls for class vote on the proposition. The vote is decided by a majority.

7. Debrief the activity. Debriefing questions vary according to the topic. Begin by discussing the results of the vote taken on the proposition. Discuss the facts and argument presented on the topic. Ask students to evaluate the strength of the positions taken and of the procedures used to develop and support a position. Also ask students to evaluate their experience with the town meeting itself. Conclude the debriefing by having students discuss the effectiveness of this activity as a tool for learning, including how well they performed their role in it. If a resource person assisted with the activity, that person should be included in the concluding discussion.

DEBATE

Debate begins with the assumption that the debater has already found a solution or approach to a specific issue. The intent of the debater is to persuade others that his or her solution or approach is the proper one.

Debate can be an effective device for encouraging students to clearly and logically formulate arguments based upon evidence. Debate teaches a means to adequately support a position on an issue. It also develops a sense of efficacy and confidence in a person's ability to sway public opinion or to change public policy.

HOW TO PROCEED

1. Clarify topic. Help students understand the topic of the debate. The topics are clearly identified in the lessons in the student text and in this edition. Formulate the topic into a resolution (resolutions always ask for a change from the status quo, e.g., Resolved: that capital punishment should be found unconstitutional by the United States Supreme Court).

2. Contact resource person. Invite someone from the community or a local interest group to serve as a resource person on the topic of the debate.

3. Assign roles. Select students to take part in the debate. Divide them into two teams, one in support of the resolution, the other opposing it. Make certain that those participating in the debate are familiar with the procedures to be followed during the debate. Select a moderator and a timekeeper.

4. Prepare presentations. Allow sufficient time for students to prepare their "constructive arguments" (argument based upon three to five major points logically developed and substantiated by factual evidence in support of a particular position). Help students see the dimensions of the problem and develop clear, logical arguments supported by evidence on the position they defend in the debate. Also, ask them to anticipate the views of the other side in preparation for their "rebuttal arguments."

Help students gain an understanding of some of the implicit values in debate such as learning to make convincing arguments from another frame of reference, as might be the case if one is debating a position that does not correspond with one's own beliefs. This furthers development of students' abilities to understand and respect the right of individuals to hold opinions and beliefs that are different from their own.

5. Arrange the classroom. The moderator and debaters are seated at the front of the audience, usually with the team in opposition to the resolution to the left of the moderator.

6. Conduct the debate. The form of debate described here is widely used, but is rather formalized. You may wish to make the procedures less formal or use some other form of debate.

a. The moderator briefly introduces the subject and the resolution to be debated and establishes the time limits to be observed by the speakers.

b. The moderator introduces the first speaker from the affirmative team and asks the speaker to present his or her constructive argument. The order in which constructive arguments will be given by each member of the team should be determined in advance of the debate. The timekeeper will inform the speaker when the time limit has been reached.

c. The moderator introduces the first speaker from the team in opposition to the resolution and asks the speaker to present his or her constructive argument.

d. The moderator next introduces the second speaker from the affirmative team. This procedure is alternated until each debater on both affirmative and opposition teams have given a constructive argument.

e. Rebuttal arguments follow the constructive arguments. At this time each debater is

given the opportunity to weaken the position of the opponents by attacking their position and by answering attacks that have been made upon his or her position. No new issues may be introduced during rebuttal arguments. Rebuttal arguments always begin with the team in opposition to the resolution. Again, follow the same alternating procedures used during constructive arguments.

f. At the conclusion of the debate, the moderator makes a few concluding remarks and the debate is ended.

7. Debrief the activity. You may wish to evaluate the success of the debating teams by informally polling the class to determine how many people agree with the team in support of the resolution and how many agree with the team in opposition to the resolution. You may then ask class members to explain whether their own positions were strengthened or changed as a result of hearing the debate and why. Also ask students to evaluate their experience with the debate process itself. Conclude the debriefing by having students discuss the effectiveness of this activity as a tool for learning, including how well they performed their role in it. If a resource person assisted with the activity, that person should be included in the concluding discussion.

CONTINUUM

The continuum is an exercise in which participants are presented with a range of possible attitudes or approaches on a controversial issue. Participants are asked to determine which element of the continuum (e.g., strongly agree or strongly disagree) most approximates their own attitude. Issues that are clearly controversial and characterized by polar position are suitable for using this method. The issues should have legitimate opposing view points, such as whether equal rights can best be achieved by an amendment or whether gun control is an effective way to stop crime. Issues that are above debate such as the morality of a holocaust or sexual abuse of children are obviously not legitimate topics for a continuum.

The continuum is a useful tool for introducing controversial issues. It can help students see the ranges of values or opinions which exist on a given topic and understand the reasoning which supports those positions. The continuum provides an orderly method for discussing controversy, especially at the early stages of a lesson when students may be expressing "gut-level" reactions rather than informed opinions.

HOW TO PROCEED

1. Identify an issue to be discussed. The issue should be one in which one can identify polar positions, such as the death penalty.

2. Before initiating the activity it is important to cultivate a classroom atmosphere of trust where opinions can be expressed freely. Being receptive and nonjudgmental is critical to open discussion.

3. The teacher should initiate the activity by describing the issue(s) in enough detail so that the polar positions are clearly understood. These should be written on the board.

4. Students should be asked to write their position on the issue (e.g., strongly agree, agree, disagree, strongly disagree, can't decide) and to list the two most compelling reasons why they believe as they do.

5. While the students are writing their statements, the teacher can draw a continuum line across the chalkboard. When the students are finished writing, the teacher can print along the continuum brief versions of some possible polar position on the issue. Ask a limited number of students to stand at the position on the continuum where they believe their position on the issue falls.

6. At this point, students should be asked to explain or clarify, but not to defend their positions. They should be encouraged to move their position along the continuum as they listen to others clarify their positions.

7. Students now can be asked to state their reasons for positioning themselves as they have. The teacher may wish to post on the board the different reasons expressed by the students. At this point, students can respond to questions concerning their reasoning, but argumentation should be discouraged.

8. To make sure that students listen to and consider opposing points of view, all students should be asked to present the arguments that, although contrary to their positions, give them pause, make them think twice, or are the most persuasive.

9. Finally, students should be asked to consider the consequences of alternative policy choices. This involves identifying the existing law or policy on the issue being considered, if one exists. The class can then discuss what impact the polar positions presented on the continuum would have on society as a whole and on individuals.

KEEPING JOURNALS

Journal writing provides a systematic way for students to maintain a personal record of summary statements, reflections, or questions about what is being learned in a particular instance. Journal writing encourages students to reflect on the "what," "why," and "how" of their own learning. Taking time to reflect is a good study habit to develop. Journals have the additional benefit of improving writing skills.

Because the content introduced in *We the People: The Citizen and the Constitution* contains many new concepts and experiences, opportunities for students to reflect on what they are learning are especially important. Some opportunities for journal writing are identified in the teacher's edition, but many more exist in this curriculum. You may want to allow a few minutes at the conclusion of a lesson or at the close of an activity for students to complete a journal entry. Encourage students to discuss some aspect of the content studied, to record a personal reaction to the lesson or the outcome of an activity, or to record questions the lesson or activity raised about an issue. Sometimes you may want to assign journal notations as homework.

Whether journals are graded is a personal choice. You should collect journals periodically, however, to offer students some feedback on the content. Writing comments and personal observations in the journals can be an effective tool in establishing a personal dialogue with students. Do encourage students to share their journals with other students and with their parents if they wish. By so doing, students demonstrate to themselves and others what they have learned.

EVALUATING STUDENT ACHIEVEMENT

The methods used to evaluate student achievement of the concepts, knowledge, and skills offered in this curriculum need to be both comprehensive and varied. The methods selected for measuring progress may range from the more traditional paper and pencil tests to performance-based assessments.

Traditional paper and pencil tests are valuable for checking knowledge and understanding of specific concepts, ideas, or procedures. For this purpose, the *We the People: The Citizen and the Constitution* program provides a multiple-choice test in the back of this book. When teachers ask students to apply their complex knowledge and skills in various contexts, teachers need to measure students' achievement in similar contexts. For example, students who participate in a simulated legislative hearing during instruction should be asked to demonstrate their knowledge and skills in a similar context during testing. Thus, *We the People: The Citizen and the Constitution* includes performance assessment activities to measure achievement of the curriculum's higher level goals and objectives. The culminating performance assessment activity for the curriculum is the simulated congressional hearing, which is fully explained in the Reference Section of this book under the title Simulated Congressional Hearing.

Performance assessment differs from traditional testing in that students are not asked to recognize and select correct answers to questions focused on discreet, isolated facts. During performance assessment, students demonstrate their knowledge and skills by addressing complex questions within a meaningful context (e.g., a legislative hearing) for which there is usually not just one correct answer. Students, therefore, construct or create appropriate answers, or a product, as a means of demonstrating what they know and what they can do.

Performance assessment is particularly well-suited to the content, skills, and learning experiences emphasized in the program. Classroom activities such as group discussions, debates, and other creative projects provide prime opportunities for integrating performance assessment as part of the learning. Other opportunities for integrating performance assessment may be found in the sections titled "Additional instructional activity."

Below are some general guidelines for performance assessment you may want to consider in designing your evaluation of student achievement in this program:

- Assess desired behavior in the context in which the behavior is used. To assess students' ability to do X, have them do X.

- Assess how well students can apply what they learned in one situation by asking them to apply similar knowledge and skills in other, similar situations. Structure situations in which students can construct or create appropriate answers, rather than select from a menu of choices.

- Assess the process and the quality of a performance or product, not the ability to identify correct answers. Stress the thinking and reasoning that supports a quality performance or product.

EVALUATING STUDENT ACHIEVEMENT (CONT'D)

- Assess how well students see the connections among a variety of related ideas and skills. For example, in preparing for a debate students should combine reading, research, writing, speaking, and critical thinking skills. Students also should see how knowledge and skills from other disciplines can help them deal with challenging topics.

- Provide the criteria for successful performance in advance and make sure that they are clearly understood. When possible, provide models of exemplary performance.

- Provide criteria for effective and successful group work. Teamwork and group interaction are important skills that are given legitimacy when students know they are being assessed.

- Structure opportunities for students to assess their own progress, to judge for themselves when they have or have not done well. This will help them internalize high standards and learn to judge for themselves when they measure up. Because most learning strategies in this text are used more than once, students will have successive opportunities to reflect on their progress.

- Offer plenty of opportunities for students to receive feedback from the teacher, their peers, and community resource people who participate in activities with the class.

REFLECTING ON THE LEARNING EXPERIENCE

At the conclusion of each unit it is recommended that students evaluate the extent to which they achieved the objectives of that particular unit. This includes thinking about the content as well as the instructional methods used to learn about that content.

Distribute "Reflecting on Your Experience," Handout D3, to each student. Handouts are in the Appendix Section at the back of this book. Ask students to answer the questions. Remind them that they should not only reflect on and evaluate their own learning experiences, but also those of the entire class. Conduct a class discussion in which students have an opportunity to share their reflections on the learning experiences offered in *We the People: The Citizen and the Constitution.*

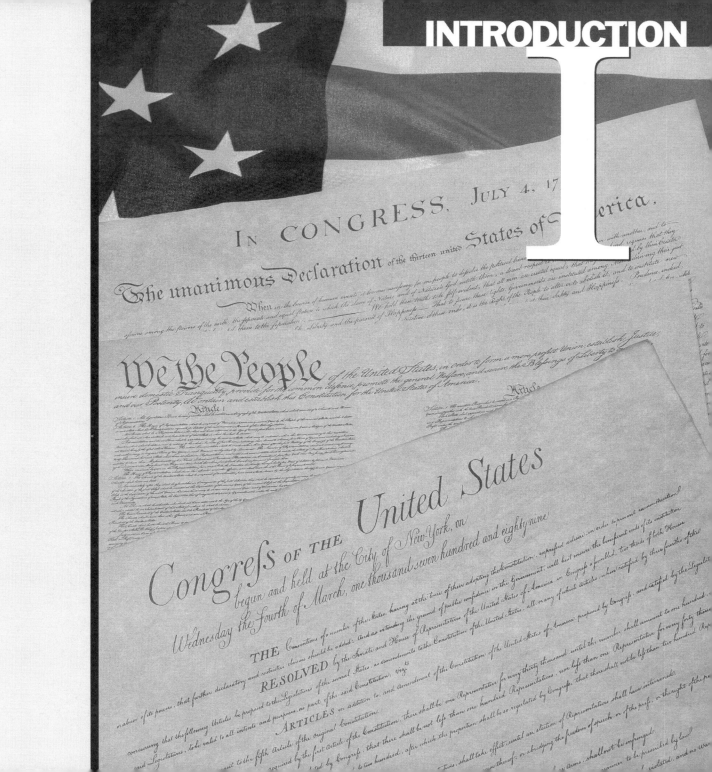

INTRODUCING THE BOOK

Inform students that they are about to begin a study of the Constitution of the United States. Explain that the text will provide them with an understanding of how the Constitution came into existence, why it took the form it did, and how it has worked for the past two hundred years.

Have students locate the **Table of Contents** and read aloud the titles to each of the units. Point out that each unit title and each lesson title asks a question. Tell students that they will learn the answers to these questions as they study each lesson. Ask students to find the Reference Section; discuss the contents of the section and explain how it can be used.

Next, have the students turn to the Introduction to the text. Read the Introduction with the class and answer any questions.

These things are true in our country because of our Constitution:

- You have the right to hold any religious beliefs you wish. You also have the right not to hold any religious beliefs at all.

- If you are arrested for a crime, you have a right to have a lawyer help defend you.

- Members of the Senate must run for election every six years.

- The president of the United States cannot stop an election from being held.

- When you become 18 years old, you will have the right to vote in all elections.

What is the Constitution?

The United States Constitution is a written plan that says what our government should do. It also says how our government is to be organized and run.

The Constitution describes what members of our government may do. It also says what they may not do. The Constitution helps prevent the government from violating our rights.

Our Constitution is the highest or supreme law of our land. Even the president, Congress, and the Supreme Court must obey the Constitution. In our country, everyone must obey the law.

Our Constitution was written in Philadelphia more than 200 years ago. We need to understand our Constitution to know our rights and responsibilities as citizens.

This book is not like most history books. Most history books tell the story of people and events of the past. This book is a history of ideas. It explains the most important ideas of our Constitution and tells you how they were developed.

This book will help you understand some of the basic ideals, or goals, of our nation. These ideals include the belief in liberty and justice for all people. You also will learn about your responsibilities as a citizen to help make these ideals a reality for everyone. The title of each lesson asks an important question about government. After you have finished the lesson, you should be able to answer the question. The answers to the questions will help you understand why the Constitution is important for you.

What basic ideas about government did the Founders have?

UNIT OVERVIEW

The lessons in this unit help students understand who the Founders were and what ideas and experiences shaped their thinking. **Lessons 1** through **3** are devoted to a consideration of the Founders' ideas about government.

Lesson 2 introduces students to the Founders' beliefs about natural rights and the purpose of government. **Lesson 3** presents another important idea that influenced the Framers–republicanism. Students also are introduced to the roles played by the ideas of the common good and civic virtue in a republican government. Students learn why the Framers were convinced that a republic was the best kind of government for Americans. **Lesson 4** introduces students to the idea of constitutionalism. They are asked to consider the rationale for limiting government powers. With this background, in **Lessons 5**, **6**, and **7** students study the events that led to the American Revolution, analyze the Declaration of Independence, and look at the first state governments.

UNIT OBJECTIVES

At the conclusion of this unit, students should be able to

1. describe the characteristics of life in the British colonies in America during the 1770s
2. explain what the Founders meant by natural rights and what they considered to be the purposes of government.
3. explain the characteristics of republican government
4. discuss the role of civic virtue and the concept of the common good
5. distinguish between constitutional government and dictatorial governments
6. explain basic ideas in the Declaration of Independence

UNIT INTRODUCTION

Read the Introduction with the class. Focus on the units' key topics. You may want to read them more than once to familiarize students with the terms.

UNIT PROJECT (OPTIONAL)

You might want to divide the class into thirteen small groups with each group assigned responsibility for researching life in one state and illustrating what they learned. For example, they might depict Founders from that state, important contributions to the American Revolution from that state, or typical scenes from that state during the 1770s.

What basic ideas about government did the Founders have?

To understand the United States Constitution, we need to know about the people who wrote it. How did they live? What experiences did they have? What were their ideas about good government? What were people like in the British colonies in America during the 1770s?

In this unit, we will study their history and their basic ideas about good government.

Studying this unit will help you understand other lessons in this book. More importantly, it will help you understand the basic principles of our government. It will help you understand why our government works the way it does.

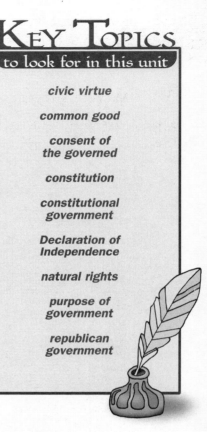

KEY TOPICS
to look for in this unit

civic virtue

common good

consent of the governed

constitution

constitutional government

Declaration of Independence

natural rights

purpose of government

republican government

Lesson 1

What were the British colonies in America like in the 1770s?

Purpose of the lesson

More than 200 years ago, there were British, Dutch, French, and Spanish colonies in North America. In this lesson, you will learn how people lived in the British colonies. We want to learn about these colonies because they became the United States of America. They were the first thirteen states. The lesson will help you know about the people who wrote our United States Constitution.

When you have finished this lesson, you should be able to explain what life was like for the average American living in the colonies. You should also be able to explain how living in the colonies influenced people's ideas about government.

5

OVERVIEW

The lesson is designed to help students learn about the people whose ideas influenced the writing of the U.S. Constitution. It begins with a brief description of British rule in the colonies and life in the 1770s. Students consider the geography of the colonies and the diversity of the people. Students examine various colonial life styles and the social, political, and economic opportunities that were available to them. The lesson concludes with an introduction to the contributions of some of the Founders.

OBJECTIVES

At the conclusion of this lesson, students should be able to

- describe who the colonists were and how they lived in the British colonies in America
- describe the opportunities available to most of the people living in the British colonies and the limitations on those opportunities
- explain what the term Founders means
- name some of the Founders and explain what they did

MATERIALS

- Globe or map of the world

TEACHING PROCEDURES

INTRODUCTORY ACTIVITY

Have students read the section and consider the objectives of the lesson. Emphasize that there were colonies in America ruled by other countries during the same period.

Write the "Terms to understand" on the board, or use a vocabulary-building activity of your choice. You may wish to have students look up the words in the glossary at the back of their text.

- colony
- diverse
- Founders
- indentured servant
- plantation
- self-sufficient
- slave
- subject

READING AND DISCUSSION

The first five sections of this lesson are devoted to knowledge acquisition through reading. Assign the class to read a section aloud or call upon individual students. You may follow a section with questions to stimulate discussion and recall. Allow students to speculate on "what do you think?" type questions. Accept reasonable responses to questions of this nature.

Who ruled the thirteen colonies?

Ask the class to look at a map of the world and locate Europe, Great Britain, and North America. Point out that the American colonies were 3,000 miles away across the Atlantic Ocean. Ask students to think about the following questions.

- What would it be like to live in a colony ruled by another country?
- Would you want to live under the rule of a king or queen? Why or why not?

What was it like to live in the colonies in 1770?

Ask students to consider the following questions.

- What were some differences between Europe and the American colonies in the 1770s?
  Most nations in Europe were much smaller than the colonies. Only the rich could afford to buy and own land. In America, land was cheap and available to almost everyone. There was work for everyone and if you worked hard, you could eat well and be healthy.

- If land and natural resources are abundant, how might this affect the way you farm and your attitude toward cutting trees for lumber or firewood?
  You might not be concerned about cutting down too many trees or how you grow crops. You might not worry about taking care of the soil.

- If transportation is very slow and there is a great distance between you and your neighbors, what might be the effect on your way of living?
  You would probably not travel or visit very much. You may not know your neighbors very well. Families would be self-sufficient and would have to find ways to meet the needs of all members of the family: build their homes, make their clothes, grow their food, milk cows, raise chickens, plant grains and vegetables, etc.

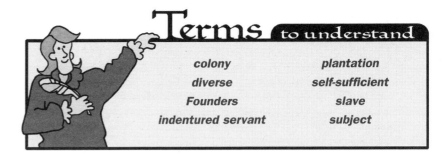

Terms to understand

colony	plantation
diverse	self-sufficient
Founders	slave
indentured servant	subject

Who ruled the thirteen colonies?

In the year 1770 our country did not exist. There was no United States of America. The people who were to create our country lived in thirteen British colonies. A **colony** is a territory ruled by another country.

How is this old map of America different from a current map of the United States?

The colonists were subjects of Great Britain. Being a **subject** means that you are under the authority of a government. Great Britain owned and ruled the colonies. The British colonies were on the Atlantic coast of North America. Great Britain was across the ocean more than three thousand miles away.

What was it like to live in the colonies in the 1770s?

When people came from Europe to America, they saw that America was different from where they had lived before. America was a very large place compared to most nations in Europe. There was a great deal of open, unsettled space. The British colonies spread from what is now the state of Maine in the north to Georgia in the south.

There was space in America for people to settle and to own land. In Europe, only the rich could afford to buy land. In the colonies, land was cheap. People came with the hope of owning their own land. Owning land meant that you could farm to support your family. The number of people who lived in the colonies grew quickly. In 1775, there were 2.5 million people. Fifteen years later, there were almost 4 million people.

Who lived in the colonies?

Since many settlers came to the colonies from Great Britain, they spoke English. They dressed like the British. They followed many of the British customs.

Some colonists were not like the British. They came from many other countries such as France, Germany, Holland, and Sweden. Each group of settlers brought with them their own customs and ways of life.

Native people and their ancestors had lived on the land for thousands of years before the colonists arrived. They had their own customs and ways of life. The settlers called these people Indians. Some American Indians accepted the settlers and lived peacefully with them. Others fought the settlers. After many battles, some Indians were moved from their land by force. Moving the Indians from their land continued for the next hundred years.

Half a million African people and their descendants also lived in the colonies. They were 20 percent of the population. Most of these people had been brought from Africa to work as slaves. **Slaves** are people who are forced to work without pay and who are not allowed to have any rights. The colonists treated the slaves as if they were property. Most of the enslaved people were in the Southern Colonies, but slavery existed in all thirteen colonies.

► How was society in the American colonies different from society in Europe?

Massasoit and his warriors.

● Do you think you would have wanted to move from Europe to the American colonies in the 1770s?

Perhaps, because there were more opportunities in the colonies for ordinary people. There was some freedom of religion and you did not have to be rich to own property. Some students may suggest that if they were rich and living in Europe, they might not want to move to a place where they would have to work hard and live away from other people.

Who lived in the colonies?

Discuss the diverse groups that lived in the colonies and the similarities and differences among them. Ask students to think about diversity in America today.

● How does the diversity of the 1770s compare to the diversity of today?

Most of the colonial immigrants were from Great Britain and other European countries. The African people came as slaves. The American Indians sometimes welcomed the newcomers and shared their land but often the colonists engaged in battles with them. Contemporary immigrants come willingly to the U.S. from all over the world, not only Western Europe. They have a wide variety of languages and customs.

● Do you think there are groups living in America now, who were not represented in the colonies in the 1770s?

There are many parts of the old world that did not contribute a significant immigrant population in colonial times but today immigrants come from every corner of the world.

LESSON 1

How did the colonists live?

Divide the class into groups of three to five students. Have students read the section in their groups. After recalling how the colonists lived, have groups discuss how their lives today are different from the lives of the colonists. Use the following guidelines.

- Apply what you learned by writing an agenda and schedule for a typical day on a farm in the Middle or New England Colonies, or on a plantation in the Southern Colonies.
- How does a day on a colonial farm or plantation compare with a typical day in the present?
- Explain why you would, or would not, like to live in the colonies.

The colonies became home for people from many places and backgrounds. The people brought with them diverse ideas. **Diverse** means to be unlike one another. People held diverse ideas about religion, government, and rights. This diversity helped create a society that was different from society in Europe.

How did the colonists live?

Most Americans in the 1770s were farmers, but not all farms were alike. In the New England Colonies, the cold climate made farming more difficult. A farm might be only a small fifty-acre patch of rocky soil. On such a farm,

▶ *What do you think life was like on a small northern farm? How was life on a large southern plantation different?*

family members did all the work themselves. Sometimes, they hired a person to help them. Some farmers had an indentured servant. **Indentured servants** were people who exchanged their work for a number of years to pay for the trip from Europe to the colonies.

In the Middle Colonies, the soil was good for growing wheat, oats, and barley. People in the Middle Colonies also raised cows, hogs, sheep, and horses. The Middle Colonies had deep rivers. The farmers used the rivers to ship their goods to market.

In the Southern Colonies, the warmer climate made farming easier. Most of the people lived on small farms much like the people in New England. Some people lived on plantations. **Plantations** are large farms that need many workers. The slaves and other workers lived on the plantations. Some plantations had hundreds of slaves.

In the 1770s, most Americans were self-sufficient. **Self-sufficient** means that people raised their own food and wove their own cloth for clothes. They built homes and barns, made their own furniture and tools, and even made their own medicines. They traded any extra farm products at a local store for those few goods they could not make for themselves.

What opportunities did people have in America?

After the reading, discuss the advantages of life in America in the 1770s.

- Why do you think most colonists were able to live so well?
  Possible responses: There was a lot of fertile land, so it was easy to grow crops. There were not very many people living in the colonies. There was work for everyone.

- Identify groups that did not share these advantages.
  Possible responses: The American Indians, enslaved people, indentured servants, or the poor.

How are the opportunities that the colonists sought in America in the 1770s different from those that people seek today?

What opportunities did people have in America?

A visitor to the colonies would have been impressed by how well the people lived. They lived better than most people anywhere else in the world. There was plenty of work for everyone. The colonists worked hard, but the land was fertile and they grew plenty of food. So most colonists ate better, grew taller, and were healthier than people in Europe.

More people in the colonies could read and write than in any other nation in the world. Many owned enough property to be able to vote. More people had the right to vote than anywhere else in the world. Most of the people had a chance to earn a good living through hard work. Wealth and family name did not mean as much in the colonies as they did in Europe.

However, not all people had the same opportunities. While some people became wealthy, some remained poor. Only adult white men who owned property could vote. In most of the colonies, women were not allowed to own property. In the few cases where women did own property, they were not allowed to vote. Slaves did not have any rights.

Despite these limits, most colonists had more rights than did people in Europe. For example, the colonists could follow their religious beliefs freely. Their rights were very important to them. By 1775, the colonists worried about how to protect their rights.

LESSON 1

IDEAS TO DISCUSS

What opportunities did this colonial farmer enjoy?

Have students read the description that Philip Taylor wrote about his life in America. Have them work with a partner to discuss the questions. Then open the discussion to the class after the partners have addressed all six questions.

1. What did Philip Taylor like about life in America?

    He had land and a comfortable home. He had some livestock and the possibility of soon owning a cow. He was free and independent because he did not work for someone else. He did not have to share his crops with a landowner or pay a tax on his property or goods. He believed he was equal to other men.

2. What rights did he enjoy?

    Freedom to own land, raise crops of his choice, make decisions about how he wanted to live. He enjoyed the rights of life, liberty, and property.

3. Do you think he would favor a law that does not permit people to buy or sell what they choose? Why?

    Probably not, because he enjoyed the freedom of making his own decisions about what he bought and sold.

4. Do you think he would favor a law that gave people rights because they were wealthy? Why?

    Probably not, because he believed he had an equal chance to better himself through hard work and careful planning. If only wealthy people had certain rights, he might not be able to improve his life.

5. Do you think he would favor a law that gave people rights because of their family or group to which they belonged? Why?

    No, because he stated that he enjoyed not having to raise his cap, in other words, to be considered a less important person than someone who happens to be from a higher social class. However, he might favor laws that gave rights to white men owning property since he was a white man who owned property.

6. What did he mean when he said, "Neither is my cap worn out from lifting it in the presence of gentlemen."?

    Philip Taylor's response illustrates the absence of social class in the colonies, unlike society in Great Britain.

Ideas to discuss

What opportunities did this colonial farmer enjoy?

One farmer who wrote about his life in the colonies was Philip Taylor. Read what he wrote. Work with a partner to answer the questions that follow. Be prepared to share your ideas with the class.

We now have a comfortable dwelling. We have two acres of land planted with potatoes, corn, and melons. I have two hogs, one ewe and her lamb. The price of cows in the spring was as high as 33 dollars. No doubt, I shall have one by fall.

I am living in God's noble and free soil, neither am I slave to others... I have now been on American soil for two and one-half years and I have not been compelled to pay for the privilege of living. Neither is my cap worn out from lifting it in the presence of gentlemen.

1. What did Philip Taylor like about life in America?

2. What rights did he enjoy?

3. Do you think he would favor a law that does not permit people to buy or sell what they choose? Why?

4. Do you think he would favor a law that gives people more rights because they are wealthy? Why?

5. Do you think he would favor a law that gives people rights because of their family or the group to which they belong? Why?

6. What did he mean when he said, "Neither is my cap worn out from lifting it in the presence of gentlemen"?

Who governed the colonies?

The American colonies were ruled by Great Britain from 1607 to 1776, more than 150 years. George III was king of Great Britain from 1760 to 1820. During much of this time, Great Britain was busy with problems in Europe. The British government did not pay much attention to the colonies. The American colonies learned to govern themselves. They had brought British customs and laws with them to America. They used these British ideas to develop their own governments. The colonists participated in their governments much more than people did in Europe.

During the 1770s, Americans thought about what kind of government they wanted. The colonists asked themselves if King George III was really protecting their rights. There were many arguments, speeches, and books about what was best for the colonies. If you had lived in America then, you would have found it an exciting time.

Who were the Founders?

There were many important leaders in early America. For example, George Washington, Patrick Henry, Abigail Adams, and Benjamin Franklin were all well known during this time.

▶ Did the colonists like being ruled by King George III? Why, or why not?

You probably have heard of these people. We call these leaders the **Founders** because they helped found, or establish, our country.

The Founders led the fight to free our country from British rule. They developed their own ideas about what type of government would be best for America. The next lessons will help you understand the ideas the Founders used to create our government.

11

READING AND DISCUSSION

Who governed the colonies?

Who were the Founders?

Have students read both sections. Hold a whole class discussion. Use the guidelines below.

- What were the effects of British policy, which ignored the colonies for most of this period?
- Think about what might happen if Britain had decided to tighten its control.
- Why do you think most of the Founders were men?

 see next student page

LESSON REVIEW

The questions in the student book are intended to assess learning and to reinforce knowledge through discussion. The questions are directly related to the lesson objectives. You may wish to include additional questions developed by yourself or by students.

1. What was life like for the average American colonist?
   Most colonists were farmers. On small farms, families did all the work themselves. On plantations slaves did the work. Because there was a lot of land and people could grow crops easily, the colonists ate well and were healthier than people in Europe. Most colonists could read and most white men were allowed to vote. Colonists in America had the freedom to follow their religious beliefs.

2. Why did so many Europeans want to come to live in the colonies?
   Land was cheap and available. By this time, religious diversity had become an important part of colonial life. Freedom of religion had replaced persecution and people from all over the world wanted to experience it. Colonial immigrants also believed they had a chance to better themselves economically and socially because wealth and family name were not as important in the colonies as they were in the Old World.

11

3. How might living in the colonies help to influence people's ideas about government?

People came to the American colonies to escape oppression in homelands ruled by monarchies. The colonists believed they had more freedom and rights than Europeans. They could make independent decisions about how to govern themselves because they were so far from Great Britain. Many colonists had ideas about government that differed from the ideas held in Great Britain and the rest of Europe. The colonists heard and discussed these ideas openly with one another.

4. What is the meaning of the term, "the Founders"?

The term refers to the people who founded, or established, the new country.

ACTIVITIES

The suggested activities are intended to extend and apply learning outside the classroom. You may have students complete one or more activities. Have them share the results with the class.

ADDITIONAL INSTRUCTIONAL ACTIVITY

Have a group of students write and present a play for their classmates. Each student should play the role of a person living in the colonies, for example: a property owner, a woman, an enslaved person, a farmer, or children of any of the above, etc.

The actors should describe their lives in America to a European who is thinking about emigrating to the colonies. One student should play the European. He or she may ask the other students questions that will provide desired information about what to expect if he or she moves to America.

Review the lesson

1. What was life like for the average American colonist?

2. Why did so many Europeans want to come to live in the colonies?

3. How might living in the colonies help to influence people's ideas about government?

4. What is the meaning of the term, "the Founders"?

Activities to do

1. Write a short story about how the colonists' American way of life might have influenced their ideas about government. Share your story with the class.

2. Go to your library or use your computer. Find information about one of the following topics:

   - What was life like for children in the colonies?

   - What was life like for Native Americans in the colonies?

   - What was life like for women in the colonies?

   - What was life like for slaves in the Southern Colonies?

   - What was life like for indentured servants?

   Share what you learned with your class.

3. Find a map of the United States today. Locate the original thirteen colonies. What were the names of the thirteen colonies? Which ones were New England Colonies, Middle Colonies, and Southern Colonies?

4. On a map of the United States, locate your state. Was your state originally a British colony? Was it a French or Spanish colony? What American Indian tribes lived there before the Europeans came? When did your state become part of the United States?

Lesson 2

Why did the Founders believe that people needed a government?

Purpose of the lesson

In this lesson, you will learn some of the Founders' most important ideas about our basic rights. You will learn the Founders' beliefs about where these rights come from. Finally, you will learn why the Founders believed that people must have government.

When you finish this lesson, you should be able to explain the Founders' ideas about our rights and the purposes of our government.

13

OVERVIEW

This lesson introduces the basic concept of the natural rights philosophy. Even though students may not be familiar with terms used to describe the philosophy, they will readily understand the ideas, if they can be related to their experiences.

Since many of the ideas in the remaining lessons are based on the concepts presented in Lesson 2, teachers will want to devote extra time to ensuring that students understand these ideas.

Students are asked to compare their own beliefs about rights with the beliefs held by the Founders. They learn that natural rights are the rights to life, liberty, and property and that the Founders were concerned about how to protect those rights.

Students explore what life might be like without any rules or laws and then compare their ideas with the ideas of John Locke. They learn how Locke influenced the thinking of the Founders and why the Founders believed that all societies need a government.

OBJECTIVES

At the conclusion of this lesson, students should be able to

- explain the Founders' beliefs about natural rights
- explain what problems might occur in a world without rules or laws and compare their own ideas with those of the Founders
- explain the influence of John Locke on the thinking of the Founders
- explain why the Founders believed that every society needs a government

TEACHING PROCEDURES

INTRODUCTORY ACTIVITIES

Have students read the "Purpose of the lesson" section and consider the objectives of the lesson.

- consent
- consent of the governed
- liberty
- life
- natural rights
- property
- social contract
- state of nature

LESSON 2

Write the "Terms to understand" on the board or use a vocabulary-building activity of your choice. The definitions for these words are in the glossary at the end of the student book. Direct students to look for these terms as they study the lesson.

IDEAS TO DISCUSS

What are your beliefs about rights?

Organize students into groups of three to five. Read the section to the class, allowing time for questions.

Ask each group to develop answers to the three questions in the activity and to write the answers on chart paper. Each group should select a recorder, to do the writing, and a reporter, to report the group's responses to the rest of the class. Each group should post its chart on the wall.

As students report their ideas, you may wish to keep a tally of the rights listed by students as rights that people should have. After all groups have reported, compare the lists of the various groups and ask students

- to state the similarities and differences among the groups' lists of rights
- how many, if any, groups chose the same right as most important

1. List the rights you think you should have.
   Why do you think it is important to have these rights?
   Some things they might list are the following: to go where you want to go; say, think, and do what you want; to choose your friends; to listen to music you like; to attend the church of your choice; to read the books you choose; to have privacy; and to be left alone when you are not doing anything wrong. These rights are important because they ensure the quality of life of the American people, and they ensure that people feel safe in their society.

2. Which rights seem most important?
   Arrange the rights you listed in order. Place the most important first.

3. Why do you think these rights are the most important?
   Accept reasonable responses.

4. Do you think people everywhere should have these rights?
   Why or why not?
   Accept reasonable responses.

Ideas to discuss

What are your beliefs about rights?

Before you learn about the Founders' beliefs about rights, let's examine your own ideas about rights. Then you can compare your ideas with theirs. You will probably find that you and the Founders have many of the same ideas.

Do you think you should have the right to believe in any religion you wish? Do you think you should have the right to speak freely?

Work with a partner or in a group of three to five students. Together answer the questions that follow. Be prepared to share your ideas with the class.

1. List the rights you think you should have. Why do you think it is important to have these rights?

2. Which rights seem most important? Arrange the rights you listed in order. Place the most important first. Why do you think these rights are the most important?

3. Do you think people everywhere should have these rights? Why or why not?

▶ What rights do all of these people have? Why do you think they have these rights?

Terms to understand

consent	natural rights
consent of the governed	property
liberty	social contract
life	state of nature

What were the Founders' beliefs about rights?

Most of the Founders believed that people have certain natural rights. Natural rights include the rights to life, liberty, and property. All persons have **natural rights** just because they are human beings. Everyone is born with these rights. No one can take these rights away. Here is what these natural rights mean.

- **Life** is the right to live without fear of being injured or killed by others.

- **Liberty** is the right to be free. Some examples of liberties are the rights to believe what you wish, to read what you want, to speak freely, and to travel wherever you want to go.

- **Property** is the right to own things such as books, a house, land, or a business. Your labor or work is also your property.

▶ *What natural rights do all people have from the time they are born?*

READING AND DISCUSSION

What were the Founders beliefs about rights?

Ask a student to read the section aloud to the class. Discuss the terms life, liberty, property, and natural rights, to be sure that students understand and can explain their meaning. You may want to ask students to think of a specific example of each concept from their own experience.

Compare the rights identified by students in the preceding activity with the natural rights identified by the Founders. Discuss the similarities and differences between the beliefs of the Founders and their own. You may wish to ask students to hypothesize as to why these similarities and differences exist.

What problems might we have protecting our rights?

Ask students to read the next section and find its main idea. Ask them why the Founders had the foresight to try to protect their own rights and the rights of others. Ask them if they think that protecting the rights of others is harder than protecting their own rights. If so, why?

▶ *Do you agree with John Locke's ideas? Why?*

What problems might we have protecting our rights?

The Founders knew that protecting the rights of the people was not an easy thing to do. Sometimes people try to take the rights of others away from them. The Founders thought they should have a plan to protect their own rights and the rights of others.

Many Founders had read a book by John Locke. John Locke was an Englishman. He lived from 1632 to 1704. Locke wrote about natural rights. His ideas help us to understand more clearly the problem of protecting the rights of people.

John Locke suggested that you imagine living in a state of nature. **A state of nature** is a situation where there is no government, no rules, no laws. Think about what your life might be like in a state of nature.

16

Ideas to discuss

What might happen if there were no rules, laws, or government?

Imagine that you live on an island far away. There are no rules, no laws, and no government. There is no one to tell you what to do.

Work with a partner or in a group of three to five students.

Together answer the following questions. Be prepared to share your ideas with the class.

1. Would anyone have the right to govern you? Would you have the right to govern anyone else? Why?

2. Would you have any rights? What might they be?

3. What might people who were smarter or stronger than others try to do? Why?

4. What might people who were not as smart as others or who were weaker than others try to do? Why?

5. What might life be like for you, your family, and everyone else in a state of nature?

▶ *What would life be like without any government? How would people protect their rights?*

17

IDEAS TO DISCUSS

What might happen if there were no rules, laws, or government?

Read the section with the class and then organize students into groups of three to five. Each group should develop answers to the five questions.

Each group member should write down her or his group's responses and be responsible for stating aloud the response to one question. In this way, all members will focus on the group discussion and be prepared for the class discussion.

Have groups share their responses with the class. You may wish to have students in each group share experiences in which a problem arose because there were no rules or people to enforce them. You might ask them to share their experiences with the class.

Possible responses to the five questions follow.

1. Would anyone have the right to govern you?
   Would you have the right to govern anyone else?
   No. The right to govern would have to be established by some means such as the rules of tradition, culture, law, or consent.

2. Would you have any rights? What might they be?
   You would have the right to do whatever you wanted. However, this right would only last until someone stopped you from doing it. In fact, your rights would not be secure.

3. What might people who were smarter or stronger than others try to do? Why?
   People could take things from you, or beat you up if they wanted to. People might come into your house and steal personal belongings. There might not be enough food because some people might steal or hide it. Someone bigger might force you to do something you did not want to do.

4. What might people who were not as smart or stronger than others try to do? Why?
   Group with others to protect one another. They might band together for power over the strong.

5. What might life be like for you, your family, and everyone else in a state of nature?

There might be some good things because you could do what you wanted to do. However, if everybody could do whatever he or she wanted, you would not be safe or secure or protected from harm.

READING AND DISCUSSION

What did John Locke say might happen if there were no rules, laws, or government?

After students read the section, ask them to compare their lists of problems from the previous "Ideas to discuss" exercise with those enumerated by John Locke. Ask them to underline or highlight, on their list, those problems that were identified by themselves and John Locke.

▶ *How does this artist's view of life in a state of nature differ from that of John Locke?*
Edward Hicks, The Peaceable Kingdom, © 1840, Holger Cahill Collection

What did John Locke say might happen if there were no rules, laws, or government?

You just had a chance to think about your rights in a state of nature. Now, you might want to compare your thinking with that of John Locke. Locke thought that life would be very difficult without laws or government. He worried about the problems that might happen. He said:

1. Some people might try to take away other people's rights. The stronger people might force the weaker people to do the things the stronger people want. The weaker people might unite against the stronger people.

2. People would have natural rights, but their rights would not be safe.

3. It would be very hard to live a safe, peaceful, and happy life in a state of nature.

Why did the Founders believe we needed a government?

John Locke wrote about how to solve the problems of life in a state of nature. He said people could make a social contract. A **social contract** is an agreement among the people to set up a government. The people agree to give up something and then they receive something in return.

The people give up some of their freedom. They **consent**, or agree, to create a government and laws. The **consent of the governed** means that the people consent to obey the laws and the government they create. The people no longer will be able to do whatever they want.

What the people gain is protection for their rights. The government protects the rights of the people. It protects their rights to life, liberty, and property. People would feel safer than they did in a state of nature. The people might live more secure and happier lives.

The Founders believed that people need government to protect their rights. Therefore, the main purpose of government, they said, is to protect a person's rights to life, liberty, and property.

▶ How do citizens show their consent to be governed?

19

Why did the Founders believe we needed a government?

Discuss the ideas that influenced the Founders in their belief that the main purpose of government is to protect a person's rights to life, liberty, and property. Make sure students understand the concept of "social contract" and the meaning of the word "consent" and how the two terms relate. You may wish to engage students in a discussion regarding how the concepts of social contract and consent can be applied in their classroom.

LESSON REVIEW

The questions in the student book are intended to assess learning and to reinforce knowledge through discussion. The questions are directly related to the lesson objectives. You may wish to include additional questions developed by yourself or by students.

1. What basic rights did the Founders believe people should have?
   They believed that all people were entitled to have their natural rights to life, liberty, and property.

2. What are natural rights? How do you get natural rights?
   Some of the most important natural rights are the right to life, the right to live without being injured or killed by others. Liberty, the right to be free—think, believe, read what you want and to speak freely. Property, the right to own things. You get these rights by virtue of being human.

3. What might life be like if there were no rules, laws, or government?
   Everybody would do what he or she wanted without respect for other people's rights. People would not be safe from harm or secure in their homes.

4. What is a social contract?
   A social contract is an agreement among the people. In a social contract the people agree to set up a government, obey its laws, and give up some things to receive protection of their rights.

5. What did the Founders think should be the main purpose of government?
   The Founders thought the main purpose of government should be to protect a person's rights to life, liberty, and property.

LESSON 2

ACTIVITIES

The suggested activities are intended to extend and apply learning outside the classroom. You may wish to have students complete one or more of the activities. Then, have them share the results with the class.

ENRICHMENT ACTIVITIES

Have students keep a list of the times that they see people's rights violated during a one-week period. They might include situations seen at school, on television, in newspapers, or in the community. Ask them to identify the right involved and explain why they believe that right was violated.

Review the lesson

1. What basic rights did the Founders believe people should have?

2. What are natural rights? How do you get natural rights?

3. What might life be like if there were no rules, laws, or government?

4. What is a social contract?

5. What did the Founders think should be the main purpose of government?

Activities to do

1. Write a paragraph explaining what life might be like in a state of nature and why we need government. Draw a cartoon to illustrate your main points.

2. Write a short story that tells how the rights to life, liberty, and property apply to you and your family. Share your story with the class.

3. Go to the library or use your computer to learn more about John Locke and his ideas. Share what you learned with the class.

4. Read the Mayflower Compact. What are the three main things the signers of the compact agreed to do? Explain how the Mayflower Compact is an example of a social contract. Share what you learned with your class.

Lesson 3

What is a republican government?

Purpose of the lesson

The Founders gained some of their ideas about government from studying history. They used this knowledge when they created our government. In this lesson, you will learn what the Founders thought about government.

When you have finished this lesson, you should be able to explain some of the advantages of a republican government.

OVERVIEW

Many of the ideas that influenced the Founders originated with the governments of the Roman Republic and the American colonies. This lesson provides students the opportunity to explore the meaning of republican government, direct democracy, common good, and civic virtue. Ask students to consider how these ideas, as they were practiced in ancient Rome and in the American colonies, influenced the thinking and behavior of the Founders.

The lesson opens with a discussion of where the Founders learned their ideas about government and how people rule themselves. Next, the lesson provides a description of republican government, the characteristics of this form of government, and the kind of citizens that make the form of government work well. Students engage in a problem-solving activity that examines the characteristics of civic virtue.

LESSON OBJECTIVES

At the conclusion of the lesson, students should be able to

- explain the differences between republican government and a direct democracy
- explain why the Founders thought republican government was the best type of government
- discuss the importance of the concepts of common good and civic virtue

TEACHING PROCEDURES

INTRODUCTORY ACTIVITY

Have students read the "Purpose of the lesson" section and consider the objectives of the lesson.

Write the "Terms to understand" on the board, or use a vocabulary-building activity of your choice. You may wish to have students look up the words in the glossary at the back of their text

- civic virtue
- common good
- direct democracy
- interests

- represent
- representatives
- republican government
- Roman Republic

READING AND DISCUSSION

Where did the Founders get their ideas about government?

How can the people rule themselves?

Have students read the first section aloud. Call upon individual students to read the next section. Make sure that they understand the principle of direct democracy, the purpose of representatives, and the elements of republican government.

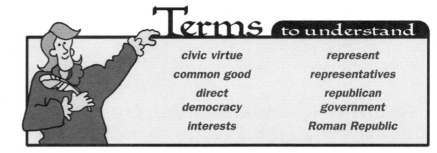

Terms to understand

civic virtue	represent
common good	representatives
direct democracy	republican government
interests	Roman Republic

Where did the Founders get their ideas about government?

The Founders studied the history of government. They knew how people in the ancient world governed themselves. The Founders liked what they read about the Roman Republic. The **Roman Republic** existed more than 2,000 years ago. Rome was the capital of the republic. Today Rome is the capital of Italy.

▶ *How many places in your everyday life do you see the word "republic"?*

A king did not rule the Roman Republic. The citizens of Rome ruled themselves. The Founders were curious about how people could rule themselves. The Founders used some of the ideas they learned from the Romans to create our government. Let's examine some of these ideas.

How can the people rule themselves?

In many of the American colonies, people lived in small towns. If there was a problem in the community, the leaders called a town meeting. The people of the town came to the meeting. They talked about the problem and decided what was best for their town. A town meeting is a form of direct democracy. **Direct democracy** means that the people themselves decide what laws they need. As communities grow larger, it becomes harder to make decisions in town meetings.

Sometimes the people choose **representatives** to make the decisions for them. This is what the people in the Roman Republic did. The government of Rome was called a republican government. The Founders read that **republican government** was one in which

- The people hold the power of government

- The people give power to leaders they elect to **represent** them and to serve their **interests**

- The representatives are responsible for helping all the people in the country, not just a few people

▷ Why would elections be an important part of a republican government?

Why did the Founders like the idea of a republican government?

These are some things that the Founders believed were advantages to a republican government.

- **Representatives are selected to serve the common good.** Representatives do not help just one person, such as a king. They do not help just one favored group of people, such as the rich or the poor. Representatives make laws to help everyone.

- **Having representatives make the laws is more efficient.** In a direct democracy, everyone helps make the laws. Making laws takes time. The people have to study

23

Why did the Founders like the idea of a republican government?
Have students read the sections to themselves. Review each advantage of republican government listed. Explain the difference between a capital "R" Republican (political party) and small "r" republican (type of government).

What is the common good?

Write the word "common good" on the board and discuss the meaning of each word and the entire phrase. Emphasize with students that "common welfare" and "common good" have the same meaning. Ask students to cite examples of the common good in their own classroom, school, and community.

What kinds of citizens make a republican government work well?

After students read the section, discuss the meaning and importance of civic virtue. Ask students why they think civic virtue is necessary in a republican form of government. Ask them to provide some examples of civic virtue in their own lives.

---

every problem to make good and fair laws. People do not have time. They have to earn a living. Representatives can make laws faster and better because it is their job.

- **The people have a say in their government.** The people do not give up their voice in government. They decide who will represent them. The people can tell their representatives what they want them to do.

- **The representatives have to listen to the people.** The people expect their representatives to make good and fair laws. If the representatives do not make good and fair laws, the people can vote them out of office. The people can choose new leaders to represent them.

What is the common good?

The main purpose of republican government is to promote the common good. The **common good** means what is best for the community as a whole. When a government tries to help everyone in a country, we say it is serving the common good. The common good is what is good for everyone in the country, not just a few people.

▶ Cesar Chavez used nonviolent actions to improve working conditions for farm workers. Is this an example of serving the common good? Why or why not?

What kinds of citizens make a republican government work well?

When you work to help others and promote the common good, you are showing **civic virtue**. The Founders thought that people must have civic virtue for a republican government to work. People with civic virtue are interested in having their government help all the people.

The Founders felt it was necessary to teach children the importance of helping others. Young people learned about civic virtue in their homes, schools, and churches. Adults also heard about civic virtue from their religious and political leaders.

The Founders thought a republican government would work in the new country. They believed that most of the people had civic virtue. They thought the people would select leaders who would work for the common good.

Ideas to discuss

How can we decide what is for the common good?

How do you decide what the common good is? When should you give up your own interests to do something that is good for everyone? Each one of us has to answer this question personally. The following exercise will help you do this.

Work with a partner. Discuss the questions. Be prepared to share your ideas with the class.

1. What might be a situation in your school in which you should try to do what is best for everyone?

2. What might be a situation in your school in which you should do something for yourself and not try to help others?

3. People often do not agree about what is best for everyone. Describe a situation in your school where people might disagree. How would you decide what the common good is in this situation?

4. What are some things that leaders in your school should do to promote the common good?

▶ How are these students promoting the common good at their school?

25

IDEAS TO DISCUSS

How can we decide what is for the common good?

Have students work with a partner and discuss the four questions. Then ask the partners to share their ideas with the class. Student responses should be specific to their school, but accept any reasonable response. Possible answers are suggested.

1. What might be a situation in your school in which you should try to do what is best for everyone?
   Students should help keep the school grounds clean, follow the school rules, obey the crossing guards, help keep the classroom orderly, etc.

2. What might be a situation in your school in which you should do something for yourself and not try to help others?
   Accept any reasonable response.

3. People often do not agree on what is best for everyone. Describe a situation in your school where people might disagree. How would you decide what the common good is in this situation?
   Accept any reasonable response.

4. What are some things that leaders in your school should do to promote the common good?
   Accept any reasonable response.

PROBLEM TO SOLVE

Why is civic virtue important?

Read the activity with the class. Then divide the class into groups of three to five. Ask each group to prepare responses to the five questions. When reporting responses to the class, ask that each student in the group be responsible for answering one of the questions aloud to the class.

Suggested possible responses:

1. In the story, what was the common good for the citizens of Rome?
   The citizens needed to protect Rome from the enemy that was burning and looting the countryside.

2. What self-interests did Cincinnatus have in this story?
   Cincinnatus owned only four acres of land and he needed to plow his fields to feed his family.

3. Do you think Cincinnatus had civic virtue? Why or why not?
   Yes, he had civic virtue. He wanted to protect his country, so he left his farm and family and went to Rome to lead the army.

4. Why is it important that citizens in a republican government have civic virtue?
   If a republican government is to work well, the citizens have to have civic virtue. They must be willing to put their personal interests aside for a time and work to make life better for everyone.

5. Describe someone you know who has civic virtue. What did the person do to cause you to think he or she has civic virtue?
   Accept any reasonable answer.

Problem to solve

Why is civic virtue important?

Read the story of "Cincinnatus, Citizen of Rome." Work in a group of three to five students. Answer the questions that follow the story. Be prepared to share your responses with the class.

Cincinnatus, Citizen of Rome

In the year 460 B.C., Rome was in great danger. The enemy surrounded the army of Rome on all sides. They were burning and looting the countryside.

The leaders of the Roman government called for a meeting. They decided to ask a farmer named Cincinnatus to help them during the crisis. Cincinnatus was a hard worker. He owned four acres of land on which to grow food to feed his family.

Cincinnatus once had been a skilled leader of the army. The government sent messengers to find him. When the messengers arrived, he was quietly plowing the fields. They asked him to serve as ruler of Rome for as long as the crisis might last.

▶ What would you have done if you were Cincinnatus? Why?

▶ *If Cincinnatus had remained as ruler of Rome, would he be practicing civic virtue? Why or why not?*

Cincinnatus loved his country. He left his plow to go to Rome to lead the army. In a battle that lasted two days, his army defeated the enemy. Cincinnatus saved the country.

The people of Rome honored and praised Cincinnatus. When the battle was over, he did not try to remain as a ruler of his country. He did not want power and fame. Instead, he returned to his home and his life as a farmer and an ordinary citizen.

1. In the story, what was the common good for the citizens of Rome?

2. What self-interests did Cincinnatus have in this story?

3. Do you think Cincinnatus had civic virtue? Why or why not?

4. Why is it important that citizens in a republican government have civic virtue?

5. Describe someone you know who has civic virtue. What did the person do to cause you to think she or he has civic virtue?

27

 see next student page

LESSON REVIEW

The questions in the student book are intended to assess learning and to reinforce knowledge through discussion. The questions are directly related to the lesson objectives. You may wish to include additional questions developed by yourself or by students.

1. What is a republican government? How is it different from a direct democracy?

   In a republican government the people choose representatives to make decisions for them. In a direct democracy, however, the people make the decisions themselves.

2. What are representatives in a republican government supposed to do?

   The representatives act and speak for the people. They make laws for all the people. They work for the common good.

3. What are the advantages of a republican government?

   The representatives serve the common good, not just one person or group, they are able to make laws efficiently, they allow people to have a say in their government, they study and read about the issues that affect the people because they have the time to do so.

4. What is the role of citizens in a republican government?

   The citizens should participate in their government and do things to promote the common good.

5. Define the term common good. Give examples of the common good in your school, community, and country.

   Common good means doing what is best for the whole community. Accept reasonable examples.

6. Define the term civic virtue. Why is it important that citizens have civic virtue?

   Civic virtue means to put the common good before your own interests. Citizens must have civic virtue for a republican government to work.

LESSON 3

ACTIVITIES

The suggested activities are intended to extend and apply learning outside of the classroom. You may wish to have students complete one or more of the activities. Then, have them share the results with the class.

Review the lesson

1. What is a republican government? How is it different from a direct democracy?

2. What are representatives in a republican government supposed to do?

3. What are the advantages of a republican government?

4. What is the role of citizens in a republican government?

5. Define the term common good. Give examples of the common good in your school, community, and country.

6. Define the term civic virtue. Why is it important that citizens have civic virtue?

Activities to do

1. What is a town meeting like? Hold a town meeting in your class to make rules for your classroom. Find a book in your library or use the computer to learn how to conduct a town meeting. Do you think it would be a good idea to hold a town meeting of your whole school to make school rules? Why or why not? Share what you learned with the class.

2. Use a dictionary. What is the difference between republican and Republican? What is the difference between democrat and Democrat? Draw a cartoon that illustrates how the terms are different. Share your work with the class.

3. As a class, write a letter or choose a representative to make a telephone call to a member of your town, city, or tribal council. Ask the council member to explain some things he or she does to promote the common good of your community. Ask if there has been a time when people's self-interest conflicted with what was thought to be the common good. What happened?

4. Make a list of things that students in your classroom can do to promote the common good in your school. What can you do to promote the common good in your neighborhood or community?

Lesson 4

What is a constitutional government?

Purpose of the lesson

You have learned what the Founders believed about natural rights, the common good, and civic virtue. In this lesson, there are two other important things to study and understand. The first is a constitution and the other is constitutional government. You will learn to explain the difference between the two.

When you have finished this lesson, you should be able to explain what you can learn about a nation by studying its constitution. You should also be able to explain what constitutional government means. Finally, you should be able to explain the difference between a constitutional government and a dictatorial government.

29

OVERVIEW

This lesson introduces students to key concepts useful in understanding the Founders' ideas about government. Students learn the meaning of the term "constitution" and what distinguishes a constitution from other rules and laws. They examine the essential characteristics that differentiate constitutional government from dictatorial government. They learn that in a constitutional government the powers of the person or group running the government are limited by a constitution that must be obeyed. Through a problem-solving activity based on an adapted excerpt from *Two Years Before the Mast*, by Richard Henry Dana, students learn about the dangers of a government with unlimited power.

OBJECTIVES

At the conclusion of this lesson, students should be able to

- define "constitution" and "constitutional government"
- explain the differences between a constitutional government and a dictatorial government
- explain the importance of limiting the powers of government

TEACHING PROCEDURES

INTRODUCTORY ACTIVITY

Have students read the "Purpose of the lesson" section and consider the objectives of the lesson.

Write the "Terms to understand" on the board, or use a vocabulary-building activity of your choice. You may wish to have students look up the words in the glossary at the back of their text.

- constitution
- constitutional government
- dictatorial government
- limit

PROBLEM TO SOLVE

Which rules or laws are about government?

Divide the class into groups of three to five students.
Read the instructions to the class.

Ask each group to make a chart with two columns on a piece of paper, or use student handout D 1. They should complete the chart as a group with each member contributing. When the groups are finished, call on students to help you fill out a similar chart drawn on the board. Ask each student to explain how and why they classified each rule and law.

RULES AND LAWS	
Explains something about how a government is to be run	**Does not explain anything about how a government is to be run**
1. law – how the federal government must protect your rights	**2.** family rule or good manners rule
5. law – how a government chooses and limits the power of its leaders – they are elected by the people for a limited time	**3.** playground rule or good manners rule
6. law – regulates and protects society	**4.** school rule

Problem to solve

Which rules and laws are about government?

Complete this exercise in groups of three to five students. Be prepared to explain your findings to the class.

Read the list of rules and laws. For each rule or law, follow these instructions. Your teacher will give you a chart. On the chart, write the number of each rule or law that explains something about how a government is to be run. Be prepared to explain the rule or law and what it regulates.

Then, write the number of each rule or law that does not explain something about how a government is to be run.

Rules and laws

1. Congress cannot make any laws that unfairly limit your right to speak freely.

2. Don't speak with your mouth full.

3. Take turns on the swings on the playground.

4. You must finish your assignment before you go out for recess.

5. The president must be elected every four years.

6. A person must be sixteen to get a driver's license.

▶ *Why is it important to know how a government is organized and how it operates?*

Terms to understand

constitution

constitutional government

dictatorial government

limit

What is a constitution?

In the previous exercise, you should have found some rules and laws that explain how a government is to be run. You also should have found some rules that do not have anything to do with how a government should be run.

When you found the rules and laws that tell how a government should be run, you found parts of a constitution. A **constitution** is a set of rules and laws that explain how a government is organized and how it should be run. Most constitutions are written. Some are partly unwritten. Some are not written at all. According to our definition, every nation has a constitution. Fair governments and unfair governments have constitutions.

Studying the constitution of a government will help you answer certain questions about that government and its citizens. Here are some of the questions a constitution usually answers.

Questions about the government

- What are the purposes of the government?

- How is the government organized? What parts does it have? What does each part do?

- How is the government supposed to carry out its business? How are rules made?

- How are people chosen to serve in the government?

Questions about citizens

- Who is a citizen?

- Are citizens supposed to have control over their government? If so, how do they control it?

- What rights and responsibilities, if any, are citizens supposed to have?

READING AND DISCUSSION

What is a constitution?

Read aloud and help students answer the two sets of questions about government and citizens. Help students understand that these are questions that all constitutions address. Hence, every nation has a constitution, whether the government is fair or unfair.

What is a constitutional government?

Have students read the section. Discuss the idea that a constitutional government is one in which there are limits on the powers of the people running the government. Furthermore, in a constitutional government, there must be ways to ensure that these limits are obeyed. Make sure that they understand that having a constitution is not the same thing as having a constitutional government.

Lead students in a discussion about rights and the role of a government. Ask students why the Founders believed a constitutional government was the best way to protect people's basic rights.

What is a dictatorial government?

Have students read the section aloud. Ask them to make a list of the differences between constitutional and dictatorial governments. Ask students to explain how limits make a government constitutional or dictatorial.

What is a constitutional government?

Just because a nation has a constitution does not mean it has a constitutional government. A **constitutional government** means that there are limits on the powers of government. A **limit** is a point beyond which someone or something cannot go. The United States Constitution says there are certain kinds of laws that Congress cannot make. The Constitution does not permit the president to do whatever he or she wants to do. In a constitutional government, the constitution sets limits on what the people who run the government are allowed to do.

It is not enough for a constitution to say what the limits on the powers

How do elections help limit the power of government?

of government are. The people who run the government must obey the constitution. A constitution also must provide ways to enforce the limits it sets forth. One way is to have regular and free elections. The citizens can vote to remove people from office if they do not obey the constitution.

What is a dictatorial government?

A **dictatorial government** means that there are no limits on the power of the people who run the government. They can do whatever they want to do.

Can you have a constitution and still have a dictatorial government? The answer is yes. A constitution might give a person unlimited power. The constitution might limit power but not have ways to enforce those limits. There might be ways to enforce the limits, but no one actually does.

Why is it important to limit the power of those who run the government?

Hitler came to power legally in 1933. He disregarded the German Constitution and opened the first concentration camp within six weeks.

32

Participating in a class activity

Why is it important to limit a government's powers?

You have learned that constitutional governments have limits on their powers. Why do we need such limits? The following story might help you understand why. It is based on a section from a book called *Two Years Before the Mast*. Richard Henry Dana (1815–1882), a famous American author, wrote the book.

It is a true story about Dana's experiences. When he was young, he worked on a ship that sailed from New England around South America to the West Coast.

▶ What would you have done if you were Sam? Why?

At that time there were no laws that placed reasonable limits on the powers of a ship's captain. Because of this story and the efforts of other people, laws were passed to limit the powers of captains.

When you have finished reading, work in groups of three to five students to answer the questions at the end of the story.

Life on a Sailing Ship

The Captain of our ship had been losing his temper frequently. He threatened to whip the cook for throwing food on the deck. He got furious when the mate bragged that he could tie knots better than the Captain could. Most of his anger, however, was directed against Sam.

Sam couldn't speak clearly, and he worked more slowly than the others. Still, he was a good sailor, and he tried to do his best. The Captain just didn't like him.

One Saturday morning, I heard the Captain shouting at someone. Then I heard the noise of a fight.

"You may as well keep still, for I have got you," said the Captain. "Will you ever talk back to me again?"

"I never did, sir," said Sam.

PARTICIPATING IN A CLASS ACTIVITY

Why is it important to limit a government's power?

Begin by having students brainstorm examples of powers that are being abused, for example: cheating, stealing someone's lunch money, bullying. Then, read the introduction to the activity with the class.

Have students read the story "Life on a Sailing Ship," which is part of the activity. Divide the class into five groups with each group taking one role: **Naval Review Board**, **Captain**, **Crew**, **Owners of the ships**, and **Author and friends**. The groups should then prepare a presentation about limiting the power of the ship's captain to give before the Naval Review Board. The group should explain its ideas from the point of view of the role they are playing. Each group should also prepare to answer questions from the Naval Review Board.

For the actual hearing, the president of the Naval Review Board will start the meeting. Each group will have 4 minutes to explain its position to the board. After each presentation, the Board members may ask questions of the group. Encourage all members of the group to participate in answering these questions. After hearing all the groups, the Naval Review Board should meet and decide what to do based on the information presented in the hearing.

Debrief

After the hearing, hold a debriefing session with the class. Use the "Talking it over" questions as the basis for the class debriefing.

1. In the story, was the government of the ship more like a constitutional government or a dictatorial government? Why?

    The government resembled a dictatorial government because there were no limits on the powers of the ship's captain.

2. What were the strongest arguments the shipowners and captains made against limiting a captain's power?

    Make sure that responses are specific to the arguments presented by the students during this simulation.

3. What were the strongest arguments the crew and the author made in favor of limiting a captain's power?

    Make sure that responses are specific to the arguments presented by the students during this simulation.

4. Do you agree with the decision of the Naval Review Board? Why?

    Accept any reasonable response.

5. Did the decision of the Naval Review Board help to protect the rights of sailors? If so, how?

    Accept any reasonable response.

6. Why do you think it is important to have a constitutional government?

    A constitutional government places limits on what the government can and cannot do. It limits the power of the government.

Participating in a class activity

"That's not what I asked you. Will you ever talk back to me again?"

"I never have," Sam said again.

"Answer my question, or I'll have you whipped!"

"I'm no slave," said Sam.

"Then I'll make you one," said the Captain. He sprang up to the deck and called the mate. "Tie that man up! I'll teach you all who is master of this ship!"

"Why are you going to whip that man, sir?" asked John.

Upon hearing this, the Captain turned to John and ordered him to be put in chains.

Watching this made me sick. I wanted to stop it. There were only a few others who felt as I did. If we tried to free John and Sam, we would lose. Then we would be accused of mutiny. Even if we won, we would have to be pirates for life. If we were ever caught, we would be punished. A sailor has no rights. He has to do what the Captain orders or become a pirate.

The Captain whipped both men without mercy. When John asked why he was being whipped, the Captain answered, "Because you ask questions." Then he whipped him harder and harder.

▶ *Should the powers of a ship's captain be limited? Why?*

I was horrified. I couldn't watch any more.

At last the Captain stopped. He turned to us. "Now you see how things are! Now you know what I am! I'm the slave driver, and you are all my slaves! I'll make you all do as I say, or I'll whip you all!"

CLASS ACTIVITY

The year is 1840. In the U.S. there are no laws that set reasonable limits on the power of a ship's captain. A Naval Review Board looks into problems that occur aboard sailing ships. Recently, a new problem came to the Board's attention. A young sailor wrote a book. In the book he raises questions about the limits on the power of a ship's captain.

The Board members will conduct a hearing. They will listen to the people affected by this problem. Then the Board will decide how to solve the problem.

First, let's look at the job of a ship's captain. Then let's look at what a ship's captain may not do.

A ship's captain has the duty and the power to

- Supervise the running of the ship
- Decide what course the ship will sail
- Assign people on board the ship to do different jobs
- Settle disagreements among sailors
- Punish sailors who break rules
- Write reports to the ship's owners
- Keep a daily log of the ship's progress

A ship's captain may not

- Risk the success of the voyage
- Punish by death sailors who have broken rules

▶ *What procedures should the review board follow when conducting a hearing?*

Participating in a class activity

GETTING READY

Your class will work in five groups. Each group should take one of the roles described below. Four groups should prepare to make a presentation to the Naval Review Board. The group should explain its ideas about limiting the power of the ship's captain. They should also prepare to answer questions from the Naval Review Board.

▶ *Why does each group have a different opinion about how much power a ship's captain should have?*

- **Naval Review Board.** Select a member of the group to be the president of the board. Study the role of each group. Prepare questions to ask each of the groups who will make a presentation to the board. The questions should help you to understand the position of each of the groups. The responses to the questions should help you reach a decision about what to do about the power of a ship's captain.

- **Captain.** Prepare arguments against any changes in the limits on the power of a ship's captain. Explain why the captains do not want their power limited.

- **Crew**. Prepare arguments in favor of limiting the power of a ship's captain. Propose specific limits on the captains' powers that you would like the Board to make.

- **Owners of the ships.** Prepare your arguments against limiting the power of a ship's captain. Explain why the owners do not want to limit the power of the captains on their ships.

- **Author and friends.** Prepare your arguments in favor of changing the power of the captains.

TAKING PART

The president of the Naval Review Board will start the meeting.

Each group has four minutes to explain its position to the board.

After each presentation, the Board members may ask questions of the group. Every one in the group should help answer the questions.

After hearing all the groups, the Naval Review Board will meet and decide what to do.

TALKING IT OVER

1. In the story, was the government of the ship more like a constitutional government or a dictatorial government? Why?

2. What were the strongest arguments the ship owners and captains made against limiting a captain's power?

3. What were the strongest arguments the crew and the author made in favor of limiting a captain's power?

4. Do you agree with the decision of the Naval Review Board?

Why? Review Board students may explain how they reached their decision.

5. Did the decision of the Naval Review Board help to protect the rights of sailors? If so, how?

6. Why do you think it is important to have a constitutional government?

▶ Why is it important to listen to all sides of an issue?

 see next student page

LESSON REVIEW

The questions in the student book are intended to assess learning and to reinforce knowledge through discussion. The questions are directly related to the lesson objectives. You may wish to include additional questions developed by yourself or by students.

1. What is a constitution?

   A constitution is a set of rules and laws that tells how a government is organized and run.

2. What can you learn about a nation's government by studying its constitution?

   How a nation is organized and run, as mandated in its constitution, will tell you about the nation's principles and ideals.

3. Why did the Founders think that it is necessary to limit the power of government?

   The Founders believed that no one person or group in a government should have all the power. This way the natural rights of the people could be protected.

4. How did the Founders think the power of government could be limited?

   The Founders believed that the way government was set up would limit its power. They believed that if the power of government was divided among different branches then each branch could check or stop the other branches from abusing its power.

5. Explain the differences between a constitution and a constitutional government.

   A constitution sets out the rules or laws that define how a government is organized and run. A constitutional government, on the other hand, means that there are limits placed on the powers of the government. Not all constitutions provide for a constitutional government.

6. Explain the differences between a dictatorial government and a constitutional government.

   A constitutional government places limits on the power of those who run the government. A dictatorial government does not place any limits on the power of those who run the government.

ACTIVITIES

The activities extend and apply learning outside the classroom. You may wish to have students complete one or more activities. Have them share their results with the class.

SUGGESTED CHILDREN'S LITERATURE

Read *Yertle the Turtle*, by Dr. Seuss, to the class. Ask students to guess what type of government is represented in the story. Ask what problems and solutions come out of the story. Have students work together to reorganize Yertle's government so that he is no longer able to abuse his power. How would the new government work?

Review the lesson

1. What is a constitution?

2. What can you learn about a nation's government by studying its constitution?

3. Why did the Founders think that it is necessary to limit the power of government?

4. How did the Founders think the power of government could be limited?

5. Explain the difference between a constitution and a constitutional government.

6. Explain the differences between a dictatorial government and a constitutional government.

Activities to do

1. Turn to the Constitution at the back of this book. Read Article 1, Section 8. What powers does Congress have? Now read Section 9. What limits does Congress have?

2. Draw a cartoon or picture that shows the difference between a constitutional government and a dictatorial government.

3. In the history of the world, there have been governments that did not have proper limits on their power. Some examples of such governments include Nazi Germany and the former Soviet Union. Find information about these governments. What are some examples of how these governments violated the natural rights of the people? Share what you learned with the class.

Lesson 5

What ideas did the Founders use in the Declaration of Independence?

Purpose of the lesson

In 1776, the American colonies broke away from British rule. They chose to be a free country. The Founders wrote a special statement to explain why they wanted to be independent. This statement is called the Declaration of Independence.

The Declaration of Independence is one of the most important writings in American history. It describes the major ideas the Founders had about government. The Declaration also lists the Founders' complaints against the British king.

When you have finished this lesson, you should be able to explain some of the main ideas in the Declaration. As you will see, they are ideas you have already studied and discussed.

OVERVIEW

Students learn about how the colonies governed themselves and the events that led to the American Revolution. They get an introduction to the Declaration of Independence and study its main ideals, arguments, and complaints. They are asked to respond to questions related to the text of the document. The lesson concludes with a problem-solving activity that reinforces some key concepts in the lesson by allowing students to write a letter or draw a picture defending the position of the Patriots.

OBJECTIVES

At the conclusion of this lesson, students should be able to

- explain why the colonists revolted against British rule
- explain the purposes of the Declaration of Independence
- explain the ideals, complaints, and arguments of the Declaration

PROCEDURES

INTRODUCTORY ACTIVITY

Have students read the "Purpose of the lesson" section and speculate as to why the colonists broke away from British rule. Then have them review the ideals of natural rights and republican government. Write those review items on the board.

Write the "Terms to understand" on the board, or use a vocabulary-building activity of your choice. You may wish to have students look up the words in the glossary at the back of their text.

- American Revolution
- Continental Congress
- Declaration of Independence
- Loyalists
- Patriots
- principles

READING AND DISCUSSION

What problems did the colonists have with the British government?

What prompted the American Revolution?

Why did the Founders write the Declaration of Independence?

Have students read these sections and look at the illustrations showing the changing relationship between the colonists and Great Britain. Each time the British tried to regain control over the colonists the Americans resisted. Colonial opposition became organized. In reviewing the events that led to the American Revolution, emphasize the British position as well as that of the colonists. Point out that many colonists, known as Loyalists, supported the British position. Ask students to describe the sequence of events that led to the Revolutionary War.

Students should understand that the Declaration of Independence was written to justify the rebellion against the British government. Have students think about the process of writing the Declaration.

Jefferson was a Founder and a member of the Second Continental Congress. He did not attend the Philadelphia Convention because he was representing the new nation as an ambassador to France.

Terms to understand

American Revolution   Loyalists

Continental Congress   Patriots

Declaration of Independence   principles

What problems did the colonists have with the British government?

For many years, the British government let the colonists govern themselves. Britain was busy fighting wars with other European countries. In the 1760s, however, Britain began to tighten its control. The British government passed new laws taxing the colonists and controlling their trade. The colonists became alarmed. They felt their rights were not being protected. The colonists did not have the right to vote for people to represent them in the British government. Some argued that the British government had no right to tax them. They said, "No taxation without representation!"

Great Britain felt it had the right to tax the colonies and control their

▶ What does this picture show about the way the British government treated the colonies at first?

trade. People in Britain were paying high taxes to support and defend the American colonies. They thought the colonists should pay their fair share of taxes since they received the benefits of being a part of Great Britain. Many Americans became angry about the new trade laws and taxes.

What prompted the American revolution?

In 1774, twelve colonies sent representatives to a meeting in Philadelphia. This meeting was called the **First Continental Congress**. The Congress tried to find ways to get the British to change the laws. It sent a protest to the British government. Congress then ordered that the buying and selling of British goods be stopped. It also began to organize a citizens' army. Soon there was talk of fighting the British.

In April 1775, the British sent soldiers to look for some colonists that they thought were rebels. When the sides met near Boston, they began shooting at each other. War between Britain and the American colonies had begun. The **American Revolution** was underway, but the colonists had not yet declared their independence.

Why did the Founders write the Declaration of Independence?

The colonists sent delegates to the **Second Continental Congress** after the first incident of the Revolution. They were still thinking about ways to get Britain to change its policies. Soon, however, they were conducting the war.

In the spring of 1776, more and more colonists were in favor of

▷ How did Great Britain's control of the colonies change in the 1760s?

What ideas about government are in the Declaration of Independence?

Read aloud the first paragraph of this section with the class. Tell students they will be working in groups of six to study the main components of the Declaration. In each group, students will carry out the following assignments:

Students 1 and 2 will read and explain the "Basic ideas about people and government" to the rest of the group's members. Students 3 and 4 will be responsible for reading and explaining "Reasons why the Founders thought they had the right to be free of British rule." Students 5 and 6 will read and explain the "Complaints against the British king."

After each pair of students has explained its assigned section to the rest of the group, review the material with the entire class. Be sure that all students understand the concepts presented in this section.

independence. Congress wanted to wait until all the states agreed before it declared independence. In the meantime, Congress appointed a committee to write a declaration. The declaration would explain to the world why the colonists were declaring independence and why they had a right to do so. The committee asked one of their members, Thomas Jefferson, to write the declaration. Jefferson was known to be an excellent writer. The **Declaration of Independence** that he wrote describes the basic principles of the new nation. **Principles** are rules or beliefs about how to behave. The Congress voted to accept the Declaration on July 4, 1776.

What ideas about government are in the Declaration of Independence?

In writing the Declaration, the Founders used some of the main ideas you have studied to explain why they wanted to be free from Great Britain. The Declaration of Independence has three parts:

1. Basic ideas about people and government

2. Reasons why the Founders thought they had the right to be free from British rule

3. Complaints against the British king

These parts of the Declaration are so important that it is worth learning more about them.

▶ *What caused the colonies to declare their independence from Great Britain?*

▶ *What did the Founders think about the role of government?*

1. Basic ideas about people and government

These include the idea that all people are "created equal." They are born with certain rights that no one can take away. Among these rights are rights to "life, liberty, and the pursuit of happiness." The purpose of government is to protect these rights.

2. Reasons why the Founders thought they had the right to be free from British rule

The Declaration also says that the power of government comes from the consent of the people. People are the masters of government and not the other way around. If a government violates the rights of its people, the people can change the government or get rid of it and create a new one.

3. Complaints against the British king

To prove that the king had violated their rights, the Founders included a long list of complaints against him. The complaints are based on the idea that government should protect the rights of the people and serve the common good.

- He refused to approve laws made by the colonists that were necessary for their common good

- He closed the colonists' legislatures when they opposed his violation of the rights of the people

- He kept a standing army in the colonies even though there was no war

- He stopped the colonists' trade with other countries

Why did some colonists reject the idea of independence?

Have students read the section. Discuss the difficulty many colonists felt in deciding whether or not to support the Revolution. Explain that most colonists considered themselves loyal subjects of Great Britain. After the Declaration of Independence was issued, the time came to choose sides and many colonists continued to remain loyal to King George III.

The Loyalists felt that Britain had supported the colonies and provided for their defense. For this reason—as well as a sense of tradition and loyalty, intensified frequently by family or official connections—many Americans were unwilling to break their ties with Britain.

On the other hand, the Patriots were those who severed their ties with Britain and followed the cause of independence.

- He taxed the colonists without their consent

- He took away the colonists' right to a trial by jury

Why did some colonists reject the idea of independence?

John Adams was one of the Founders who strongly supported the Declaration of Independence. He said that not everyone wanted the colonies to become independent from Great Britain. At the time the Declaration was written, he said that about one-third of the colonists wanted independence. They were called the **Patriots**. They agreed with the ideas and arguments in the Declaration of Independence.

Adams said that about one-third of the colonists had not made up their minds about independence. Finally, about one-third of the colonists did not want to become independent. They were called **Loyalists** because they believed the colonies should stay loyal or faithful to the king.

Many Loyalists were large landowners or wealthy merchants. They thought their businesses would be hurt. Other Loyalists had been appointed to their jobs by the king. If the colonies became independent, they would lose their jobs. Even if the

Loyalists did not like British taxes and other limits on their freedom, they did not think that breaking with Great Britain was the way to solve those problems.

Many Loyalists joined the British army and fought for the king. Some Loyalists moved back to Great Britain. Others went to Canada or to the West Indies. Those who stayed in the colonies had a hard time. Sometimes their property was taken from them. Some Loyalists were treated cruelly or put in jail.

▶ *Why did the Loyalists oppose independence?*

Ideas to discuss

Why should you support the idea of independence?

Imagine that you are a Patriot. You want to convince everybody that they should support the idea of independence from Great Britain. You have some friends and neighbors who are Loyalists and some who do not want to choose sides.

Work in groups of two to three students to write a letter to the newspaper in your colony. Explain why the colonies should become independent. Use the ideas, reasons for independence, and complaints stated in the Declaration of Independence.

▶ What were some reasons for the colonies to stay loyal to Great Britain?

▶ What were some reasons for the colonies to become independent?

IDEAS TO DISCUSS

Why should you support the idea of independence?

After clarifying the positions of both Patriots and Loyalists, divide the class into small groups and have them discuss the pros and cons of being independent from Britain.

Each group should then write a letter to the newspaper explaining why the Patriot cause is just or not. The class as a whole might decide that the arguments are not strong enough to merit a war for independence. Or, they might be persuaded to give strong support for the arguments about going to war presented by the Patriots.

 see next student page

LESSON REVIEW

The questions in the student book are intended to assess learning and to reinforce knowledge through discussion. The questions are directly related to the lesson objectives. You may wish to include additional questions developed by yourself or by students.

1. Why did the Founders feel that the British government was not protecting their rights?

    The colonists did not have a vote in Parliament. Parliament was passing more laws to restrict their freedom. The King was not serving the common good of the colonies.

2. Why did the Founders write the Declaration of Independence?

    The Founders wanted to formally state that the colonies were free and independent of British rule and domination. They also wanted the rest of the world to know the ideals upon which they were establishing their government.

3. According to the Declaration of Independence, why do people set up a government?

    People set up a government to protect their natural rights of life, liberty, and the pursuit of happiness.

4. According to the Declaration of Independence, how do governments get their power?

   Governments get their power from the people who consent to be governed.

5. According to the Declaration of Independence, what action may people take if government does not protect their rights? How is this right related to the idea of consent of the governed?

   If a government does not protect the rights of the citizens, the citizens have a right to change or abolish the government. The King had tried to take away the people's rights. Since he had broken the contract with the people, they were free to set up their own government. The people gave their consent to set up the new government.

6. Why did some people in the colonies not support the Declaration of Independence?

   Some people in the colonies felt that they should remain loyal to Britain. Most of them were either landowners or wealthy merchants who benefited from their alliance.

7. How important are the ideals of the Declaration of Independence to you today?

   Why? Accept any reasonable response.

ACTIVITIES

The suggested activities are intended to extend and apply learning outside the classroom. You may wish to have students complete one or more of the activities. Then, have them share the results with the class.

SUGGESTED CHILDREN'S LITERATURE

Have students read (or read to the class) one of the following books by Jean Fritz: *Can't You Make Them Behave, King George?* or *Would You Please Sign Here, John Hancock?*

Review the lesson

1. Why did the Founders feel that the British government was not protecting their rights?

2. Why did the Founders write the Declaration of Independence?

3. According to the Declaration of Independence, why do people set up a government?

4. According to the Declaration of Independence, how do governments get their power?

5. According to the Declaration of Independence, what action may the people take if government does not protect their rights? How is this right related to the idea of consent of the governed?

6. Why did some people in the colonies not support the Declaration of Independence?

7. How important are the ideals of the Declaration of Independence to you today? Why?

Activities to do

1. Some laws that the British passed were the Tea Act of 1773, the Quartering Act, and the Coercive Acts. Learn more about these laws. Write a speech explaining either why these laws violated the rights of the colonists or why they were necessary.

2. Women played an important part in the Revolutionary War. Choose one of these women. Write a report about her accomplishments for your class.

   - Abigail Adams
   - Lydia Darragh
   - Nancy Hart
   - Sybil Ludington
   - Mercy Otis Warren
   - Molly Pitcher
   - Deborah Samson
   - Phillis Wheatley
   - Elizabeth "Betty" Zane

3. How did American Indians help the colonists in the Revolutionary War?

4. Find out about African Americans who fought in the Revolutionary War. Which side did they fight for? Explain why. Read your report to the class.

Lesson 6

What were the first state governments like?

Purpose of the lesson

When the American colonies became independent from Great Britain, they needed new governments. Colonial leaders set about writing constitutions for their new states. In this lesson, you will learn about the new state governments.

When you finish this lesson, you should be able to explain some important ideas used in the state constitutions. You should also be able to explain how the state constitutions protected the rights of citizens.

47

OVERVIEW

This lesson looks at how the people governed themselves after gaining their independence from Great Britain. Students will learn that the American people were loyal to their states and set up new state governments that reflected the ideas and beliefs they all shared about government.

OBJECTIVES

At the conclusion of the lesson, students should be able to

- explain how the people governed themselves following the American Revolution
- explain the people's ideas about government and how these ideas protected the rights of the people

TEACHING PROCEDURES

INTRODUCTORY ACTIVITY

Have students read the "Purpose of the lesson" section and consider the objectives of the lesson.

Write the "Terms to understand" on the board, or use a vocabulary-building activity of your choice. You may wish to have students look up the words in the glossary at the back of their text.

- bill of rights
- checks and balances
- executive branch
- higher law
- judicial branch
- legislative branch
- separation of powers

READING AND DISCUSSION

How did the people govern themselves after declaring their independence from Great Britain?

What kind of state governments did the people create?

Point out to students that most of the Americans did not see themselves as united in one nation. Ask students to speculate on what potential problems the newly independent states might encounter with this attitude. Have them share their responses with the class, for example: the states would be unable to settle conflicts among themselves; they might not be able to regulate trade among the states, or with foreign countries; and they might have different currencies.

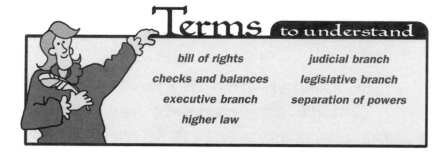

Terms to understand

bill of rights	judicial branch
checks and balances	legislative branch
executive branch	separation of powers
higher law	

How did the people govern themselves after declaring their independence from Great Britain?

In 1776, British government in the colonies came to an end. The colonies were now free and independent states. They were free to rule themselves. To do so, each state had to set up a new government. A few states wrote constitutions before the Declaration of Independence. Most of the states wrote their constitutions some months later.

At that time, most Americans did not think of themselves as one nation. They were loyal to their states. Some people believed that the states should be united. They needed a way to control trade among the states and with other countries. They also needed a way to manage conflicts that might arise among the states. A national government could help do these things.

A closer look at the state governments the people set up will help us to better understand the United States Constitution. First, we will look at the state governments. In the next lesson, we will look at the national government.

What kind of state governments did the people create?

The people in the states put into practice the ideas and beliefs they shared about government. They used the following ideas in their state constitutions. You studied most of them in earlier lessons.

Ideas about natural rights

- The purpose of government is to protect a person's rights to life, liberty, and property.

Ideas about republican government

- All power comes from the people. The people give some of their power to the government. The people elect members of government to represent them.

Ideas about constitutional government

- The constitution limits the power of people in the government.

- The constitution is a **higher law**. This means that lawmakers cannot make laws that violate the constitution. It also means that all people in government must obey the constitution.

- One way to limit power is by **separation of powers**. This means that power is divided among three branches. The three branches are the legislative, the executive, and the judicial.

The state constitutions gave most of the power to the **legislative branch**. It made the laws. The people elected representatives to make the laws. People believed that it was the safest branch in which to place most of the power. It was the branch closest to the people. Therefore, it was most likely to protect the rights of citizens.

The **executive branch** carried out and enforced the laws. The state executive was the governor. People believed that they should not trust the

▶ *How does this picture illustrate the idea of separation of powers and checks and balances?*

How did the state constitutions protect the rights of the citizens?

Have students work in pairs and read the sections. Have them write discussion notes to share with the class. Lead a class discussion emphasizing the ideas and terms presented in this and the previous section. These same ideas will play a big role in the Philadelphia Convention of 1787.

governor with too much power. It was not so easy for the people to control the governor. Once elected, a governor did not need to be close to the people.

The **judicial branch** decided what the laws mean. This branch settled conflicts. It decided what to do with people who did not follow the law. The people did not want to give the judicial branch too much power. They remembered how the king's judges had treated them in the British courts.

The state constitutions also set up a system of **checks and balances**. The three branches checked, or stopped, each other when necessary. In this way, they kept each branch from gaining too much power.

How did the state constitutions protect the rights of citizens?

Most states wrote declarations, or bills of rights. A **bill of rights** is a list of the rights of citizens. It was usually the first part of a state's constitution. These are some rights of citizens that most states wrote into their constitutions. The right to

- vote in free and frequent elections

- freedom of speech and of the press

- representation on tax matters

- have a lawyer if accused of a crime

- trial by jury

- protection from illegal search and seizure

- protection from cruel and unusual punishment

Some state constitutions did not allow the state to keep a militia in time of peace. A militia is a group of citizens who receive military training. Most of the state constitutions also did not allow the state to force people to let soldiers live in their houses.

▶ *What ideas about rights were included in the state constitutions?*

Ideas to discuss

What did the Massachusetts Constitution say about education?

The Massachusetts Constitution was adopted in 1780. Many people think it was the best of the state constitutions. Ideas found in the Massachusetts Constitution were used in writing the United States Constitution.

The Massachusetts Constitution also had something the others did not have. It said that each town must provide free public education to all children. It also said that all children must attend school.

Work with three or four other students. Discuss the questions that follow. Then compare the answers of your group with those of your classmates.

1. Why do you think Massachusetts required each town to pay for the education of its children?

2. Should all children be required to attend school?

3. Should people who do not have children be required to pay taxes to support schools?

4. Most states now have laws about school attendance. What do the laws of your state require?

5. Do you think other laws about schools are needed? Why are they needed?

▶ Why does education remain such an important issue for government?

IDEAS TO DISCUSS

What did the Massachusetts Constitution say about education?

Read the opening paragraph in this section. Have students work in groups of three or four to answer the questions posed in the section. Groups should share their responses with their classmates.

1. Why do you think Massachusetts required each town to pay for the education of its children?

    The state wanted to make sure that every child had the opportunity to receive an education.

2. Should all children be required to attend school?

    Students might place age limits for entering school and for the right to discontinue going to school. Otherwise, accept any reasonable response.

3. Should people who do not have children be required to pay taxes to support schools?

    Responses should provoke discussion of different opinions.

4. Most states now have laws about school attendance. What do the laws of your state require?

    This question would be an excellent way to have students conduct research in the computer lab, if your school has one equipped with the internet. Otherwise, make available a copy of your state's education code regarding compulsory education.

5. Do you think other laws about schools are needed? Why are they needed?

    Accept any reasonable response. Safety issues may be considered important.

LESSON 6

LESSON REVIEW

The questions in the student book are intended to assess learning and to reinforce knowledge through discussion. They are directly related to the lesson objectives. You may wish to include additional questions developed by yourself or by students.

1. What were some important ideas in the new state constitutions?
   The state constitutions included ideas about governing with checks and balances and separation of powers; ideas about natural rights and republican government; and bills of rights.

2. How did the state constitutions organize their governments?
   They established executive, legislative, and judicial branches of government.

3. How did the state constitutions limit the powers of their governments?
   They used the ideas of separation of powers and checks and balances.

4. Why do you suppose most state constitutions began with a bill of rights?
   They wanted to protect the individual rights of their citizens, such as the right to vote, to have freedom of expression and the press, etc.

ACTIVITIES

The suggested activities are intended to extend and apply learning outside the classroom. You may wish to have students complete one or more of the activities. Then, have them share the results with the class.

Review the lesson

1. What were some important ideas in the new state constitutions?

2. How did the state constitutions organize their governments?

3. How did the state constitutions limit the powers of their governments?

4. Why do you suppose most state constitutions began with a bill of rights?

Activities to do

1. Suppose that we did not have a national government. Each state would be a separate country. Each state might have its own army, its own money, and its own trade rules. Make a list of problems that might occur in this situation.

2. Find a copy of your state constitution. What is in the first part of the constitution? Does it have a bill of rights? Does the constitution say anything about education? Report your findings to your class.

3. Find one or more American Indian tribal constitutions. How are they similar or different from the United States Constitution?

How did the Founders write our Constitution?

UNIT TWO

UNIT OVERVIEW

This four-lesson unit describes the Articles of Confederation and discusses their importance. It explores the events that led to the Philadelphia Convention, the nature of the delegates, and how the convention was organized. Students explore two major conflicts facing the Framers—representation in Congress and slavery. Students learn how the Framers resolved these conflicts through compromise.

UNIT OBJECTIVES

At the conclusion of this unit, students should be able to

1. describe the Articles of Confederation, discuss achievements under the Articles, explain the weaknesses of the Articles, and describe the concerns that led to the Philadelphia Convention.

2. identify the Framers and describe some important delegates at the Philadelphia Convention. They should also be able to explain how the convention was organized.

3. describe the conflicts about slavery and representation and be able to explain how the Framers settled these conflicts at the convention.

How did the Framers write our Constitution?

Since they had declared their independence, the Founders needed to create a new government for all the states of the new nation. They did this by creating our first constitution, known as the Articles of Confederation. The problems of the national government under the Articles of Confederation led the Founders to decide to write a new constitution.

The United States Constitution was written by the delegates who attended the Philadelphia Convention. These delegates are known as the Framers of the Constitution. The convention lasted from May to September 1787. The fifty-five Framers worked together for four months. The new Constitution they wrote has lasted more than 200 years!

Some of the Framers were from states with large populations and some from states with small populations. Some were from the North, which had few slaves, and some from the South, where there were many slaves. These differences led to disagreements about what should be in the new Constitution.

KEY TOPICS
to look for in this unit

Articles of Confederation

Framers

Great Compromise

Philadelphia Convention

three-fifths clause

This unit will help you understand why the Framers wrote the United States Constitution the way they did. You will read about the agreements and disagreements among the Framers. You will learn how the Framers made compromises to solve their disagreements.

Lesson 7

What was the first national government like?

Purpose of the lesson

After the Declaration of Independence was signed, the Founders needed to create a new government for all the states of the new nation. They did this by creating our first constitution. It was called the Articles of Confederation.

When you finish this lesson, you should be able to describe the national government under the Articles of Confederation. You should also be able to explain how the problems of the new government led the Founders to decide to write a new constitution.

OVERVIEW

Students will learn that most of the Founders feared a strong national government. As a result, the government they established under the Articles of Confederation had limited powers. Students will explore the achievements and problems of the national government under the Articles. They will see how the weaknesses of that government led many people to urge that the Articles of Confederation be strengthened. This lesson will help students understand the reason for the Philadelphia Convention of 1787.

OBJECTIVES

At the conclusion of this lesson, students should be able to

- explain how the founders' fear of strong government shaped our first national government
- define the articles of confederation
- describe some achievements of the government under the articles of confederation
- describe some problems of the united states under the articles of confederation

TEACHING PROCEDURES

INTRODUCTORY ACTIVITY

Have students read the "Purpose of the lesson" section and consider the objectives of the lesson.

Write the "Terms to understand" on the board, or use a vocabulary-building activity of your choice. You may wish to have students look up the words in the glossary at the back of their text.

- Articles of Confederation
- confederation
- delegate
- Northwest Ordinance
- ordinance
- separation of powers
- Shays' Rebellion

READING AND DISCUSSION

What kind of national government did the Founders create under the Articles of Confederation?

Have students read aloud the first two paragraphs in this section. Emphasize that a confederation is a loose union of states with equal power.

As students read the rest of the lesson, have them write down how the main fears of the people were addressed in the Articles of Confederation.

Have students work with a partner and share their ideas. Ask students whether the Articles of Confederation addressed the fears. Write their responses on the board. Keep the responses available for viewing as you go through the remainder of the lesson.

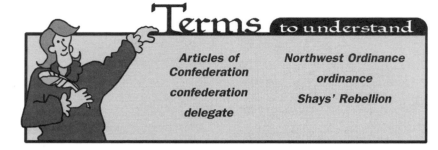

Terms to understand

Articles of Confederation

confederation

delegate

Northwest Ordinance

ordinance

Shays' Rebellion

What kind of national government did the Founders create under the Articles of Confederation?

At the start of the Revolutionary War, the Second Continental Congress talked about a plan to set up a national government. At that time, the Congress was more concerned about fighting the war, so it took no action.

After the Declaration of Independence was signed, the Second Continental Congress sent the plan to the states. Congress asked the states to approve it. This first plan of government for the United States was the **Articles of Confederation**. The Articles set up a loose union of states with equal powers. We call such a union a **confederation**.

▶ *If you had been a member of the Second Continental Congress, which would have been more important to you: setting up a national government or fighting the war against Great Britain? Why?*

56

▶ *How did the Articles of Confederation organize the first national government?*

The Founders faced two main problems when they wrote the Articles of Confederation.

1. The people feared a strong national government. They just had a revolution to get rid of a strong British government. They did not want another one like it. They felt that a strong national government might take away the rights of the states and the people.

2. The people feared that some states would have more power than other states in the new government.

These fears influenced the Founders who wrote the Articles of Confederation. Therefore, they chose to set up a weak national government. It was a government with very limited powers.

Under the Articles, there were neither national courts nor a president. The power of government was in the Congress. The Articles did not give Congress very much power, either. For example, Congress could not raise money to run the government by directly taxing the people. Congress had to ask the states for money. The states gave money if and when they wanted to. The states made sure they kept most of the power for themselves.

Each state had one vote in Congress. The size of a state's population did not matter. States with more people had the same vote as states with far fewer people. The Congress could not

What was accomplished under the Articles of Confederation?

Emphasize that the national government was responsible for a number of important accomplishments as students do the reading. The national government kept the states together during the war against Great Britain; it successfully managed the war for independence; made a treaty with Great Britain to end the war; got states to respect certain laws made in other states; kept states from conducting foreign affairs, such as making treaties and declaring war; and passed the Northwest Ordinance. Explain the importance of the Northwest Ordinance in dealing with slavery, education, and the incorporation of new states.

do anything important without having the approval of all the state governments.

After much debate, the states approved the Articles of Confederation. The Articles were in effect for seven years. Let's look at what the people were able to do under the Articles.

What was accomplished under the Articles of Confederation?

Even with their weaknesses, the Articles of Confederation were useful to the new nation. The national government was able to accomplish the following tasks:

- keeping the states together during the war against Great Britain

- winning the war for independence

- making a peace treaty with Great Britain

- preventing each state from conducting its own foreign affairs, making treaties, and declaring war

The government under the Articles of Confederation passed the **Northwest Ordinance of 1787**. An **ordinance** is an order or law made by a government. This government order was a plan for adding new states. It

▶ *Which new states were created as a result of the Northwest Ordinance of 1787?*

allowed people living in the Northwest Territories—the land between the Mississippi River, the Great Lakes, and the Ohio River—to organize their own governments. When a territory had a large enough population, it could join the Union. The new states would be equals of the original states, not colonies. The Ordinance said that part of all public lands must be set aside for public schools. It declared slavery unlawful in any new state in the Northwest Territories. The Ordinance also guaranteed freedom of religion, speech, and press.

What problems did the national government have under the Articles of Confederation?

When the Revolution was over, each state acted as a separate country. Each had its own interests. People did not think of themselves as citizens of the United States. They thought of themselves as citizens of their own states, such as Virginians, New Yorkers, or Georgians. Often the state governments did not cooperate with each other to solve common problems.

The national government under the Articles was weak. It did not have the power to unite the states. It did not have money and it did not have the authority to get it. There were no courts to settle disputes among the states.

By 1786, there was little trade between the states or with other nations. It was hard for Americans to make a living. Many businesses were failing. Many people were in debt. Soldiers who had fought in the Revolutionary War still had not been paid.

▶ What was the function of Congress under the Articles of Confederation?

What problems did the national government have under the Articles of Confederation?

Then have students read the next section. Go back to students' responses regarding the problems faced by the Founders when they wrote the Articles.

Ask students if they understand the problems that the Founders faced and the successes and failures of the Articles as a solution.

Why was Shays' Rebellion an important event?

Have students read about Shays' Rebellion and ask them why they think property owners were so frightened by what happened in Massachusetts. Remind students that the Founders thought that the purpose of government is to protect people's rights, including the right to property.

▶ *Why did Daniel Shays and his followers rebel? What did they hope to gain?*

Why was Shays' Rebellion an important event?

The states had their own problems. In Massachusetts, many farmers did not have any money. They could not trade their products in other states or countries. When they could not pay their bills, they lost their farms and homes. Some were put in prison because they could not pay their bills. Many people protested because they felt this situation was unfair.

In November 1786, more than one thousand angry farmers gathered under a leader named Daniel Shays. They were ready to fight the Massachusetts government. They shut down the courts to prevent the government from taking their property and jailing them. They tried to capture weapons to use in their struggle.

State troops stopped **Shays' Rebellion**. Many people were frightened by the rebellion. They worried that it might spread to other states.

How might the national government under the Articles of Confederation be improved?

The Founders knew that the Articles of Confederation had many weaknesses. The national government under the Articles was not effective. It was time to make improvements. Congress agreed and called for a meeting to be held in Philadelphia in 1787.

Each state was asked to send delegates. A **delegate** is someone whom you trust to represent your interests. The delegates were supposed to suggest ways to improve the Articles. Once they all got together, something else happened. They decided to put the Articles aside and start over again. The delegates then began to write a new constitution.

▶ *What did the delegates to the Philadelphia Convention decide to do about improving the Articles of Confederation?*

How might the national government under the Articles of Confederation be improved?

Emphasize that the call for the Philadelphia Convention was for delegates to revise the Articles of Confederation. The delegates decided to ignore their instructions and write a new constitution. At this point, students should have an understanding of the Founders' ideas about government and the events that led to the Philadelphia Convention.

 see next student page

LESSON REVIEW

The questions in the student book are intended to assess learning and to reinforce knowledge through discussion. The questions are directly related to the lesson objectives. You may wish to include additional questions developed by yourself or by students.

1. Why did the Founders create a weak national government?
   The Founders feared that a strong national government would take away the rights of the people. Some states feared that other states would acquire too much power and oppress them.

2. What did the first national government accomplish under the Articles of Confederation?
   The national government kept the states together during the war against Great Britain; won independence; made a treaty with Great Britain to end the war; got states to respect certain laws made in other states; kept states from conducting foreign affairs, such as making treaties and declaring war; and passed the Northwest Ordinances.

3. What were some problems under the Articles of Confederation?
   Each state acted as a separate country. The national government was very weak, it had no money or power, it could not control the states, and it had no courts to settle disputes among the states.

4. Describe Shays' Rebellion. Why was it important?

Massachusetts farmers did not have any money to pay their bills and were losing their farms. They gathered under the leadership of Daniel Shays and marched to fight the Massachusetts government. The rebellion brought out the weaknesses of the Articles of Confederation and the need for a stronger national government.

5. What did the Northwest Ordinance of 1787 require of new states?

It required that part of all public lands must be set aside for public schools. It declared that slavery was unlawful in any new state and it guaranteed freedom of religion, speech, and the press.

6. Why did the Founders decide to have a meeting?

Congress called the meeting in 1787 to look for ways to improve the Articles of Confederation.

ACTIVITIES

The suggested activities are intended to extend and apply learning outside the classroom. You may wish to have students complete one or more of the activities. Then, have them share the results with the class.

Review the lesson

1. Why did the Founders create a weak national government?

2. What did the first national government accomplish under the Articles of Confederation?

3. What were some problems under the Articles of Confederation?

4. Describe Shays' Rebellion. Why was it important?

5. What did the Northwest Ordinance of 1787 require of new states?

6. Why did the Founders decide to have a meeting?

Activities to do

1. Learn more about the Northwest Ordinance. How did it help to provide education for all people? What rights did it protect? How did it prevent slavery? What effects did it have on the American Indian tribes?

2. Learn more about Shays' Rebellion. Write a letter to the newspaper from the point of view of a farmer. Write a letter from the point of view of a property owner who was against the uprising.

3. Create a short play that shows one of the problems under the Articles of Confederation. Perform your play for the class.

4. Find out about other nations that are establishing new governments. Do their constitutions have any of the same problems as the Articles of Confederation? Use the internet or go to your library for your research. Share what you learn with the class.

Lesson 8

How was the Philadelphia Convention organized?

Purpose of the lesson

In this lesson, you will learn about some important Framers who attended the Philadelphia Convention. You will also learn about some decisions that were made at the beginning of the convention.

When you have finished this lesson, you should be able to explain the purpose of the Philadelphia Convention. You should also be able to explain what decisions the Framers made before writing the Constitution.

63

OVERVIEW

This lesson introduces students to the men who attended the Philadelphia Convention, their backgrounds, and their goals. These men are known as the Framers of the Constitution. The unit covers the reasons why Congress called for the convention and examines the preliminary decisions made by the delegates.

Before looking at the lives of the Framers, students engage in a discussion activity that asks them to consider how they would choose delegates to write a constitution for their student government. When students have completed this activity, they should be able to relate their answers to what actually happened at the Philadelphia Convention.

OBJECTIVES

At the conclusion of this lesson students should be able to

- name some of the important Framers at the Philadelphia Convention and the role that each man played
- name some Founders not present in Philadelphia and explain their absence
- name some segments of the population that were not represented at the Philadelphia Convention and suggest reasons for their exclusion
- describe some of the agreements that the delegates made at the beginning of the Philadelphia Convention

TEACHING PROCEDURES

INTRODUCTORY ACTIVITY

Have students read the "Purpose of the lesson" section and consider the objectives of the lesson.

You may wish to review the Articles of Confederation to ensure that students have a firm understanding of the Articles' weaknesses because this knowledge is the foundation of the information in Lesson 8.

Write the "Terms to understand" on the board, or use a vocabulary-building activity of your choice. You may wish to have students look up the words in the glossary at the back of their text.

- Framers
- Philadelphia Convention

IDEAS TO DISCUSS

Who should participate in creating a government?

Organize the class into groups of three to five students and have them read the section. The members of each group should discuss the questions and write their answers on chart paper. Groups may select a recorder from their members to report their responses to the whole class.

Ideas to discuss

Who should participate in creating a government?

Suppose a group of students at your school were given the task of creating a constitution for your student government. Meet in groups of about five students. Discuss the following questions. Be prepared to report your answers to the class.

1. Who should attend the meeting? Should each class have the right to send delegates? Why or why not?

2. Should some classes be able to send more delegates than others? Why or why not?

3. How should class delegates be selected? Why?

4. What qualifications should delegates have? Why?

5. What responsibilities should delegates have? Why?

6. Which basic ideas about government that you have studied did you apply in answering these questions?

▶ Who should have the right to participate in your school government?

Terms to understand

Framers

Philadelphia Convention

Who were the Framers?

The delegates to the Philadelphia Convention are known as the **Framers** of the United States Constitution. They are called the Framers because they organized and wrote our Constitution. Many of the Framers had been leaders during the American Revolution. About three-fourths had served in Congress. Most were leaders in their states.

The delegates were not chosen from all parts of the American population. Some were rich, but most were not. There were no poor people, no indentured servants, or young people. All the Framers were men. Their average age was forty-two. There were no women among the delegates. There were no free black men or slaves. There were no American Indians. Poor farmers—such as those who took part in Shays' Rebellion—were not present, nor were the citizens of Rhode Island. People in Rhode Island were so much against changing the Articles of

▶ *Who were the delegates to the Philadelphia Convention?*

65

READING AND DISCUSSION

Who were the Framers?

Have students read the section. Discuss the biographies of the three persons mentioned in the reading. You might wish to ask students to identify common traits and/or some differences among the Framers.

What type of government did George Washington think the country needed?

Confederation that they refused to send any delegates!

Three important delegates to the convention were George Washington, James Madison, and Benjamin Franklin. George Washington was from Virginia. He was probably the most respected man in the country. As commander in chief of the American army during the Revolution, he was a great hero to most people. By 1787, he had retired to his plantation and would have liked to remain there. His friends urged him to attend the convention. They said his support was necessary to get a new constitution accepted by the people. Because

Washington thought a stronger national government was necessary, he went to Philadelphia.

James Madison is often called the "Father of the Constitution." His ideas about government greatly influenced the other delegates. He had already developed a written plan for the new government that he brought to Philadelphia. It was known as the Virginia Plan, and it called for a strong national government. He helped put together compromises that solved some of the disagreements among the Framers. Madison took notes during the meetings. Much of what we know about the Philadelphia Convention is based on his notes.

Why is James Madison called the "Father of the Constitution"?

Benjamin Franklin attended the convention as a delegate from Pennsylvania. He was 81 years old and in poor health. Like Washington, he was highly respected by Americans. He had been a printer, inventor, and writer. He had also helped our country develop good relations with other nations. At the convention, he encouraged the delegates to cooperate with each other and work hard to settle their differences. His support of the Constitution was important to the other delegates.

 *What role did Benjamin Franklin play at the Philadelphia Convention?*

If you had been a delegate to the Philadelphia Convention, what role might you have played? Why?

LESSON 8

Who were some important Founders who were not at the convention?

Have students read the section aloud. Ask them to consider why there were no women, African Americans, Native Americans, or poor farmers at the convention. Discuss with students why some prominent Americans did not attend the convention and why some other well-known Americans refused to attend the convention.

Who were some important Founders who were not at the convention?

At the time of the **Philadelphia Convention**, Thomas Jefferson and Thomas Paine were in France. Jefferson had written the Declaration of Independence. Paine had written *Common Sense*, an important book that helped get support for the Revolution. John Adams, a leader during the Revolution, was in Great Britain.

Other well-known Americans refused to go to the convention. Patrick Henry of Virginia was one of them. He feared that the delegates would try to create a strong national government. After the convention, Henry worked hard to convince the people to reject the Constitution.

▶ *Why did Patrick Henry not support the new Constitution?*

▶ *What did Thomas Paine contribute to the struggle for independence?*

▶ *Why did Thomas Jefferson not attend the Philadelphia Convention?*

68

What decisions did the delegates make at the start of the convention?

At the start of the convention, the Framers agreed on four things.

1. George Washington would serve as president of the convention.

2. Each state, large or small, would have one vote at the convention.

3. They would not do what Congress had asked them to do. They would not try to improve the Articles of Confederation. The Articles had too many weaknesses. They decided to write an entirely new constitution.

4. They would keep their discussions private. They decided that whatever was said at the meeting would remain a secret for thirty years.

There were good reasons for secrecy. The Framers believed they needed to speak freely. If people told others what they said, they would not feel as free to discuss their ideas. They would be less likely to change their minds during debate.

The Framers wanted the people to accept the new constitution. They feared that the people might not if they knew all the disagreements the Framers had during the writing.

Once the Framers reached these agreements, it was time to get down to work. It was time to create a constitution. In the next lessons, you will learn about some of the disagreements the Framers had and how they solved them.

▶ Why did the delegates to the Philadelphia Convention decide to keep their discussions private?

What decisions did the delegates make at the start of the convention?

Discuss the four agreements made by the delegates. Ask students if the delegates were justified in ignoring their instructions to amend and improve the Articles of Confederation. Through class discussion encourage students to think about whether the Framers were correct in keeping the convention proceedings secret for 30 years.

 see next student page

LESSON REVIEW

The questions in the student book are intended to assess learning and to reinforce knowledge through discussion. The questions are directly related to the lesson objectives. You may wish to include additional questions developed by yourself or by students.

1. Why did Congress call for the Philadelphia Convention?
   Congress realized that there were weaknesses in the Articles of Confederation and that these weaknesses needed to be corrected.

2. Describe the members of the Philadelphia Convention as a group.
   Most delegates were young (average age 42). Many had been leaders during the American Revolution and had served in the Continental Congress. Some had signed the Declaration of Independence and most of the delegates were leaders in their states. All of them were men. None were poor.

3. Who were some of the important Framers? Why are they called Framers?
   Benjamin Franklin, James Madison, and George Washington. They were called Framers because they "framed," or wrote, the Constitution.

4. At the start of the meeting, what important decisions
did the Framers make? Why?

*George Washington would serve as president of the convention.
Each state, large or small, would have one vote at the convention.
They would not do what Congress asked them to do. They would not
try to improve the Articles of Confederation, because the Articles had
too many weaknesses. They decided to write an entirely new constitution.
They would keep their discussion private and not reveal what was
said for 30 years. They wanted to be able to speak freely.*

ACTIVITIES

The suggested activities are intended to extend and apply learning
outside the classroom. You may wish to have students complete one
or more of the activities. Then, have them share the results with the class.

SUGGESTED CHILDREN'S LITERATURE

Have students read *Shh! We're Writing the Constitution* by Jean Fritz
(New York: Putnam, 1987) for a more detailed description of the
Framers and the convention proceedings.

Review the lesson

1. Why did Congress call for the
Philadelphia Convention?

2. Describe the members of the
Philadelphia Convention as
a group.

3. Who were some of the
important Framers? Why
are they called Framers?

4. At the start of the meeting,
what important decisions did
the Framers make? Why?

Activities to do

1. Imagine that you are a newspaper
editor in 1787. Write an article
in which you support or oppose
keeping the debates secret.

2. Learn more about the Framers
who are discussed in this lesson
or other Framers. Role-play a
television show and interview
the Framers.

3. Draw a picture showing the
Framers at work during
the convention.

4. Draw a cartoon of Benjamin
Franklin. Show him acting as
a peacemaker and soothing the
hurt feelings of the delegates
after a heated debate.

Lesson 9

How many representatives should each state have in Congress?

Purpose of the lesson

The delegates to the Philadelphia Convention agreed to write a new constitution. They wanted the new constitution to provide a stronger national government. One difficult thing they had to decide was how many representatives each state would be allowed to send to Congress. In this lesson, you will discuss this question. You will learn how the Framers solved the problem.

When you have finished this lesson, you should be able to explain why the Framers organized our Congress the way they did.

71

OVERVIEW

After reaching agreement on the basic ideas of the kind of government the Framers desired, the delegates soon ran into disagreements about how many representatives each state should be able to send to Congress. This lesson examines the conflicts about representation in the legislative branch of the new national government and describes how the conflict was resolved.

After being introduced to the conflicts between the large and small states, students engage in a problem-solving activity in which they examine the population data of 1787, consider arguments on both sides of the conflict, and try to reach an agreement on the best way to solve the problem. Finally, they learn about the concept of compromise and how the Great Compromise solved the problem of representation.

OBJECTIVES

At the conclusion of this lesson, students should be able to

- explain what basic ideas about government the Framers agreed upon
- explain why representation was an issue at the convention
- explain the arguments of the small states and the large states on the issue of representation
- describe the key features of the Great Compromise

MATERIAL NEEDED

Handout D 2 (optional)

TEACHING PROCEDURES

INTRODUCTORY ACTIVITY

Have students read the "Purpose of the lesson" section and consider the objectives of the lesson.

Write the "Terms to understand" on the board, or use a vocabulary-building activity of your choice. You may wish to have students look up the words in the glossary at the back of their text.

- Great Compromise
- House of Representatives
- Senate

READING AND DISCUSSION

What was the conflict between the large states and the small states?

Have students read the section and discuss the concerns of both the large and small states about representation to Congress. Divide the class into two groups of unequal size (one very small with some common interests and one much larger). Ask each group to select two representatives to make decisions for the group.

Tell students that they will be deciding the amount of free time they will have during the next school day. Provide hypothetical choices for a number of free periods, for example, two in the morning versus one at end of the school day or one after lunch. Even though the groups differ in size, only the four representatives are allowed to make decisions for the class. All students are bound by the decision of the representatives. Discuss why this arrangement is fair or unfair.

Terms to understand

Great Compromise   Senate

House of Representatives

What was the conflict between the large states and the small states?

How many representatives should each state be able to send to Congress? This was one of the hardest questions that the Framers had to answer.

Delegates from states with small populations were afraid. They did not want the larger states to have more votes in Congress than they had. If that happened, the large states would have more power. They would control the new national government.

Delegates from small states argued that each state should have the same number of representatives in Congress. Delegates from states with large populations said that was not fair. A state with more people should have more votes in Congress.

During the long debates, the Framers could not reach a decision on this issue. Neither side was willing to give in. The delegates were almost ready to quit and go home. Finally, they formed a special committee to try to find a solution. One delegate from each state was on the committee.

▶ Why were states with small populations afraid of states with large populations?

72

Problem to solve

How many representatives in Congress should each state have?

Work in small groups of delegates. Each group should study the bar graph on the next page. You may draw a chart like the one on page 75 or your teacher might give you a handout. Read the questions and write your answers on your chart.

Step 1 There are seven small states and six large states. Which states are they? Write their names in column one on your chart.

Step 2 Look at the graph and figure out the population of each state. Write these numbers in column two on your chart.

Step 3 Suppose each state sends only one representative to Congress, write the number one in column three on your chart.

Step 4 Now, suppose it is decided that each state would have one representative for every 30,000 people in the state. How many representatives would each state have? Divide the population by 30,000. Write these numbers in column four on your chart.

Step 5 Add the numbers in each column. Put your answers in the total boxes.

Discuss and answer the following questions.

A. If it were decided that there should be one representative for each state, how many representatives would all the small states have together? How many would all the large states have together?

B. If it were decided that representation should be based on the population of each state, how many representatives would the small states have together? How many would the large states have together?

C. In each state, how many people would each representative represent?

D. Why would the small states favor the idea of having one representative for the whole state?

E. Why would the large states favor the idea of having one representative for every 30,000 people in the state?

PROBLEM TO SOLVE

How many representatives in Congress should each state have?

Ask students to imagine that they are delegates to the Philadelphia Convention and are responsible for deciding how many representatives each state should be able to send to Congress.

Each group should study the bar graph on the next page and figure out the approximate populations of the states. At this point, you may wish to distribute Handout D 2, copies can be made from the master in the Appendix section at the back of this book. Have students answer questions A–E based on the information provided on the graph. Our figures were obtained online from the 1790 Census Data, Fisher Library, University of Virginia. Note that our figures are for the total population including slaves.

MAKE A DECISION

The whole class should take part in the discussion and listen to each group's point of view. Then they should reach an agreement on the best way to solve the problem.

1. Should the number of representatives that each state sends to Congress be based on population? Or, should each state send only one representative to Congress?

   If representation was to be based on population, the large states could get Congress to serve their interests at the expense of the interests of the small states. Although this could mean that decisions would reflect the interests of a majority, the interests of the minority might not be served or protected.

   If representation was to be based on one representative per state, the small states could get Congress to serve their interests at the expense of the interests of the large states. It could even result in a minority of the entire population controlling Congress at the expense of the majority.

2. What would happen if you divide Congress into two parts, or houses, so that in one house each state would have one representative, and in the other house each state would have representatives based on its population?

   Introduce the idea of compromise. Explain that two houses in Congress might satisfy the interests of both sides.

3. What would be some advantages of dividing Congress into two houses as described above? What might be some disadvantages?

   Advantages might include the fact that the small states would have more power in one house and the large states more power in the other house. Since both houses had to agree to pass a law, each house would have the power to check the power of the other house. This might slow down decision-making and result in more thought being given to making laws. It could also result in each house having to compromise and take the interests of the other house into account.

   Disadvantages might include the problem that laws that favor the interests of majorities might not be passed. They could be checked by the house in which small states were represented. Also, having just one house might make it easier to make decisions because there would not be another house that had to agree with whatever law was being proposed.

Problem to solve

Make a decision based on your discussion.

1. Should the number of representatives that each state sends to Congress be based population? Or, should each state send one representative?

2. What would happen if you divide Congress into two parts or houses, so that in one house, each state would have one representative, and in the other house, each state would have representatives based on its population?

3. What might be the advantages of dividing Congress into two houses as described above? What might be the disadvantages?

   Explain your group's point of view to the class. Give reasons for your group's decisions. The whole class should take part in the discussion and reach an agreement on the best way to solve the problem of representation in Congress.

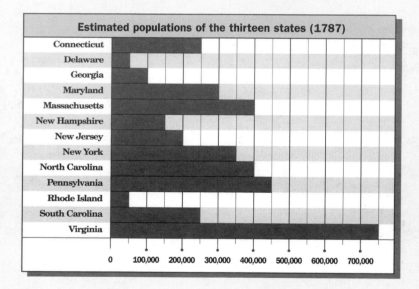

Estimated populations of the thirteen states (1787)

Connecticut, Delaware, Georgia, Maryland, Massachusetts, New Hampshire, New Jersey, New York, North Carolina, Pennsylvania, Rhode Island, South Carolina, Virginia

0, 100,000, 200,000, 300,000, 400,000, 500,000, 600,000, 700,000

HOW MANY REPRESENTATIVES SHOULD A STATE HAVE?

Small States

Step 1	Step 2	Step 3	Step 4
List the small states	List the population	List one representative for each state	List the number of representatives by population (30,000 people = 1 representative)
1.			
2.			
3.			
4.			
5.			
6.			
7.			
Step 5 TOTALS			

Large States

Step 1	Step 2	Step 3	Step 4
List the large states	List the population	List one representative for each state	List the number of representatives by population (30,000 people = 1 representative)
1.			
2.			
3.			
4.			
5.			
6.			
Step 5 TOTALS			

---

1. States are listed here in alphabetical order.
   Students may prefer to list them according to their populations.
2. For step 4, ask students to divide the state populations by 30,000.
   Approximate numbers are sufficient to illustrate the issue.
3. Direct students to add the numbers in the columns and write their sums in the total boxes.
4. Compare the charts.

Small States

Step 1	Step 2	Step 3	Step 4
List the small states	List the population	List one representative for each state	List the number of representatives by population (30,000 people = 1 representative)
1. Connecticut	250,000	1	8
2. Delaware	50,000	1	1
3. Georgia	100,000	1	3
4. New Hampshire	150,000	1	5
5. New Jersey	200,000	1	6
6. Rhode Island	50,000	1	1
7. South Carolina	250,000	1	8
Step 5 Totals	1,050,000	7	32

Large States

Step 1	Step 2	Step 3	Step 4
List the large states	List the population	List one representative for each state	List the number of representatives by population (30,000 people = 1 representative)
1. Maryland	300,000	1	10
2. Massachusetts	400,000	1	13
3. New York	350,000	1	11
4. North Carolina	400,000	1	13
5. Pennsylvania	450,000	1	15
6. Virginia	750,000	1	25
Step 5 Totals	2,650,000	6	87

READING AND DISCUSSION

What was the Great Compromise?

Ask students to read the section. Discuss the nature of compromise and how a compromise is reached. Then ask students to give examples of compromise from their own lives.

Explain to students that some of the compromises the Framers came up with were quite complicated. Write the main concepts of the Great Compromise on the board.

Direct students to consider how the formula for representation in the Senate protects the interests of the states with small populations, while the formula for representation in the House protects the interests of the states with large populations.

What was the Great Compromise?

Compromise is a way of dealing with a problem. Each side must be willing to give up something in order to solve the problem. Both sides have to agree on the solution. The Framers knew that they had to find a way to solve the problem of representation. They wanted a compromise the delegates would accept.

They appointed a committee to make a plan. The result of the committee's work is known as the **Great Compromise**.

It is the plan the delegates accepted for representation in Congress. These are the main parts of the Great Compromise.

- Congress would have two parts, or houses: the **Senate** and the **House of Representatives**.

- Each state, large or small, would have two representatives in the Senate.

- In the House of Representatives, the number of representatives from each state would be based on the number of people living in that state.

▶ How does this picture show representation in the Senate? How would this plan help the smaller states?

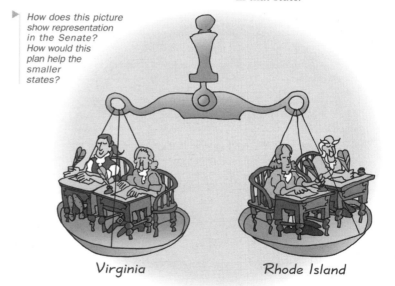

Virginia

Rhode Island

Senate

This agreement meant that each state would have equal power in the Senate. The states with more people would have more power in the House of Representatives. A law could not be passed unless a majority in both houses voted for it. This meant that large and small states could check each other's power. The Great Compromise protected the interests of both small and large states.

Some Framers did not like the compromise. It was hard for them to give up what they wanted. Nevertheless, the delegates voted and the Great Compromise was agreed upon.

▶ *How does this picture show representation in the House of Representatives? How would this plan help the larger states?*

Rhode Island

Virginia

House of Representatives

LESSON REVIEW

The questions in the student book are intended to assess learning and to reinforce knowledge through discussion. The questions are directly related to the lesson objectives. You may wish to include additional questions developed by yourself or by students.

1. Why was it hard for the Framers to agree on how many representatives a state should be able to send to Congress?

   The delegates from small states knew that if large states were given more representatives (more votes) in Congress, they would have more power. The small states wanted each state to have the same number of representatives. The large states felt they should have more representatives because they represented more people. Also, there were 7 small states and only 6 large states. The large states did not want the small states to control Congress.

2. How did the Great Compromise solve the problem of representation in Congress?

   Each state, large or small, would have two representatives in one house. In the other house, representation would be based on population, giving more representatives to large states. No law could be passed without the majority consent of both houses; in this way, the interests of both the large and small states were protected.

ACTIVITIES

The suggested activities are intended to extend and apply learning outside the classroom. You may wish to have students complete one or more of the activities. Then have them share the results with the class.

SUGGESTED CHILDREN'S LITERATURE

Read aloud the chapter "The Melody Lingers On" from *55 Men: The Story of the Constitution* (Harrisburg, PA: Stackpole Books, 1986, originally published in 1938). The chapter discusses the issues in this lesson.

Review the lesson

1. Why was it hard for the Framers to agree on how many representatives a state should be able to send to Congress?

2. How did the Great Compromise solve the problem of representation in Congress?

Activities to do

1. Find the names of the people who represent your state in the United States Senate.

2. How many representatives does your state have in the United States House of Representatives? What is the number of your congressional district? Who is your representative? Does everyone in your class have the same representative? Why or why not?

3. Find a map of the United States that shows the number of representatives the states have in the House of Representatives.

   Which states have the most members in the House of Representatives? Which have the fewest? How many people does one representative represent? See if you can find your congressional district on the map.

4. Think of a problem in your school that causes disagreements among your classmates. Make a list of things to consider when you compromise or negotiate. What things should you do? What things should you not do? Then, try working out a compromise with your classmates.

Lesson 10

What did the Framers do about the problem of slavery?

Purpose of the lesson

The Framers at the Philadelphia Convention faced another important issue. That issue was the question of slavery. Many colonists had depended on the labor of enslaved people for more than 150 years. The delegates from the Northern and Southern states could not agree about what to do. In this lesson, you will learn about the compromise the Framers reached on this issue.

When you have finished this lesson, you should be able to explain why the Framers agreed to the three-fifths clause.

79

OVERVIEW

This lesson deals with the controversy about slavery that divided the delegates from the Northern and Southern states. Students will read about the development of slavery in America and why it was more prevalent in the South than in the North. They will learn about the compromises made to convince Southern delegates to support the Constitution. They should understand that the compromises made at the convention did not solve the problem of slavery, but were necessary to keep the nation together. Without these compromises, it was unlikely that a number of Southern states would have agreed to support the Constitution.

OBJECTIVES

At the conclusion of this lesson, students should be able to

- explain why people in the North and South had different attitudes about slavery
- describe the disagreements about slavery that confronted the Framers
- describe the compromises that were made at the convention to deal with the problem of slavery

TEACHING PROCEDURES

INTRODUCTORY ACTIVITY

Have students read the "Purpose of the lesson" section and consider the objectives of the lesson. Remind students about the compromise the Framers made about the issue of representation. Point out that they also had to reach a compromise about another very important issue—slavery.

Write the "Terms to understand" on the board, or use a vocabulary-building activity of your choice. You may wish to have students look up the words in the glossary at the back of their text.

- abolish
- Civil War
- slave trade
- three-fifths clause

READING AND DISCUSSION

What was the slave trade?

Have students read the section. Discuss with them the characteristics of American slavery, making sure students understand that the people enslaved were considered to be property and had no rights. Point out to the class that in 1787 there were slaves in the North as well as in the South. The southern states, however, were economically dependent on slavery.

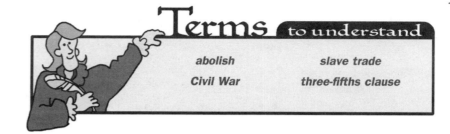

Terms to understand

abolish	**slave trade**
Civil War	**three-fifths clause**

What was the slave trade?

When our nation was founded, the slave trade had been practiced in many parts of the world for thousands of years. People in America had kept men, women, and children as indentured servants from the time of the first British colonies. But, the first people brought to the colonies specifically to be slaves were Africans.

Some of these African people were captured in tribal wars and sold to slave traders. Others were captured by the slave traders, themselves. The slave traders brought the Africans to the colonies in large sailing ships. Life aboard the ships was terrible. Many people died. Once in the colonies, the slave traders sold the people they had captured and transported.

In America, slaves were treated as if they were property, something that you can own, and buy and sell. Families were often broken up, and children were sold separately from their parents.

When the Founders signed the Declaration of Independence, there were about 500,000 people kept as slaves in the colonies. Before the Revolutionary War, there were slaves in every colony, in both the North and South.

Most people in the Southern states were farmers. Ninety percent of the slaves were in the Southern states. Plantation owners used the people that they kept as slaves to work their land. Crops such as cotton, rice, and indigo required a lot of labor. Plantation owners became dependent on slave labor for their profits.

People in the Northern states made their living in a number of different ways. They worked as farmers, fishers, merchants, and bankers. Others owned shops or worked in them. Most people in the North did not own slaves. Some Northerners, however, made their living in the **slave trade,** buying people in Africa and selling them to Southerners.

80

What did the Framers think about slavery?

The Framers came to Philadelphia with different opinions about slavery. Many of the delegates, including some from the South, believed that keeping people as slaves was wrong.

Most Southern delegates, however, wanted to protect the slaveholders. The large plantation owners depended upon slave labor for their living. These delegates said they would not support the Constitution if it abolished slavery. To **abolish** means to put an end to something. They said their states would refuse to be part of the new national government. The Framers had three main questions to resolve.

1. Should they allow the slave trade to continue?

2. Should they count slaves as part of a state's population? If they did, it would increase the number of representatives from Southern states in Congress. This would give the Southern states more power.

3. What should happen to slaves who ran away to states that did not allow slavery?

Let's look at how the Framers dealt with these questions.

What compromises did the Framers make?

After long, hard debates and discussions, the Framers agreed on several compromises about slavery. The compromises were accepted by both the Northern and Southern states. The main purpose of these compromises was to get the Southern states to agree to be part of the new government. As with all compromises, neither side got everything it wanted.

$100 REWARD!
RANAWAY

From the undersigned, living on Current River, about twelve miles above Doniphan, in Ripley County, Mo., on 2nd of March, 1860, A NE GRO MAN, about 30 years old, weighs about 160 pounds; high forehead, with a scar on it; had on brown pants and coat very much worn, and an old black wool hat; shoes size No. 11.

The above reward will be given to any person who may apprehend this said negro out of the State; and fifty dollars if apprehended in this State outside of Ripley county, or $25 if taken in Ripley county.
APOS TUCKER.

▶ *Do you think that runaway slaves caught in free states should have been returned?*

81

What did the Framers think about slavery?

After students read the section, emphasize that many of the Framers were aware of the contradiction between the principles of natural rights and the institution of slavery. The problem at the convention was the need to balance the belief that slavery was wrong with the need to win the support of delegates from the Southern states.

Review the three main problems about slavery that the Framers needed to solve. Explain the need for compromise. Ask students to work in pairs or small groups to discuss how they think the Framers might solve these issues.

What compromises did the Framers make?

Ask students to read the section. Relate each compromise to one of the problems listed in the previous section. Make sure that students understand what the Northern and Southern states gave up and what they gained in the process of compromise.

Slave populations of the thirteen original states (from the 1790 census)

*Total state population in **black***
State population of slaves in red

Connecticut	**237,655**
	2,764
Delaware	**59,096**
	8,887
Georgia	**82,548**
	29,264
Maryland	**319,728**
	103,036
Massachusetts	**378,556**
	0
New Hampshire	**141,899**
	158
New Jersey	**184,139**
	11,423
New York	**340,241**
	21,324
North Carolina	**395,005**
	100,572
Pennsylvania	**433,611**
	3,737
Rhode Island	**69,112**
	948
South Carolina	**249,073**
	107,094
Virginia	**747,550**
	292,627

The Northern states agreed that the Constitution would allow slavery to continue. The national government was not allowed to end the slave trade until 1808. Slaves who escaped to other states had to be returned.

The Southern states agreed that Congress would have the power to control trade between the states. This would help Northern businesses.

Finally, Northern and Southern delegates agreed upon another compromise. The **three-fifths clause** gave Southern states the right to count three-fifths of their slaves for the purpose of representation in Congress. In this compromise, the Southern states could send more representatives to Congress than if they were not allowed to count any slaves at all. They also had to pay more direct taxes than if they had not counted the slaves as part of the population.

Because of this compromise, the Southern states agreed to support the Constitution. They would be part of the new nation. The Constitution nowhere uses the word "slave." Some people say this is because the Framers were ashamed of slavery.

How did the three-fifths clause work for representation and direct taxes?

Free persons

POPULATION COUNT

 = 5

Enslaved persons

POPULATION COUNT

 **= 3**

How did slavery end in the United States?

Slavery continued in the United States for almost another eighty years. It ended only as a result of the Civil War. The **Civil War** was the war between the Northern and Southern states.

Soon after the Civil War, the Constitution was changed. The Thirteenth Amendment freed people from slavery. Other amendments gave former slaves the rights of citizens. However, these amendments did not end the unfair treatment of the newly freed slaves.

How did slavery end in the United States?

You might find it helpful to construct a timeline illustrating the following events in the history of slavery.

1619	First slaves brought to the British Colonies in America
1776	Declaration of Independence
1787	Philadelphia Convention
1860 –1865	Civil War
1866	Thirteenth Amendment abolishes slavery

Point out to students that slavery continued in this country for almost 80 years after the Philadelphia Convention. Although many Americans objected to slavery, it became part of the economic way of life in much of the South. It took the Civil War, much bloodshed, and the Thirteenth Amendment to end slavery.

LESSON REVIEW

The questions in the student book are intended to assess learning and to reinforce knowledge through discussion. The questions are directly related to the lesson objectives. You may wish to include additional questions developed by yourself or by students.

1. Why did the Northern and Southern states have different ideas about slavery?

   The Southern states had an agriculture-based economy. Slave labor was used to make the plantations profitable. If the slaves were freed, the plantation owners and the whole Southern economy would have suffered financial losses. The economy in the North was more varied. People made their living in a variety of ways that did not depend on the labor of enslaved people.

2. What compromise did the Framers reach about slavery?

   The Framers decided that the Congress would allow the slave trade to continue until 1808. The Southern states agreed to allow Congress to have the power to regulate commerce among the states and with other countries. The Framers agreed to count three-fifths of the slave population (or three-fifths of an enslaved person) for the census.

3. Why did the Framers compromise on this important issue?

   The Framers believed that without the compromise the Southern states would not have joined the union.

ACTIVITIES

The suggested activities are intended to extend and apply learning outside the classroom. You may wish to have students complete one or more of the activities. Then have them share the results with the class.

ADDITIONAL INSTRUCTIONAL ACTIVITY

As an option for authentic assessment, you may want to have students role-play newspaper reporters interviewing Americans in 1787 about slavery. Divide the class into small groups. One group will play the role of newspaper reporters. The other group will represent different points of view, such as Northern and/or Southern opponents of slavery, and religious leaders opposed to slavery. The activity can be performed as a skit and students might be asked to write a newspaper article.

Review the lesson

1. Why did the Northern and Southern states have different ideas about slavery?

2. What compromise did the Framers reach about slavery?

3. Why did the Framers compromise on this important issue?

Activities to do

1. Imagine you are a delegate to the Philadelphia Convention. Write a letter home to your family in which you explain your position on the slavery question.

2. Learn what life was like on-board a slave ship. Share what you learned with the class.

3. Imagine you help a runaway slave escape to freedom. Write a story about what you would do. In your story, describe what the Constitution says about returning runaway slaves.

UNIT 3

How does the Constitution organize our government?

UNIT 3

OVERVIEW

This unit of six lessons describes the way in which the Framers organized our national government. Students will analyze the basic ideas in the Preamble to the Constitution. Students also will learn that one of the Framer's major concerns was to create a strong national government while, at the same time, limiting the powers of that government to protect the rights of the people. To accomplish this task, the Framers separated the powers of the national government into three branches. Students will study these three branches—the legislative, executive, and judicial—and learn how each can check the powers of the other so that no one branch can totally dominate the government. Students will also learn how the Framers created a federal system of government that further limited the power of the national government.

OBJECTIVES

At the conclusion of this unit, students should be able to

1. explain the basic ideas in the Preamble to the Constitution
2. define separation of powers and checks and balances
3. explain the reasons that make separation of powers and checks and balances beneficial
4. describe the powers and responsibilities of the legislative, executive, and judicial branches of our national government
5. describe some ways in which the powers of each branch are limited
6. define a federal system of government
7. describe how powers are distributed in a federal system of government

INTRODUCTION

Read the Introduction with the class. Working in groups of three, have students offer some solutions to the problem presented in the introduction to the unit. Have each group share their solutions with the whole class.

Next, have students focus on the unit's key topics. You may want to read them more than once to familiarize students with the terms. Emphasize that these ideas ensure that the government does not become the master of the people. The Framers planned a national government that would have limited powers.

How does the Constitution organize our government?

In most other nations in 1787, the government was the master of the people. The government held all the power. Even today, many governments are still the masters of their people. People living under these governments have very few of the rights we have.

The Framers knew when they created our government that they faced a difficult problem. They wanted to create a stronger national government. But, they also worried about creating a government with too much power. A government with too much power might become our master instead of our servant.

Try to imagine how you would solve this problem if you were one of the Framers. Suppose you were creating a new government for our country. You know you have to give the government power over your life, liberty, and property. You are afraid of giving the government so much power.

How can you plan your government so it will remain the servant of the people? How can you organize it so that its powers will be limited and it will not become your master? In this unit, you will learn how the Framers solved this problem.

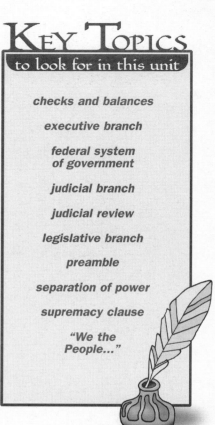

KEY TOPICS
to look for in this unit

checks and balances

executive branch

federal system of government

judicial branch

judicial review

legislative branch

preamble

separation of power

supremacy clause

"We the People..."

Lesson 11

What basic ideas about government are included in the Preamble to the Constitution?

Purpose of the lesson

The Framers wrote an introduction, also called a **preamble**, to the Constitution. The Preamble states the purposes of our Constitution. It includes some basic ideas about government that you have studied in this book. When you finish this lesson, you should be able to explain these ideas.

OVERVIEW

This lesson explores some ideas in the Preamble to the Constitution. Students learn the importance of the words, "We the People." The lesson emphasizes that the power to govern belongs to the people who have created a government to protect their rights and promote their welfare. Students read the Preamble and develop definitions for the six key phrases in the document.

OBJECTIVES

At the conclusion of this lesson, students should be able to

- explain the purpose of the Preamble to the Constitution
- explain the meaning of key phrases in the Preamble

TEACHING PROCEDURES

INTRODUCTORY ACTIVITY

Have students read the "Purpose of the lesson" section and consider the objectives of the lesson.

Write the "Terms to understand" on the board, or use a vocabulary-building activity of your choice. You may wish to have students look up the words in the glossary at the back of their text.

- a more perfect union
- blessings of liberty
- common defense
- domestic tranquility
- general welfare
- justice
- ordain
- posterity
- preamble

LESSON 11

IDEAS TO DISCUSS

What do you think should be the purposes of government?

Have students work with a partner or in groups of three to five. Students should read the six questions and discuss possible answers. They should be encouraged to examine their own experiences and to form reasoned opinions. Have each group or pair share their responses with the class. Possible answers are suggested.

1. What is a purpose?
   The goal, the point that is intended, or the reason to do something is a purpose.

2. Why is it important to know what your own purposes are?
   You need to know what your purposes are so that you know what you want to achieve or do.

3. Why is it important to know what the purposes of a government are?
   The people who are to be governed can only be assured that their rights will not be abused or taken away when they know what the government intends to do and how it will rule.

4. List five or six purposes that you think our government should have.
   - *protect the people's rights*
   - *make sure there is a fair system of laws*
   - *provide order for the people*
   - *protect the country during wartime*
   - *promote the common good*
   - *ensure domestic tranquility*
   - *protect the environment*
   - *educate the people*
   - *accept other reasonable responses*

5. Explain why you think each of the purposes you have listed for government is important.
   Responses should be specific to the purposes students gave in number 4.

Ideas to discuss

What do you think should be the purposes of government?

Before you learn about the purposes stated in the Preamble, let's examine your own ideas. Then you can compare your ideas with those in the Constitution. You might find that you and the Framers have many of the same ideas.

Work with a partner or in a group of three to five students. Discuss the questions that follow. Be prepared to share your ideas with the class.

1. What is a purpose?

2. Why is it important to know what your own purposes are?

3. Why is it important to know what the purposes of a government are?

4. List five or six purposes that you think a government should have.

5. Explain why you think each of the purposes you have listed for government is important.

▶ *The Federal Power Commission approved the construction of the Diablo Dam in Washington in 1927. Do you think government should regulate this type of project? Why or Why not?*

Terms to understand

a more perfect union

blessings of liberty

common defense

domestic tranquility

establish

general welfare

justice

ordain

preamble

Why does the Preamble say "We the People... do ordain and establish this Constitution for the United States of America"?

In 1787, the Framers wrote and signed the Constitution. The Preamble to the Constitution says that "We the People of the United States... do **ordain** (give official approval) and **establish** (accept) this Constitution for the United States of America." This means that the Constitution was approved by the people of the United States and that they agreed to live under the government it created. Each generation of Americans—including yours—must give its approval or consent to live under the government created by the Constitution.

- How do you and other Americans show that you consent to be governed under the Constitution?

- How do you, as one of the people, ordain and establish the Constitution?

There are many ways of answering these questions. One way is by willingly obeying the laws. Another way to show your consent is by repeating the Pledge of Allegiance. When you are older, you can give your consent by voting, serving on a jury, or holding public office. You also give consent when you take part in solving your community's problems. Taking your place as a citizen, one of "We the People," means that you consent to live under the Constitution.

▶ How can citizens show that they give approval to be governed by the Constitution?

89

READING AND DISCUSSION

Why does the Preamble say "We the People... do ordain and establish this Constitution..."?

Read the first paragraph of this section aloud with students. Then lead a discussion using the questions and examples presented in the second paragraph. Make sure that students understand the concepts of "ordain" and "establish."

LESSON 11

PROBLEM TO SOLVE

What ideas are expressed in the Preamble?

Have the class work in groups of three to five students. Assign each group one of the purposes of our national government. Students are responsible for explaining their assigned purpose and should give examples of how our national government tries to accomplish the purpose.

The three questions at the end of the problem-solving activity will help each group to focus on their part of the activity. The activity presents the opportunity for groups to not just answer the questions but to engage in the exercise in a variety of ways: drawing a poster; preparing a short dramatic skit; conducting an imaginary radio call-in show; or conducting an imaginary interview with a member of Congress, the president of the United States, or a justice of the U.S. Supreme Court.

Problem to solve

What ideas are expressed in the Preamble?

The Preamble to the Constitution explains who created the Constitution and the basic purposes of our government. "We the People…" are the first words in the Preamble. These words are very important. They show that the power to govern belongs to the people. The people established the Constitution. They used it to create a government to protect their rights and their welfare.

▶ Why are the first words of the Constitution, "We the People," so important?

The ideas in the Preamble are so important that you should study them carefully. To do this, first read the entire Preamble.

Preamble to the Constitution of the United States

We the People of the United States, in order to form a more perfect union, establish justice, insure domestic tranquility, provide for the common defense, promote the general welfare, and secure the blessings of liberty to ourselves and our posterity, do ordain and establish this Constitution for the United States of America.

The Preamble is made up of many words that might be hard to understand when you first read them. But if you study them, you will find they are not that difficult.

Let's examine the basic ideas in the Preamble to see how important they are to all of us. To do this, your class may work in small groups. Each group should study one part of the Preamble.

▶ *Which words in the preamble give government the right to organize military forces?*

We the People...

Group 1 do ordain and establish this Constitution for the United States of America.

Group 2 establish justice...

Group 3 insure domestic tranquility...

Group 4 provide for the common defense...

Group 5 promote the general welfare...

Group 6 secure the blessings of liberty...

Each group should answer the following questions about the part it is studying. Be prepared to explain your group's answers to the rest of the class.

1. What do the words that your group studied mean? Give an example.

2. Why is the part of the Preamble that your group studied important?

3. What does the part your group studied have to do with protecting your rights and the common good?

91

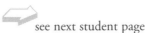 see next student page

LESSON REVIEW

The questions in the student book are intended to assess learning and to reinforce knowledge through discussion. The questions are directly related to the lesson objectives. You may wish to include additional questions developed by yourself or by students.

1. Some people have said the most important words in our Constitution are the first three words of the Preamble. These are the words, "We, the People." Explain why you agree or disagree with this opinion.

   The people have created the government and are its ultimate source of authority. The people consent to be ruled by the government they have created. They give power to both the national and state governments and retain all other power for themselves.

2. In your own words, explain what establishing justice means. Why is this an important purpose of government?

   Establishing justice means that the laws of the government must be fair and all the people must be treated in a fair manner.

3. Explain the difference between ensuring domestic tranquility and providing for the common defense.

   To ensure domestic tranquility means to keep peace and order within the borders of the United States. To provide for the common defense means to protect the United States and its citizens from those who might want to wage war against the United States.

4. What is the general welfare? What are some ways to promote the general welfare?

   General welfare means the same thing as the common good. That is, what is good for all the people of a community or nation. Some ways to promote the general welfare include paying taxes, obeying the law even though you may not agree with it, getting your immunization shots to protect the community from diseases. In Lesson 15, you will find a more in-depth discussion concerning how one can determine what is the common good.

5. What are some of the blessings of liberty that you enjoy? How can you help to make sure that one day your children will also enjoy them?

This phrase refers to providing the people with the protections and freedoms of a constitutional democracy, not only for themselves but also for their children and future generations.

6. How can you and other Americans show that you consent to live under the Constitution?

You can show your consent by obeying the laws of the government, serving on a jury, supporting and monitoring elected leaders, and participating in the election process.

ACTIVITIES

The suggested activities are intended to extend and apply learning outside the classroom. You may wish to have students complete one or more of the activities. Then, have them share the results with the class.

Review the lesson

1. Some people have said the most important words in our Constitution are the first three words of the Preamble. These are the words, "We the People." Explain why you agree or disagree with this opinion.

2. In your own words, explain what establishing justice means. Why is this an important purpose of government?

3. Explain the difference between ensuring domestic tranquility and providing for the common defense.

4. What is the general welfare? What are some ways to promote the general welfare?

5. What are some of the blessings of liberty that you enjoy? How can you help to make sure that future generations will also enjoy them?

6. How can you and other Americans show that you consent to live under the Constitution?

Activities to do

1. The people who worked on writing the Preamble were William Samuel Johnson, Alexander Hamilton, James Madison, Rufus King, and Gouverneur Morris. Learn more about these men. Share what you learned with the class.

2. Work with a partner to create a skit. One of you should portray Patrick Henry who said the Framers did not have the right to speak the language of "We the People" instead of "We the States."

The other student should portray Gouverneur Morris defending the position of the Framers in the use of the words "We the People." Perform your skit for the class.

3. Create six symbols to represent each of the six parts of the Preamble. In your own words, write a sentence that tells what each symbol means. Use the six symbols to create a bulletin board for your classroom.

Lesson 12

How does the Constitution limit the powers of our government?

Purpose of the lesson

The Framers wanted to limit the powers of our national government. They wanted to be sure that no one group of people in government would have too much power. So, they divided the powers of government among three groups or branches. In this lesson, you will learn more about the separation of powers and checks and balances.

When you have finished this lesson, you should be able to explain why the Framers separated the powers of our government. You should also be able to explain how the Constitution balances and checks the powers of each branch of government.

OVERVIEW

This lesson is designed to help students understand how the Framers wrote the Constitution so that it would limit the powers of the national government. The lesson opens with a discussion activity that helps students think about how they would organize a government for their class.

Introduce students to the concepts of separation of powers and checks and balances. Explain that by dividing and balancing power between the three branches of government, giving each branch a way to check on the power of the others, no one branch can completely control the government.

OBJECTIVES

At the conclusion of this lesson, students should be able to

- explain why the Framers thought it was necessary to limit the powers of the national government
- explain the concepts of separation of powers, balancing powers, and checking powers
- describe briefly the function of each of the branches of our government

TEACHING PROCEDURES

INTRODUCTORY ACTIVITY

Have students read the "Purpose of the lesson" section and consider the objectives of the lesson.

Write the "Terms to understand" on the board, or use a vocabulary-building activity of your choice. You may wish to have students look up the words in the glossary at the back of their text.

- balancing powers
- branches
- checking power
- executive power
- judicial power
- legislative power
- separation of power
- United States Supreme Court

IDEAS TO DISCUSS

How would you organize your government?

Organize the class into groups of three to five students and have them read the activity. Each group should answer the questions and share their answers with the class. You might wish to extend the discussion by analyzing your school and/or class government. Students should be encouraged to think about how power is limited when it is shared by different groups. They should be asked why it is necessary to limit the power of government. Students should be reminded that one of the key characteristics of a constitutional government is that its powers are limited. Possible answers are suggested; however, accept any reasonable response.

1. Suppose you decide to give all the powers of your class government to one group of students. What would be the advantages and disadvantages of doing this?

    Advantages: work might be done more quickly since the involvement of fewer people means that there might be fewer opinions about how to solve problems. Disadvantages: most students would not have their ideas represented, the group might not want to share any of their power, and they might make rules that are unfair to some students.

2. Suppose you decide to give the power to three different groups of students. You divide the powers of your government among them. What would be the advantages and disadvantages of doing this?

    Advantages: the interest of more students would be considered. Disadvantages: it might take longer for all three groups to make a decision.

Ideas to discuss

How would you organize your government?

Suppose you want to create a government for your class. Think how you might organize that government. It would need to have the following powers:

1. Power to make rules. This is called **legislative power**.

2. Power to carry out and enforce the rules. This is called **executive power**.

3. Power to settle disagreements about the rules. This includes the power to say what the rules mean. This is called **judicial power**.

Think about how you might distribute these powers in your class government. Work in small groups and answer the questions below. Be prepared to share your answers with the class.

1. Suppose you decide to give all the powers of your class government to one group of students. What would be the advantages and disadvantages of doing this?

2. Suppose you decide to give the power to three different groups of students. You divide the powers of your government among them. What would be the advantages and disadvantages of doing this?

▶ *How might you use the idea of separation of powers to organize a school government?*

Terms to understand

balancing powers	judicial power
branches	legislative power
checking power	separation of powers
executive power	United States Supreme Court

What ideas did the Framers use to limit the power of government?

When the Framers organized our national government, they knew they needed to limit its powers. The Framers did this by dividing the government into three parts. They called these parts the three **branches** of government. They gave certain powers to each branch.

- Legislative branch. The Framers gave this branch the power to make laws. They called our national legislature Congress. Congress has two parts or houses. They are the Senate and the House of Representatives.

- Executive branch. The Framers gave this branch the power to carry out and enforce the laws made by Congress. The president is the head of this branch.

- Judicial branch. The Framers gave this branch the power to settle disagreements about what the laws mean. The **United States Supreme Court** is the highest court in this branch.

What else did the Framers do to limit the power of government?

The Framers knew that governments often gain too much power. When they do, they can violate the rights of the people. They work for the selfish interests of a few people instead of for the common good. They do not treat people fairly.

The Framers wanted to make sure this could not happen. They separated and balanced the powers among the different branches. Then they gave each branch a way to check the use of power by the other branches. The Framers believed that the way they organized the government was the best way to protect the rights and welfare of the people.

95

READING AND DISCUSSION

What ideas did the Framers use to limit the power of government?

Have students read this section aloud. Write the terms "separation of powers" and "checks and balances" on the board and explain to the class that these are the important ideas they will be studying. Students should be able to draw some parallels between the ideas they presented during the previous activity and the goals of the Framers.

What else did the Framers do to limit the power of government?

Explain that dividing the powers of government into separate branches is not sufficient for controlling the power of each branch. Remind students that when the scale is out of balance, one branch can gain too much power. When this happens, the rights of the people might be in danger.

The Framers knew from history that constitutional governments are often divided into different branches. **Separation of powers** means to divide the power of government among its branches. The Framers used the idea of separation of powers as one way to limit the power of government.

The Framers also knew that it was not enough just to separate the powers of government. If you gave too much power to one branch, it might control the others. The Framers believed that the powers of government needed to be balanced among the different branches. **Balancing powers** means that no one government branch is given so much power that it can completely control the other branches.

▶ *How is power balanced among the different branches of government?*

96

The Framers used one more way to limit the power of government. They gave each branch ways to check the other branches. **Checking powers** means that each branch can stop the other branches from making final decisions or from taking certain actions. For example, Congress has the power to make laws. The president can stop or control this power by refusing to approve a bill passed by Congress. But, the bill might still become law. Two-thirds of the members of Congress would have to vote to make it a law. Suppose the bill does become law. The judicial branch has the power to check Congress and the president. If a case is brought before them, the courts have the power to say that a certain law is not allowed by the Constitution.

▶ *How does the judicial branch check the power of the executive and legislative branches?*

LESSON 12

LESSON REVIEW

The questions in the student book are intended to assess learning and to reinforce knowledge through discussion. The questions are directly related to the lesson objectives. You may wish to include additional questions developed by yourself or by students.

1. What are the three branches of our government? What power does each branch have?

   The legislative branch makes the laws. The executive branch enforces the laws. The judicial branch settles disagreements about what the law means.

2. Why did the Framers separate the powers of our government?

   The Framers wanted to be sure that the powers of government were limited to prevent any abuse of power.

3. Why did the Framers balance the powers of government?

   The Framers balanced the powers of government to prevent any one branch from having too much power and taking control of the other two branches.

4. Why did the Framers provide ways for each branch of our government to check the powers of the other two branches? Give an example of how one branch can check the power of another.

   By allowing each branch to check the power of the other branches, the Framers provided a measure to ensure that no one branch of government became too powerful. The president can check the power of Congress by refusing to sign a bill passed by Congress. Congress can check the power of the president by voting to pass the bill over the president's objection, if they have two thirds of the members' approval. The U.S. Supreme Court can check the power of the Congress by declaring a law unconstitutional.

ACTIVITIES

The suggested activities are intended to extend and apply learning outside of the classroom. You may wish to have students complete one or more. Then, have them share the results with the class.

Review the lesson

1. What are the three branches of our government? What power does each branch have?

2. Why did the Framers separate the powers of our government? How are they separated?

3. Why did the Framers balance the powers of our government?

4. Why did the Framers provide ways for each branch of our government to check the powers of the other branches? Give an example of how one branch can check the power of another.

Activities to do

1. Write a short letter to a friend. Describe what you have learned about the separation of powers and checks and balances. Tell why you think these ideas are important. Share your letter with the class.

2. Draw a diagram. In your diagram, show your understanding of how separation of powers and checks and balances work. Share your diagram with the class.

3. Find newspaper or magazine articles that report examples of the use of checks and balances. Share your articles with the class.

4. Watch the news on television. Report to the class any story about one branch of government checking another branch.

Lesson 13

What is the legislative branch?

Purpose of the lesson

You have learned that the legislative branch makes our laws. Our national legislature is Congress. In this lesson, you will learn about the powers of Congress. You will learn something about how Congress makes laws. You will also learn how our Constitution limits the powers of Congress.

When you have finished this lesson, you should be able to describe how Congress is organized, what powers it has, and how its powers are limited. You should also be able to explain how a law is made.

99

OVERVIEW

This lesson examines the legislative branch in a way that requires student involvement, creative decision-making, and analysis of a "real-life" situation.

Students should first examine the organization of the two houses of Congress, the powers of Congress, the procedures for making a law, and the limitations on the power of Congress. Students then read about the responsibilities of a representative. They are presented with a dilemma on how a representative should vote when faced with a conflict between the common good and the economic needs of her particular state.

OBJECTIVES

At the conclusion of this lesson, students should be able to

- explain the function of the legislative branch
- describe the procedure for making a law
- describe the powers of Congress and the limitations on those powers

TEACHING PROCEDURES

INTRODUCTORY ACTIVITY

Introduce this lesson by asking students what they know about the legislative branch of government. Write their ideas on the chalkboard to compare their findings with what they learn in the lesson. Then have students read the "Purpose of the lesson."

Write the "Terms to understand" on the board, or use a vocabulary-building activity of your choice. You may wish to have students look up the words in the glossary at the back of their text.

- Article I
- bill
- Congress
- unconstitutional
- veto

READING AND DISCUSSION

What is Congress?

Have students read "What is Congress?" and continue the exercise by comparing what they read with the ideas that they volunteered at the start of the lesson.

Terms to understand

Article I	unconstitutional
bill	veto
Congress	

What is Congress?

Congress is the legislative branch of our national government. It makes our nation's laws. As you have learned, the Framers created two houses of Congress. The two houses are the Senate and the House of Representatives.

Senate

Senators must be at least thirty years old. They must have been citizens of the United States for at least nine years, and they must live in the state that they represent. Senators are elected to serve for six years.

Each state sends two persons to the Senate. Today, the United States Senate has 100 senators.

House of Representatives

Representatives must be at least twenty-five years old. They must have been citizens for at least seven years, and they must live in the district they represent. Representatives are elected to serve for two years.

The number of representatives each state can send to the House is based on its population. Currently, each member of the House represents about 650,000 people. When the Constitution was written, each member represented 30,000 people. The total number of representatives is now limited to 435. There are five representatives from other parts of our country: the District of Columbia, American Samoa, the Commonwealth of Puerto Rico, Guam, and the United States Virgin Islands. In 2003, California had the most people. California sent fifty-two representatives to the House. Wyoming had the smallest population. Wyoming and six other states each sent one representative to the House.

100

What powers does Congress have?

Article I of the Constitution lists the powers of Congress. Some of these powers are very specific. For example, Congress has the power to

- tax the people
- raise an army and navy to defend our nation
- declare war
- create a court system
- coin money

Other powers of Congress are very general. The Constitution gives Congress the power to

- pass all laws that are necessary and proper to carry out its responsibilities. For example, Congress passed the Civil Rights Acts to prevent unfair discrimination against some citizens.

- provide for the general welfare of the United States. For example, Congress created the National Institutes of Health to support medical research on health issues and to find cures for those who are sick.

▶ What does the legislative branch do?

What powers does Congress have?

Read the section and refer students to Article I, Section 8 of the Constitution. Review some of the powers of Congress listed there. Students should also review what they learned about the "general welfare" in Lesson 11 and apply this concept to the power that Congress has to promote the general welfare.

LESSON 13

How does Congress make a law?

Students should read the section "How does Congress make a law?" Review the three steps described and discuss the difference between a bill and a law.

How does Congress make a law?

Congress provides for the general welfare by passing laws that help people. Suppose that you, a member of Congress, the president, or some group with an interest, has an idea for a new law. How does the idea become a law? Here are the basic steps that must be followed.

1. **Write a bill.** A member of Congress must agree that the idea is good. Then, he or she writes a proposal for the law, which is called a bill. A **bill** is a proposed law.

2. **Go to committee.** Congress has committees that deal with different areas of the people's needs. A committee will examine the bill. The members of the committee discuss the bill, and then, they might rewrite it, change some parts, or decide that it is not a good bill.

3. **Get a majority vote of Congress.** When the bill is ready, the member of Congress who wrote the bill must get a majority of members to vote for it. If the member is a senator, the bill goes to the Senate first. If she or he is a representative, it goes to the House of Representatives first. Then the bill goes to the other house for a vote.

4. **Get the president to approve the bill.** If the bill passes in both houses, Congress must send the bill to the president. If the president approves the bill and signs it, it becomes a law. If the president refuses to sign the bill and sends it back to Congress, this is a **veto**. The bill can still become a law, if two-thirds of all the members of Congress vote to pass it over the president's veto.

▶ *What steps does Congress need to follow to make a new law?*

Why are the powers of Congress limited by the Constitution?

How does the Constitution limit the powers of Congress?

The Constitution and Bill of Rights limit the powers of Congress. They list the kinds of laws that Congress may not make. For example, Congress may not make a law that unfairly and unnecessarily limits your freedom to speak.

Suppose Congress passed a bill saying you cannot criticize the national government. Then the president signed the bill and it became a law. How might this law be overturned? How are your rights protected?

The Supreme Court has the power to declare a law made by Congress unconstitutional. **Unconstitutional** means that that the Constitution does not give Congress the right to pass such a law. If the Supreme Court says this, then the law cannot be enforced. It is no longer a law. This is another check on Congress.

What are the responsibilities of senators and representatives?

Members of Congress are responsible for making laws that protect our rights and promote our welfare. To make laws, members of Congress first must learn about the problems of our country. There are groups with special interests that try to convince members of Congress to make laws that benefit their groups. Congress must find ways to deal with the problems that concern these groups, as well as the people as a whole. Senators and representatives talk to the people in their states and districts. They read letters sent by citizens. They listen to debates and attend committee meetings.

Making good laws is not easy. A bill might help some people while it hinders others. Members of Congress must decide whether to vote for or against each bill. The next class participation activity will help you understand how difficult it can be to decide if a bill deserves support.

How does the Constitution limit the powers of Congress?

What are the responsibilities of senators and representatives?

Have students read the next section, "How does the Constitution limit the powers of Congress?" Point out that Article I of the Constitution and the power of the Supreme Court to declare a law unconstitutional are the major means of limiting congressional powers. Remind students that these limits are part of the system of checks and balances that they studied in Lesson 12.

In the next section, "What are the responsibilities of your senators and representative?" discuss how members of Congress can respond to the needs of their constituents. Students should be encouraged to think about the following questions:

- What happens when constituent needs conflict with what a member of Congress believes to be right?
- What happens when constituent needs conflict with the common good?

CLASS PARTICIPATION ACTIVITY

How should Representative Smith vote?

Read the instructions for the activity to the class. Divide the class into groups of three to five students. One group should role-play representative Smith and her staff. The other groups role-play people in Representative Smith's state and include such divergent groups as tobacco growers, citizens for freedom, citizens for a smoke-free environment, and citizens for better health.

Groups should read the story and answer the questions that follow it. The groups will need to discuss the problem and develop a position based on their roles. All members should be ready to make a presentation before Representative Smith and her staff.

The "Talking it over" section is important for debriefing students on the process in which they have engaged. They should be encouraged to listen to and rearticulate arguments made by the other groups.

Participating in a class activity

How should Representative Smith vote?

Suppose that Representative Smith is visiting your community to seek advice and opinions. She has arranged a public hearing on Thursday night at seven o'clock. She has invited the people who live in her district to attend the hearing. She is hoping for a good turnout. Representative Smith wants to find out if she should vote for a bill that would prevent smoking in public places.

GETTING READY FOR THE PUBLIC HEARING

Read the story and answer the questions that follow it. Prepare to play the role of one of the groups described after the story. Each group should prepare a presentation to make at the public hearing. Representative Smith and her staff will ask your opinion about a bill in Congress.

Representative Smith makes a decision

Smoking cigarettes is a national problem. Studies have shown that smoking is dangerous to everyone's health. Even breathing smoke from someone else's cigarette is dangerous. Each year, thousands of Americans die from smoking cigarettes.

Many farmers in Representative Smith's congressional district are involved in growing tobacco. Many other people make their living by working in factories that make tobacco products.

There is a bill in Congress that would forbid smoking in public places. Representative Smith knows smoking is dangerous and costly. She also knows that if she votes for the bill, the tobacco industry will suffer. Many people will lose their jobs, and some businesses will fail.

Representative Smith must decide how to vote on the bill. Should she vote against the bill to protect the jobs of the people in her district? Should she vote for the bill because she believes smoking is dangerous to people's health? The public hearing will help Representative Smith decide how to vote.

Representatives are supposed to support laws that protect people's rights. They are also supposed to support laws that serve the common good.

1. What rights are involved in this situation?

2. Which rights do you think are most important? Why?

3. What is the common good in this situation? Explain your answer.

▶ To make a good and fair decision, what issues does Representative Smith have to consider?

Participating in a class activity

Group 1: Representative Smith and Her Staff

Representative Smith must decide if she will vote "yes" or "no" on the bill. Before she decides, she and her staff want to know what the people in her district think about the problem. Representative Smith wants to speak with the groups that have valuable information about the situation. After she hears from the people she represents, she will make a decision.

Group 2: Tobacco Growers and Processors

You earn a living by growing and processing tobacco, just as your families have done for generations. If Representative Smith supports the bill, many people will lose their jobs. Some people will lose their businesses and their way of life.

Group 3: Citizens for Freedom

You believe that adults should be allowed to make their own lifestyle choices. You think that this bill would limit people's freedom to make their own decisions about their health and smoking.

Group 4: Citizens for a Smoke-Free Environment

You think that smoking in public places is a serious problem. Smoking in public violates the rights of nonsmokers who are forced to breathe secondhand smoke.

Group 5: Citizens for Better Health

You think that putting limits on smoking in public would help improve everyone's health. All citizens carry the costs of health care.

TAKING PART IN THE PUBLIC HEARING

A member of each group may tell Representative Smith the group's opinion about the proposed law. That member may also give her advice on how to vote on the issue. Then, Representative Smith and her

Why is it important for Representative Smith to listen to the ideas of the people in her district? How is this related to the idea of republican government?

staff will discuss the problem, decide what to do, and explain their decision.

TALKING IT OVER

1. Do you agree with Representative Smith's decision? Why or why not?

2. Why might citizens disagree about which responsibility is more important for their representative to carry out?

3. In what other ways could Representative Smith carry out her responsibilities in this situation?

4. Did you change your own opinion after listening to all the groups? If you did, what argument convinced you?

 see next student page

LESSON REVIEW

The questions in the student book are intended to assess learning and to reinforce knowledge through discussion. The questions are directly related to the lesson objectives. You may wish to include additional questions developed by yourself or by students.

1. What information will you find in Article I of the Constitution?
   Article I states that Congress has two houses and it lists the powers of Congress.

2. What does the legislative branch of our government do?
   The legislative branch makes the laws.

3. Name the two houses of Congress.
   The two houses of Congress are the Senate and the House of Representatives.

4. Make a list of some of the powers that the Constitution grants to Congress.
   - *tax the people*
   - *create the court system*
   - *declare and wage war*
   - *coin money*
   - *provide for the common defense*
   - *raise an army and navy*

5. Explain the steps by which a bill becomes a law.
   - *(1) Write the bill*
   - *(2) Go to committee*
   - *(3) Get a majority vote of both houses of Congress*
   - *(4) Get the president's approval*

6. What are some limits on the powers of Congress?
   - *(1) The president must approve the bills passed by Congress.*
   - *(2) The United States Supreme Court can declare a law unconstitutional.*
   - *(3) Article I establishes specific powers that are denied to Congress.*

ACTIVITIES

The suggested activities are intended to extend and apply learning outside the classroom. You may wish to have students complete one or more of the activities. Then, have them share the results with the class.

Review the lesson

1. What information will you find in Article I of the Constitution?

2. What does the legislative branch of our government do?

3. Name the two houses of Congress.

4. Make a list of some of the powers that the Constitution grants to Congress.

5. List and explain the steps by which a bill becomes a law.

6. What are some limits on the powers of Congress?

Activities to do

1. Find a recent newspaper article about Congress. Be prepared to talk about the issues in the article with your class.

2. The Constitution says that every ten years, the government must count the number of people in the country. This is called a census. Find out how the census is used to determine how many representatives a state may send to the House of Representatives.

3. Decorate your classroom by creating a picture gallery that shows the current senators from your state and the representative from your district. Write something about each person, and include this information in your gallery. Learn about some of the bills your senators and your representative have written or sponsored. Ask your teacher to invite your member of Congress to your classroom.

4. Divide your class into two "houses." Ask each student or small group of students in each house to write a bill proposing a policy for your classroom. The writers of each bill should present it to their own house for a vote. If it passes, then it should be presented to the other house for a vote. If the bills pass in both houses, send them to your teacher, who will act as president and approve or veto the bill.

Lesson 14

What is the executive branch?

Purpose of the lesson

You already learned that the executive branch carries out and enforces the laws passed by Congress. The president is the head of the executive branch. In this lesson, you will learn about the powers of the president. You will also learn how Congress can check the powers of the president.

When you have finished this lesson, you should be able to describe how the executive branch is organized. You should be able to identify the powers of this branch. You should also be able to explain some of the limits on its powers.

OVERVIEW

This lesson introduces students to the executive branch of our national government. They learn about the concerns of the Framers in balancing the need for an effective president with the fear of giving too much power to one person.

Students should learn how the powers of the presidency are limited by Congress. This lesson concludes with an examination of how the first Congress organized the executive branch.

OBJECTIVES

At the conclusion of this lesson, students should be able to

- explain the concerns of the Framers when they created the executive branch
- describe the powers of the president
- describe the ways in which Congress limits the president's powers

INTRODUCTORY ACTIVITY

Students should be able to understand how the powers of the presidency are limited by Congress. They should recognize that limiting the powers of the presidency is the result of the Framers' concern about balancing the need for an effective president with the fear of giving too much power to one person. The lesson concludes with an examination of how the first Congress organized the executive branch.

Write the "Terms to understand" on the board, or use a vocabulary-building activity of your choice. You may wish to have students look up the words in the glossary at the back of their text.

- appoint
- Article II
- budget
- commander in chief
- impeach
- treaty

Reading and discussion

How did the Framers create the executive branch?

What are the powers and duties of the president?

Ask students why the Framers were so afraid of a strong president. Discuss George III and the colonies' experiences with him. You may wish to review the complaints against the king from the discussion in Lesson 5.

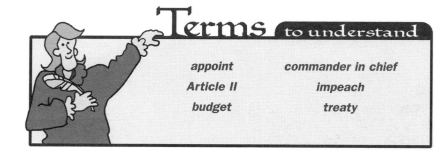

Terms to understand

appoint	commander in chief
Article II	impeach
budget	treaty

How did the Framers create the executive branch?

The executive branch of our government carries out and enforces the laws passed by Congress. For example, Congress might pass a law to build a highway across the country. The executive branch has to carry out the law.

The president of the United States is the head of the executive branch. The Framers had many discussions about how much power to give to the president. They did not want to make the executive branch too weak or too strong.

The Framers wanted to do two things. They wanted to give the president enough power to carry out and enforce the laws. But, they did not want to give the president too much power. If they did, a president might be able to gain unlimited power. With unlimited power, the president might become a dictator.

Article II of the Constitution establishes the executive branch. Article II lists the duties and powers of the president.

What are the powers and duties of the president?

The Framers gave the president many powers and duties. Some of these powers and duties are listed below.

The president has the power to

- act as the **commander in chief** of the armed forces. The military must obey the orders of the president.

- make treaties. A **treaty** is an official agreement between two or more countries. Treaties must have the advice and consent of the Senate.

- appoint ambassadors, with the consent of the Senate. The job of an ambassador is to represent the

110

To what types of positions can the president appoint people?

Judge J. Harvie Wilkinson, President George W. Bush and Secretary of the Treasury John Snow.

United States in another country. To **appoint** means to choose or name someone for an office or duty.

- appoint judges to the Supreme Court, with the consent of the Senate; appoint other officials of the United States.

- grant pardons for crimes against the United States.

The president must protect the Constitution. The president must also carry out the duties of the office. The president has the duty to

- act as the head of the executive branch. There are many

departments, or offices, within the executive branch. The president must make sure that these departments carry out and enforce the laws.

- suggest laws and policies. The president may ask the Congress to pass certain laws. Every year the president prepares a **budget**. The budget is a plan for how to spend the nation's money. The budget goes to Congress for approval.

- set policy for dealing with other countries in the world. The president is responsible for dealing with other countries.

What types of treaties might a president sign with another country?

Boris Yeltsin (Russian President) and President Bill Clinton.

How does the Constitution limit the powers of the president?

Have students read the next section. Outline on the board the powers and duties described in the reading. Outline the ways in which Congress can limit the president's powers. Remind students that these limits are part of the system of checks and balances they have studied.

How does the Constitution limit the powers of the president?

The Framers were careful to limit the powers of the president. They made the president share most powers with Congress. Here are some examples of how Congress can check the powers of the president.

- **Appointment.** The president has the power to appoint people to important jobs in the executive and judicial branches. The Senate has to approve the person before he or she may have the job.

- **Treaties.** The Senate must approve any treaty, agreed to by the president, before it can take effect.

- **War.** The president can conduct a war. Only Congress, however, can declare a war. The president commands the armed forces, but Congress controls the money needed to support the armed forces.

- **Veto.** The president has the power to veto a bill. Congress has the power to approve the same bill in spite of the president's veto, if two-thirds of each house agree.

- **Impeachment.** To **impeach** means to charge a public official with wrongdoing in office. It also means to bring the official to trial. The House of Representatives has the power to impeach the president. If tried and found guilty by the Senate, the president can be removed from office.

In the next lesson, you will learn how the Supreme Court checks the power of the president.

▶ *How can Congress limit the powers of the president?*

▶ *Why do you think departments were created to help the president?*

How is the executive branch organized?

George Washington was elected the first president of the United States. The Framers knew that the president would need help in running the executive branch. But, the Framers did not have a plan. The Constitution does not say how the executive branch should be organized. Instead, the Framers left it up to President Washington and Congress to decide how to organize the executive branch.

Washington and Congress worked together to decide what advisors the president would need. Congress created four departments to help the president.

- **Department of State** – to handle relations with other countries

- **Department of the Treasury** – to handle the money of the federal government

- **Department of War** – now called the **Department of Defense**, to handle the defense of the nation

- **Attorney General** – now the head of the **Department of Justice**, to be the chief law enforcement officer

The people in charge of these departments act as advisers to the president. These advisers became known as the president's cabinet. The cabinet now includes the vice president and the heads of fifteen executive departments.

How is the executive branch organized?

Have students discuss how the executive branch has grown since George Washington was president. Students might be asked to collect news articles dealing with one or more cabinet members.

LESSON 14

LESSON REVIEW

The questions in the student book are intended to assess learning and to reinforce knowledge through discussion. The questions are directly related to the lesson objectives. You may wish to include additional questions developed by yourself or by students.

1. What are some duties and powers of the president of the United States?

   The president can grant pardons, make treaties, name ambassadors, act as commander in chief, and nominate judges to the Supreme Court. Some of the duties of the president include being the head of the executive branch, proposing laws and policies, and setting policies for dealing with other countries in the world.

2. Explain four ways that Congress can check the power of the president.

   1. Senate must approve presidential appointments.
   2. Senate must approve treaties.
   3. Only Congress can declare and wage war.
   4. Congress can approve a bill with a 2/3 vote when the president does not sign the bill.

3. What does the president's cabinet do?

   The members of the cabinet act as advisers to the president.

4. Who holds each of the offices in the United States today: the president, the vice-president, the secretary of state, the secretary of the treasury, the secretary of defense, the attorney general?

   With each new presidential election be sure to keep students informed of the office holders in the current administration.

ACTIVITIES

The suggested activities are intended to extend and apply learning outside of the classroom. You may wish to have students complete one or more of the activities. Then, have them share the results with the class.

Review the lesson

1. What are some duties and powers of the president of the United States?

2. Explain four ways that Congress can check the power of the president.

3. What does the president's cabinet do?

4. Who holds each of these offices in the United States today: the president, the vice-president, the secretary of state, the secretary of the treasury, the secretary of defense, the attorney general?

Activities to do

1. What are the qualifications for being president of the United States? To answer this question, see the Constitution, Article II, Section One, part 5.

2. Article I, Section One, says that the president is to be elected by "electors" appointed in each state. How many electors does your state have? How are they chosen? Find more information about the process for electing the president. Share what you learn with the class.

3. Today there are fifteen members of the president's cabinet. Find the names of the fifteen cabinet offices.

   Create a chart that that shows the president's cabinet. On the chart, explain what each member does.

4. Find newspaper articles about a duty that the president is carrying out. Be prepared to share the articles with your class. Use the articles to create a class bulletin board.

5. Find newspaper articles about Congress or the Supreme Court checking something the president wants to do. Write a report that explains what is happening. Use quotes from the article. Present the report to the class.

Lesson 15

What is the judicial branch?

Purpose of the lesson

The judicial branch is the system of courts of law. The courts decide what laws mean and settle disagreements about them. In this lesson, you will learn about the duties and powers of the judicial branch. You will learn how this branch is organized.

When you have finished this lesson, you should be able to describe how the judicial branch is organized and some of its powers. You should also be able to explain some of the limits on its powers.

115

OVERVIEW

This lesson examines the judicial branch and the power of judicial review. Students learn that the courts protect the rights of the people against any unconstitutional actions by the president or Congress. The power of judicial review is an important check by the judiciary on the other two branches of government. Students will read about an actual case, *Chicago v. Morales*, 527 U.S. 41 (1999), to see how the Supreme Court used its power of judicial review to strike down an unconstitutional city law.

OBJECTIVES

At the conclusion of this lesson, students should be able to

- describe the functions of the judicial branch
- explain how members of the judiciary are selected
- define judicial review and explain its importance

INTRODUCTORY ACTIVITY

Have students read the "Purpose of the lesson" section and consider the objectives of the lesson.

Write the "Terms to understand" on the board, or use a vocabulary-building activity of your choice. You may wish to have students look up the words in the glossary at the back of their text.

- appeal
- associate
- federal courts
- interpret
- judicial review

READING AND DISCUSSION

What does the judicial branch do?

How is the judicial branch organized?

How are judges in the federal courts selected?

Read aloud the following excerpt from the Constitution: "Congress shall have Power... [to] provide for the... general welfare of the United States."

1. Ask students if the meaning of this phrase is clear. Why might people argue about what it means?

   General welfare and common good refer to the same idea, that is, what is good for all of the people of a community or nation. Although people might agree in general that providing for the general welfare is a good thing to do, there are at least several problems that arise. First is the question of exactly what is meant by general welfare. Does it mean, for example, what is good for an entire population, a super majority, or a simple majority? Second, how can one determine what is good for everyone? And third, exactly what serves the general welfare in particular cases? For example, it might be easy to agree that clean air is in everyone's interest. However, suppose strict laws against air pollution result in thousands of people losing their jobs. Would such laws serve the general welfare?

2. Who should decide what the words in the Constitution mean?
   Students might suggest the judicial branch or the Supreme Court.

Explain that one function of the judicial branch is to settle disputes about the meaning of the Constitution and federal laws. Have students read the section and then discuss the role of the courts.

Have the class read the next two sections. Ask why judges are appointed rather than elected.

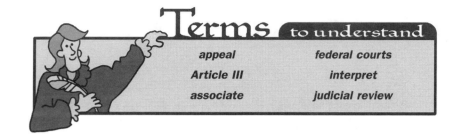

Terms to understand

appeal	federal courts
Article III	interpret
associate	judicial review

What does the judicial branch do?

The role of the courts is to **interpret** the law. To interpret is to decide the meaning of the law and the Constitution.

The courts settle conflicts between individuals and between the states. The courts also decide if someone is guilty of breaking the law. The courts are responsible for deciding how a guilty person should be punished.

The federal courts are the courts of the national government. The **federal courts** deal with problems between states. Federal courts also handle cases that deal with the Constitution and the laws made by Congress.

How is the judicial branch organized?

The judicial branch of the national government is composed of lower courts and the Supreme Court of the United States. The Supreme Court is the highest court of our national government. We call the nine judges on the Supreme Court "justices." The head of the Supreme Court is the Chief Justice of the United States. **Article III** of the Constitution describes the responsibilities and powers of this branch.

How are judges in the federal courts selected?

The Framers believed that if the people elected federal judges, the judges might not make fair decisions. They might favor the people who voted for them. For this reason, federal judges are appointed to office. The president appoints all the judges in the federal courts. The Senate must approve each appointment.

Federal judges usually serve in office until they retire or die. Congress has the power to remove federal judges if they are found guilty of serious crimes.

Ideas to discuss

What could you do if the government took away some of your rights?

Suppose you thought that one of your rights guaranteed by the Constitution was being abused by government officials. What could you do about it? In what ways might the courts help protect your rights?

▶ What could you do if you felt you were unfairly sent to jail?

▶ What does the United States Supreme Court do?

IDEAS TO DISCUSS

What could you do if the government took away some of your rights?

Have students work in small groups to share their thoughts on the questions in this section. Ask students to explain their ideas to the class.

LESSON 15

What is the power of judicial review?

For our purpose here, student readings and problem solving are limited to issues involving the federal courts. A definition of the concept of judicial review, however, may prove useful.

> Judicial review is the power of the judiciary, or the courts, to determine whether the acts of other branches of the government are in accordance with the Constitution. All courts, federal and state, may exercise the power of judicial review, but the Supreme Court of the United States has the final judicial decision on whether laws or actions of local, state, or federal governments violate or conform to the U. S. Constitution, the highest law of the land.

Patrick, John J. *The Supreme Court of the United States: A Student Companion.* Second Edition, p. 180. Copyright 2001. Oxford University Press, New York.

What is the power of judicial review?

Judicial review is one of the most important powers of the judicial branch. **Judicial review** is the power of the courts to decide whether the United States Constitution allows a certain law or action of government. Judicial review gives the federal courts the power to

- declare that a law made by Congress is not constitutional

- declare that an action taken by the president is not constitutional

- declare a state law unconstitutional, if it conflicts with the laws made by Congress or with the Constitution

Suppose Congress passed a law that said you must practice a certain religion. The Constitution says Congress cannot do this. You would go to federal court and say that Congress has no right to tell you to belong to a certain religion. The court would review your case. The court has the power to say that the law made by Congress is unconstitutional. If the court does this, the law would not be enforced.

▶ *How does the United States Supreme Court check the powers of Congress?*

What are the limits on the power of the federal courts?
Discuss the meaning of judicial review and remind students of its importance in protecting our constitutional rights.

Legislative Branch   Judicial Branch

▶ *How is the idea of judicial review related to the idea of separation of powers and checks and balances?*

What are the limits on the power of the federal courts?

The Constitution says that judges shall hold their offices "during good behavior." Congress has the power to impeach, try, and remove judges from office.

The Constitution does not give the courts the power to enforce their decisions. The president is responsible for enforcing the decisions of the courts.

The Constitution also says that judge's salaries cannot be reduced during their time in office. This means that they cannot be punished for the decisions they make.

119

LESSON 15

PROBLEM TO SOLVE

How would you decide this case?

The case of *Chicago v. Morales* provides students with an opportunity to see how the Supreme Court used its power of judicial review.

Read the opening paragraph of the problem solving section aloud with students. Ask students to read the entire case summary that follows. Then divide the class into three groups. One group will represent judges, one group will represent attorneys for the city of Chicago, and one group will represent attorneys for Jesus Morales.

Have each group read their assigned role. If they are playing the role of attorneys, they should develop arguments for their side. If they are role-playing judges, they should develop questions to ask of the attorneys during the hearing. Then divide the three large groups into small groups that consist of one judge, one attorney representing the city of Chicago, and one attorney representing Mr. Morales.

Each small group will conduct a hearing with the judge calling the hearing to order. The judge then asks the attorney for Chicago to present his or her arguments. Next, the judge asks the attorney for Mr. Morales to present his or her arguments. The judge may interrupt the presentation at any time to ask questions of the attorneys. The attorneys should speak only to the judge and not to each other. After listening to both sides of the case, the judge should consider the issue and make a decision about how the settle the case. The judge should then be prepared to explain the reasons for his or her decision.

For more detailed instructions see the section on holding a Pro Se Court in the interactive teaching strategies section, page xxiv.

If students are curious about the outcome of the actual case, they can compare their reasoning with that of the Supreme Court. The case is available on the internet.

Problem to solve

How would you decide this case?

Suppose that you are a justice of the United States Supreme Court. This case has come to you on appeal from a lower court. **Appeal** means to request that a case from a lower court be heard again. Work in a group of five students. First, read the case. Then consider the arguments made by both sides. When you finish, the group should decide how it would rule. Not every member of the group has to agree with the decision. The members who agree should write their ideas on a sheet of paper. The members who disagree should do the same. Be prepared to share your decision with the class.

Chicago v. Morales

Police may not arrest people until they commit a crime. In Chicago, the city government was trying to deal with an increase in gang activity. To help the police, the city government passed a law. The new law made loitering by gang members a crime. The law stated that loitering meant, "to remain in one place with no apparent purpose."

If a police officer saw two or more people loitering, the officer was to order them to move away from the area. Anyone who did not move was in violation of the city law. The person could be put in jail for up to six months. The person might also have to pay a fine or do community service. A person who was able to prove that he or she was not a gang member was to be set free.

▶ *Do you think that laws against loitering violate a person's rights? Why?*

▶ *What issues should the court consider in this case?*

A police officer saw Jesús Morales standing with six other people who might be gang members. The officer ordered them all to move on. When the officer came back a little later, the people were still there. The officer then arrested them.

Jesús Morales took his case to the state courts. He claimed that the law violated his rights to move about freely and to associate with others. To **associate** means to join with others as a partner, member, or friend. Morales also argued that the law was unfair. It punished people not for what they have done but for who they are. The state courts ruled in favor of Morales.

The city of Chicago took the case to the United States Supreme Court. The city argued that street gangs scare people and they make the community unsafe. Giving the police power to arrest loitering gang members helps to prevent crime. The law, the city said, does not violate the right to associate with others. It is directed only at loitering. Otherwise, people may associate with whomever they want.

In this case, the Supreme Court has to weigh the rights of individuals against the need of the city to prevent crime. If you were a member of the Supreme Court, how would you decide this case?

LESSON 15

LESSON REVIEW

The questions in the student book are intended to assess learning and to reinforce knowledge through discussion. The questions are directly related to the lesson objectives. You may wish to include additional questions developed by yourself or by students.

1. What is the role of the judicial branch of our government?
   The judicial branch interprets the laws and settles disputes about them.

2. What is the highest court in the judicial branch?
   The United States Supreme Court is the highest court in the judicial branch.

3. Why are Supreme Court justices and other federal judges appointed rather than elected?
   The Framers believed that if federal judges were elected they might cater to the will of the people who voted for them. They were concerned about the judicial branch showing fairness to all the people.

4. What is judicial review? Why is it one of the most important powers of the judicial branch?
   Judicial review is the power of the courts to decide if a law or action of government is permissible under the Constitution. Judicial review is important because it allows the Supreme Court of the United States to exercise the power to say that an action taken by the president or a law made by Congress is unconstitutional. This power also applies to the actions of all state and local governments. It protects the rights of the people.

ACTIVITIES

The suggested activities are intended to extend and apply learning outside of the classroom. You may wish to have students complete one or more of the activities. Then, have them share the results with the class.

Review the lesson

1. What is the role of the judicial branch of our government?

2. What is the highest court in the judicial branch?

3. Why are Supreme Court justices and other federal judges appointed and not elected?

4. What is judicial review? Why is it one of the most important powers of the judicial branch?

Activities to do

1. Find a recent article in a newspaper that discusses a case the Supreme Court is hearing. Be prepared to explain the article to your class.

2. With your teacher's help, invite an attorney or a judge to come to your classroom. Ask her or him to discuss how our court system works. Prepare your questions before the guest's visit.

3. Learn the names and something about the current United States Supreme Court justices or some famous justices of the past.

Lesson 16

How did the Constitution create a federal system of government?

Washington, D.C.

Purpose of the lesson

The Constitution created a new system of government. We call it a federal system. In this lesson, you will learn what a federal system is and how it works. You will learn how power is delegated to the national and state governments. You also will learn which powers both governments share.

When you have finished this lesson, you should be able to describe our federal system. You should also be able to explain some of the powers that are given to our national and state governments. You should also be able to explain some of the limits on the powers of our national and state governments.

123

Overview

This lesson is intended to introduce students to our federal system of government. Students learn what a federal system of government is and why the Framers chose to create this system. Students are then given examples of how federalism works. They learn that in the inevitable conflicts between the state and federal government, the authority of the Constitution is superior to the power of the state.

Objectives

At the conclusion of the lesson, students should be able to

- explain the concept of a federal system of government
- give examples of how powers are distributed in the federal system
- describe reasons why the Framers created this new system of government

Teaching procedures

Introductory activity

Have students read the "Purpose of the lesson" section and consider the objectives of the lesson.

Write the "Terms to understand" on the board, or use a vocabulary-building activity of your choice. You may wish to have students look up the words in the glossary at the back of their text.

- delegate
- federal government
- federal system
- supremacy
- supremacy clause

READING AND DISCUSSION

What new system of government did the Framers create?

As students read the section, remind them that the power of government belongs to the people. When the Framers wrote our Constitution, they were concerned about how to distribute this power. They attempted to answer the questions: How much power should be delegated to the national government? How much should be delegated to the states and how much should be retained by the people?

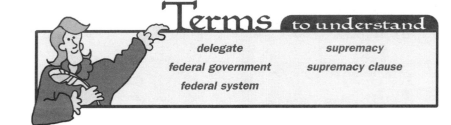

Terms to understand

delegate	supremacy
federal government	supremacy clause
federal system	

What new system of government did the Framers create?

When the Framers wrote our Constitution, they created a **federal system** of government. Our national government is also called the **federal government**. In our federal system, the powers of our national and state government come from the people.

"We the People" delegate some powers to our national government. To **delegate** means to entrust to someone else. We delegate some powers to our state governments. We delegate some powers to be shared by both the national and state governments. Finally, we keep some powers for ourselves.

▶ *What powers should be shared by the national and state governments? Why?*

State capitol building in Carson City, Nevada.

Ideas to discuss

What is a federal system?

With a partner, look at the illustration below. It shows how our federal system of government works. Then, answer the questions and be prepared to share your answers with the class.

1. Where does power come from in our federal system of government?

2. To whom is power delegated?

3. Why do you think the Framers chose a federal system of government?

4. What are some advantages of a federal system of government? What might be some disadvantages?

▶ *In a federal system how do the people delegate their power?*

125

IDEAS TO DISCUSS

What is a federal system?

Have students work with a partner to answer the questions and be prepared to share their responses with the class.

1. Where does power come from in our federal system of government?
   The power comes from the people.

2. To whom is power delegated?
   Some power is delegated to the federal government and some to the state governments, some powers are delegated to both governments (shared powers) and some powers are retained by the people.

3. Why do you think the Framers chose a federal system of government?
   The Framers wanted to ensure that the people could keep the government from becoming too powerful and that the people would have a say in what both the state and federal governments do. The people delegate their power to both levels of government.

4. What are some advantages of a federal system of government? What might be some disadvantages?
   Advantages: no one level of government can become too powerful. The rights of the people are protected. Disadvantages: It is not always clear which level of government has the final say on some issues.

LESSON 16

READING AND DISCUSSION

Where have people delegated power?

Be certain that students understand the different types of power given to the federal and state governments.

▶ *Why do you think the federal government is in charge of running the postal service?*

How have the people delegated power?

Here are some examples of how the people delegate power in our federal system.

Powers to the national government

We give some powers to our national government. These include the power to

- Tax the people to support the national government

- Declare and conduct war

- Control trade between the states and with other nations

- Create post offices

- Coin money

Powers to the state governments

We give some powers to our state governments. These include the power to

- Tax the people to support the state government

- Create public schools

- Control trade within the state

▷ *Why do you think each state has the power to make its own traffic laws?*

- Make motor vehicle and traffic laws

- Make laws regulating marriage and divorce

Powers the national and state governments share

The national and state governments share certain powers. These include power to

- Tax the people

- Borrow money

- Provide for the health and welfare of the people

- Make laws

- Create a court system

Powers kept by the people

We keep certain powers and rights for ourselves. These include the right to

- Practice our religious beliefs or not hold any religious beliefs

- Express our opinions in speech or writing or by other peaceable means

- Join with others to ask our government to do or not do certain things

▷ *Why is it important that the people keep certain powers in a federal system of government?*

127

Which level of government has the most power?

What limits does the Constitution place upon national and state governments?

The supremacy clause makes the Constitution the supreme law of the land; therefore, neither Congress nor state governments can make laws that are in conflict with the Constitution.

Students should understand what limits are placed on both the national and state governments.

▶ *May government officials spend tax monies any way they wish? Why or why not?*

Which level of government has the most power?

The Constitution says, "This Constitution, and the laws of the United States...shall be the supreme law of the land...." We call this the supremacy clause. **Supremacy** means to be highest in rank. The **supremacy clause** says that the states cannot make laws that are in conflict with the United States Constitution. States also cannot make laws that are in conflict with the laws made by Congress.

What limits does the Constitution place upon national and state governments?

A constitutional government means that the powers of government are limited. The Constitution limits the powers of both the national and state governments.

Limits on the powers of the national government

These are some examples of limits on the powers of the national government. The national government may not

128

- make laws that favor trade in one state over the others

- spend money unless there is a law giving it approval to do so

- tax goods that are leaving the country

Limits on the powers of the state governments

These are some examples of limits on the powers of the state government. The state governments may not

- coin or print money

- engage in war unless actually invaded or in immediate danger of being invaded

- make treaties with other nations

Limits on both national and state governments

These are some examples of limits on the powers of both the national and state governments. They may not

- deny people the right to freedom of religion and expression

- deny people the equal protection of the laws

- deny a trial by jury to those accused of a crime

Is the way the Constitution organizes and limits powers enough to protect our rights?

You now understand something about how the Framers wrote the Constitution to organize our government. We have a national or federal government. We have state governments, and we have local governments in our towns and cities.

Many Framers believed this way of organizing our government was enough to protect our rights. Some Americans were worried that the new Constitution gave too much power to the national government. They refused to accept the Constitution unless a bill of rights was added to it.

▶ *Why are individual states not allowed to print their own money?*

129

Is the way in which the Constitution organizes and limits powers enough to protect our rights?

Emphasize that the role of the national government has greatly increased during the course of our history. The Framers would be surprised at how complex our society has become and how the role of the national government has increased.

 see next student page

LESSON REVIEW

The questions in the student book are intended to assess learning and to reinforce knowledge through discussion. The questions are directly related to the lesson objectives. You may wish to include additional questions developed by yourself or by students.

1. Where does our government get its powers?
   The people are the highest authority.

2. Explain how our federal system of government works.
   In this system of government, the people decide where to place their power. They delegate some powers to the national government, some to state governments, and they keep some powers for themselves.

3. What are some powers the constitution grants to the national government?
   The national government is granted the power to tax the people, declare and conduct war, create post offices, control trade among states and with other nations, and coin money.

4. What are some of the powers the constitution grants to the states?
   Some powers granted to the state governments are the power to control trade within their borders, tax residents, create public schools, make motor vehicle and traffic laws, and make laws to regulate marriage and divorce.

5. What are some powers that the national and state governments share?
   Both governments share the powers to make laws, tax people, borrow money, create court systems, and provide for the common good of the people.

6. What are some examples of rights that the people keep for themselves?

The people keep the power to hold certain rights for themselves such as the right to select their careers, travel, choose their friends, and exercise all other rights not forbidden by law.

7. What are some limits on the powers of the national government?

No one religion can be established by the state, the people have rights to free expression, assembly, and petition of the government. Ex post facto [after the fact] laws cannot be passed, writs of habeas corpus [protection against illegal imprisonment] cannot be suspended, the national government cannot exercise power that belongs to the states.

8. What are some limits on the powers of the state governments?

State governments may not coin money, make treaties with other nations, or engage in war.

9. What is the supremacy clause?

The supremacy clause states that the Constitution is the supreme law of the land.

ACTIVITIES

The suggested activities are intended to extend and apply learning outside of the classroom. You may wish to have students complete one or more of the activities. Then, have them share the results with the class.

Review the lesson

1. Where does our government get its powers?

2. Explain how our federal system of government works.

3. What are some powers that the Constitution grants to the national government?

4. What are some powers that the Constitution grants to the states?

5. What are some powers that the national and state governments share?

6. What are some examples of rights that the people kept for themselves?

7. What are some limits on the powers of the national government?

8. What are some limits on the powers of the state governments?

9. What is the supremacy clause?

Activities to do

1. Make a chart that shows what might happen if a state violates the supremacy clause.

2. Draw your own picture or cartoon that shows how our federal system of government works.

3. Use the internet. Look for newspapers from different states. Find examples of the use of power by federal, state, and local governments. Be prepared to explain the examples to your class.

**How does
the Constitution
protect our
basic rights?**

UNIT 4

OVERVIEW

This unit explains how the Bill of Rights was adopted and looks at five basic rights protected under the Constitution: freedom of expression, freedom of religion, equal protection, due process, and the right to vote. The unit addresses the importance of these rights and examines situations in which issues have been raised with regard to their interpretation. Lesson 19 focuses on the changes made by the Supreme Court in interpreting the equal protection clause and how these changes have extended the right of equal protection to groups denied that protection in the past. Lesson 21 focuses on how the right to vote has been expanded by amendments to the Constitution.

OBJECTIVES

At the conclusion of this unit, students should be able to

1. explain what the Bill of Rights is, why it was added to the Constitution, and how it applies to actions of either the national or state governments
2. explain the meaning of the five key rights which are guaranteed by the Constitution: the rights to freedom of expression, freedom of religion, equal protection of the law, due process of law, and the right to vote
3. explain the importance of these basic rights in a democratic society

INTRODUCTION

Read the unit introduction with the class. Make sure they understand the way the Constitution organizes government and the Bill of Rights protects individual rights. It is the power of the Supreme Court to interpret the meaning of the Constitution. In this way, the courts help to protect rights.

You may wish to introduce the key topics in this unit by asking students to share what they know about each of the concepts and write their responses on chart paper. As students study the lessons in the unit, the lists can be added to and changed as knowledge increases.

UNIT PROJECT (OPTIONAL)

You might assign partners to work together on a collage as a unit project. You can allow each group to focus on a particular right in the unit or allow them to cover all five rights on their collage. You will need to collect magazines and newspapers ahead of time. Provide the groups with a folder or envelope to store their clippings and a box in the room where these folders/envelopes can be kept.

How does the Constitution protect your basic rights?

Many Founders were worried that the rights of the people were not well protected by the new Constitution. They said they would not help to get the Constitution approved unless a bill of rights was added. The other Founders agreed to add one when the first Congress met, and that is exactly what happened.

The **Bill of Rights** is the name of the first ten amendments to the Constitution. This part of the Constitution was added in 1791. Since that time, other amendments have been added. Many of the amendments give rights to people who were not given these rights in the original Constitution. For example, the Nineteenth Amendment, added in 1920, gave women the right to vote.

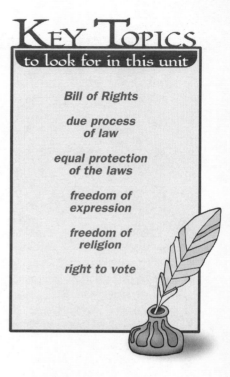

KEY TOPICS
to look for in this unit

Bill of Rights

due process of law

equal protection of the laws

freedom of expression

freedom of religion

right to vote

Lesson 17

How does the Constitution protect your right to freedom of expression?

Purpose of the lesson

The Founders believed that freedom of expression is important for all citizens. In this lesson, you will learn the meaning of freedom of expression. You will learn why freedom of expression is important to you and to our nation. You will also learn about when it might be reasonable to limit this freedom.

When you have finished this lesson, you should be able to explain what freedom of expression means and list some of its benefits. You should also be able to describe situations in which it is fair and reasonable to limit your right to freedom of expression.

OVERVIEW

The Founders chose to amend the Constitution through the addition of the Bill of Rights. They placed great importance on the right to freedom of expression. In this lesson, students will first read sections dealing with the forms of expression protected by the Constitution, the benefits resulting from freedom of expression, and the need to protect this right. The lesson ends with a problem-solving activity that explores the limits to free expression.

OBJECTIVES

At the end of this lesson, students should be able to

- state the various forms of expression covered by the First Amendment
- describe the benefits of freedom of expression to the individual and to a democratic society
- discuss and explain what they might consider reasonable limits on freedom of expression

INTRODUCTORY ACTIVITY

Ask students to give examples of freedom of expression. Ask them to suggest why freedom of expression is important to them as individuals and to our nation. Explore the possibility of situations occurring that necessitate the limiting of freedom of expression. Write students' ideas on the board or chart paper and compare their responses to those in the lesson.

Write the "Terms to understand" on the board, or use a vocabulary-building activity of your choice. You may wish to have students look up the words in the glossary at the back of their text.

- assembly
- expression
- petition
- speech

READING AND DISCUSSION

What is freedom of expression?

Write the word "expression" on the board. Ask students to explore its meaning. Emphasize that expression refers to all the ways that people communicate their ideas, opinions, and actions.

Explain the four types of freedoms of expression listed. If you conducted the previous activity and recorded student ideas, ask them to review the list and decide if any categories of expression have been omitted.

Brainstorm other examples of "expression" and add them to the original list. If you did not have students give examples previously, or write their ideas down, simply begin the brainstorming process here. Explore derivative forms of speech, e.g., political buttons, t-shirts with slogans, protest signs, and picketing.

As an extended activity, have students draw a picture of one or two of the freedoms of expression.

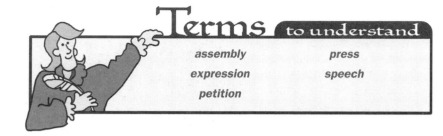

Terms to understand

assembly	press
expression	speech
petition	

What is freedom of expression?

Suppose someone asked you to name the freedoms that you think are very important. Most Americans would say that it is important to have freedom of

- **Speech** – the right to talk about your beliefs, ideas, or feelings

- **Press** – the right to read and write whatever you wish

- **Assembly** – the right to meet with others to discuss your beliefs, ideas, or feelings

- **Petition** – the right to ask your government to correct things that you think are wrong or to do things you believe are needed

▶ *What is a petition? How is signing a petition a form of expression?*

134

The rights to freedom of **speech**, **press**, **assembly**, and **petition** are all a part of **freedom of expression**. **Expression** means to communicate your beliefs, ideas, or feelings to others. The First Amendment of the Bill of Rights protects our right to freedom of expression.

Our Constitution limits the powers of our government in order to protect these freedoms. Under our Constitution, the government cannot interfere with these rights except under very special circumstances.

What are the benefits of freedom of expression?

Freedom of expression is important to all people who live in a democracy.

Freedom of expression supports our democracy. Our democratic system of government depends on the people's ability to make good decisions. To make good decisions, you need to be able to get enough information to make up your mind. You need to hear and discuss different ideas and opinions. Discussing different points of view will help you in many ways. You can make reasonable choices about supporting leaders. You also will know which laws deserve your support.

▶ Why is freedom of the press so important?

Freedom of expression helps us grow as individuals. When you express your thoughts and listen to the ideas of others, you learn and become more mature. Hearing and discussing different points of view help you make thoughtful choices about what you think is right. You mature as a person when you make choices for yourself rather than just accepting what others tell you.

Freedom of expression advances knowledge. It is easier for you to make new discoveries and gain new knowledge when you can suggest ideas and exchange information freely. Even if some ideas do not work, they

135

What are the benefits of freedom of expression?

Assign students to read the next two sections aloud. Review the benefits of freedom of expression and the historical incidents of intolerance toward freedom of expression. One example is the nonviolent civil rights demonstration that took place in 1963, in Birmingham, Alabama, which led to Rev. Martin Luther King Jr. being jailed.

Why was freedom of expression important to the Founders?

At this point, you may want to talk about the concept of "costs." Students learned about the benefits of freedom of expression. The historical examples reveal that sometimes costs or negative outcomes occur when citizens exercise their right to freedom of expression. Some other negative outcomes or costs might be demonstrations becoming disruptive, people being injured, or people expressing ideas that are abhorrent to the majority of citizens. Ask students to balance these costs to the individual or to the public against the benefits enumerated.

▶ *What benefits do individuals and society gain from the right to freedom of expression?*

provide a way of testing the truth of other ideas.

Freedom of expression makes peaceful change in society possible. If you are free to try to persuade others to change things, you are less likely to use violence. We have improved many things in our country by using our right to freedom of expression. If we may criticize things we cannot change, we may be willing to have patience until we can get them changed.

Why was freedom of expression important to the Founders?

The Founders of our nation knew it was necessary to protect freedom of expression. Throughout history, governments had often tried to stop people from spreading new ideas or criticizing government actions.

Some people in the American colonies had suffered—and in some cases died—for expressing their ideas. Three examples are Mary Dyer, John Buckner, and John Peter Zenger.

Mary Dyer lived in Massachusetts. In 1660, the Puritan leaders had her put to death. The Puritans said that she taught people that slavery, war, and the death penalty were wrong.

John Buckner was a printer in Virginia. In 1682, he used his press to print the laws of the colony. The governor of Virginia said that Buckner did not have permission to print the laws. He banned all printing presses in the colony. The governor said, "Printing has encouraged [the people] to learn and even criticize the best government. God, keep us from free schools and printing."

John Peter Zenger was a newspaperman in New York. In 1735, he wrote an article saying that the government was dishonest. The governor had Zenger arrested and thrown in jail. After a long trial, the court set Zenger free. The jury decided that what Zenger had said was true.

These are some reasons why the Founders and others believed it was necessary to protect freedom of expression. It is why they insisted that this protection be in the Constitution.

Should freedom of expression ever be limited?

Sometimes it is reasonable and fair to limit freedom of expression to protect other rights and interests. For example, you may not shout "Fire!" in a crowded theater just to frighten

▷ How did John Peter Zenger's arrest help the Founders decide that freedom of expression is important?

Should freedom of expression ever be limited?

Considering the costs, why is freedom of expression still an important right? Have students read the section. Discuss why, on occasion, it might be necessary to limit freedom of expression.

people when there is no fire. Someone might get hurt rushing to get out of the theater.

Most people believe that there should be some limits to the right of freedom of expression. In some cases, limits to free expression actually may protect your right to speak.

For example, in your class there may be a rule that says you have to raise your hand before you may speak. The purpose of this rule is to make it possible for others who want to speak to have a fair turn.

▶ *Should people be able to express their ideas loudly even in the middle of the night? Why?*

Ideas to discuss

When are other rights and interests more important than freedom of expression?

Freedom of expression is so important that it is not easy to answer this question. Discuss the situations below. You will discover other important rights and interests of society. These other rights and interests must be balanced with our right to freedom of expression.

Work with a partner or in small groups. Read all the situations or the ones assigned to your group. Then answer the three questions about the situations you have read. Be prepared to share your group's ideas with the class.

1. What rights and interests might be endangered in this situation?

2. Should this kind of expression be limited? Why?

3. What rule can you make to limit this kind of expression?

- You learn some of our nation's military secrets. Should you be able to sell the secrets to another country?

- People are very angry about the results of a trial in your community. You want to stand in front of the crowd and shout, "Let's go and shut down the courthouse right now!"

- You are thinking about telling lies in a court of law to protect your friend.

- You want to use a loudspeaker in the middle of the night in your quiet neighborhood.

- A parent goes into a kindergarten class and starts swearing.

- You think that someone you work with is a bad person. So, you tell lies about her that harm her reputation. You cause her to lose her job.

IDEAS TO DISCUSS

When are other rights and interests more important than freedom of expression?

Have students work in small groups or with a partner. Ask them to answer the questions about each of the six situations described and to share their ideas with the class.

LESSON 17

PROBLEM TO SOLVE

Should freedom of expression be limited in this case?

Divide the class into groups of five students each. Explain that they will serve as justices of the Supreme Court and will make a decision about a legal case. Have students read the summary of *Feiner v. New York* (1951) and the two opinions that follow it. The groups should discuss both opinions and decide which one they agree with. Each group should write down its decision and reasons for selecting that opinion. Students may select one member of the group to report to the class.

Problem to solve

Should freedom of expression be limited in this case?

Suppose you are a justice of the United States Supreme Court. Read the case below. Then work with a group of five students. Read and discuss the opinions that follow the case. Decide which opinion you would agree with or develop your own opinion. Be prepared to explain your reasons to the class.

Feiner v. New York (1951)

On the evening of March 8, college student Irving Feiner stood on a wooden box on a street corner in Syracuse, New York. He was addressing a racially mixed crowd of about seventy-five people. The police received a telephone call about the meeting, and two police officers were sent to find out what was happening.

Feiner urged the African Americans in the crowd to take up arms and fight for equal rights. He urged them to attend a meeting later that night to talk about equal rights. Feiner told the crowd that the president of the United States, the mayor of the city, and other public officials were bums. His words gave the impression that he was trying to get the people to become violent and to fight for their rights.

The crowd became restless. Feelings both for and against the speaker were rising. For thirty minutes, the police made no effort to interfere with the speech, but they were concerned about the crowd. There was some pushing and shoving, and as Feiner continued to speak, one man threatened him with violence.

The officers asked Feiner three times to get off the box. Then they demanded that Feiner stop talking. Finally, the officers arrested Feiner and charged him with disorderly conduct. This law makes it a crime to encourage people to use violence. The officers said that they had acted to control the crowd, to keep the peace, and to prevent injury.

At his trial, the state court found Feiner guilty and sentenced him to prison. Feiner appealed the decision. Feiner said that the police were trying to silence his views in violation of his right to freedom of speech.

Do you think Feiner's speech was a lawful speech? Did it go beyond persuasion, and did he try to encourage a riot? Did the police violate Feiner's right of free speech?

Opinion 1: The police did not violate Feiner's right of free speech.

The officers making the arrest were responsible for keeping law and order. They were not trying to keep Feiner from expressing his views and opinions. The way Feiner acted and the immediate danger of the audience becoming violent were reasons enough for the police to arrest him. Freedom of speech does not include the right to try to make people use violence or to riot.

Opinion 2: The police did violate Feiner's right of free speech.

The facts do not show any immediate danger of a riot or disorder. It is not unusual that some people at public street meetings push, shove, or disagree with the speaker. The police had a duty to protect Feiner's right to speak. The crowd was restless, but the police did not try to quiet it. One man threatened Feiner, but the officers did nothing to discourage this man. Instead, the police acted only to stop Feiner's speech.

▶ *When do you think the government should have the power to limit your right to freedom of expression?*

LESSON REVIEW

The questions are intended to assess learning and reinforce knowledge through discussion with students. You may wish to include additional questions developed by yourself or students.

1. What are the four types of free expression? Give examples of each. Where in the Constitution will you find the right to freedom of expression?

   The four types of expression are speech (the right to say what you want), press (the right to read and write what you wish), assembly (the right to meet with others to talk about what you wish), and petition (the right to ask our government to correct something that you think is wrong). You can find the right to freedom of expression in the First Amendment.

2. Why did the Founders believe it is important to protect free expression?

   The Founders knew from experience that some governments had tried to keep people from speaking out against government policies. They also knew of people who had suffered great injustice and harm because they expressed their ideas.

3. List four benefits of freedom of expression. Give examples of each. Which do you think is most important? Why?

   Freedom of expression helps our democracy work well, helps us grow as individuals, helps to advance knowledge, and helps to make peaceful change in society possible through the free exchange of information and new ideas. We listen, understand different points of view, and can make choices that are more informed.

4. In what kinds of situations do you think it is fair and reasonable to limit freedom of expression?

   Give examples. Accept any reasonable responses and examples.

ACTIVITIES

The suggested activities are intended to extend and apply learning outside the classroom. You may wish to have students complete one or more of the activities. Then have them share the results with the class.

Review the lesson

1. What are the four types of free expression? Give examples of each. Where in the Constitution will you find the right to freedom of expression?

2. Why did the Founders believe it is important to protect free expression?

3. List four benefits of freedom of expression. Give examples of each. Which do you think is most important? Why?

4. In what kinds of situations do you think it is fair and reasonable to limit freedom of expression? Give examples.

Activities to do

1. Learn about the policies in your school district or the rules at your school that regulate how students may exercise freedom of expression. Share what you learned with the class.

2. Make a poster that shows the four parts of freedom of expression. In your poster, show people exercising these rights. Share your poster with the class.

3. Imagine that a group with unpopular opinions wants to hold a meeting at a public park in your community. Most of the people in your community do not agree with the views of this group. The people fear that the meeting might become disorderly and disturb the peace. Work with a partner. One of you should prepare a discussion in favor of allowing the group to hold the meeting. The other should prepare a discussion against allowing the group to hold the meeting. Both of you should present your opinions to the class and then let the class decide.

4. Find a newspaper article that shows someone exercising the right to freedom of expression. Write a short essay that explains the benefits of this right to you and your community.

Lesson 18

How does the Constitution protect your right to freedom of religion?

Purpose of the lesson

The Founders thought the right to freedom of religion was so important that they placed it at the beginning of the Bill of Rights. In this lesson, you will learn why the Founders thought this freedom was so important. You will learn how the Constitution protects religious freedom. You will also study situations in which religious freedom may be limited when it conflicts with other important rights and interests.

When you have finished this lesson, you should be able to explain the importance of freedom of religion. You should also be able to explain when it might be reasonable to limit this freedom.

143

OVERVIEW

In this lesson, students learn how the First Amendment protects freedom of religion. They are introduced to two key concepts: the "establishment clause" and "free exercise" clause. Students read sections on why freedom of religion was so important to the Founders and explore the distinction between limiting religious beliefs and limiting religious practices. Finally, students examine conflicts about the establishment clause and participate in a discussion activity that deals with religion in public schools.

OBJECTIVES

At the conclusion of this lesson, students should be able to

- explain the meaning of the freedom of religion clauses in the Constitution
- explain why the Founders placed so much importance on protecting freedom of religion
- understand that there are conflicts about the interpretation of freedom of religion clauses and explain some of the conflicts related to religion in the public schools
- explain the distinction between freedom of religious beliefs and freedom of religious practices and state some reasons for the distinction

INTRODUCTORY ACTIVITY

Write the words "freedom of religion" on the board or chart paper. Ask the class to brainstorm what that phrase means. List all possibilities. Now have students read the "Purpose of the lesson" and consider the lesson objectives.

Write the "Terms to understand" on the board, or use a vocabulary-building activity of your choice. You may wish to have students look up the words in the glossary at the back of their text.

- discriminate
- establishment clause
- free exercise clause
- freedom of belief or conscience
- tolerant

READING AND DISCUSSION

How does the First Amendment protect freedom of religion?

Have students read each section. You may wish to take some time to go over the Amendment language quoted in the lesson and emphasize that this is an example of how government power is specifically limited in the Constitution.

Review definitions of the "establishment" and "free exercise" clauses, then have students compare these concepts to the ideas they volunteered in the introductory activity.

Ask students to suggest examples of each clause.

Terms to understand

discriminate

establishment clause

free exercise clause

freedom of belief or conscience

tolerant

How does the First Amendment protect freedom of religion?

The first words of the Bill of Rights protect your right to freedom of religion. They say, "Congress shall make no law respecting [about] an establishment of religion, or prohibiting the free exercise thereof." These words show how important freedom of religion was to the Founders. Here is what these words mean.

- Congress may not establish (set up) an official religion for our country or favor any one religion over others. This is the **establishment clause**.

- Congress may not stop you from holding any religious beliefs you choose or from having no religious beliefs at all. The government may not unfairly or unreasonably limit your right to practice any religious beliefs you wish. This is the **free exercise clause**.

▶ Why did the Founders think that freedom of religion needed to be protected in the Bill of Rights?

144

Why was freedom of religion so important to the colonists?

Many colonists came from Europe to the New World in search of religious freedom. Two such groups were the Puritans and the Pilgrims. They controlled the government and the religious practices of the Massachusetts Bay Colony.

Those who disagreed with the beliefs of the Puritans were sometimes persecuted or even executed. Others, such as the Puritan minister Roger Williams, were forced to leave the colony.

Roger Williams and his wife Mary believed that the church and the government should be separate. Williams wanted the church to be tolerant of the beliefs of others. To be **tolerant** means being willing to let other people hold opinions that are different from one's own. These ideas angered the Puritan leaders. So, they forced Roger and Mary Williams and their followers to leave. The group left and founded the colony of Rhode Island.

By the end of the American Revolution, there were people of many different religions in America. There were Baptists, Catholics, Jews, and Quakers, for example. All believed they had as much right as anyone else to practice their religions. As a result,

What religious conflicts did the colonists have before the Constitution was written?

Americans got used to living with people of different religious beliefs. People began to believe that others should have the same rights they wanted for themselves.

Why was freedom of religion so important to the Founders?

Leaders such as Thomas Jefferson and James Madison thought it was unfair to **discriminate** against people because of their religious beliefs. To discriminate against people means to treat some people unfairly. They thought such discrimination took away the rights of the people and was dangerous to the common good.

Why was freedom of religion so important to the Founders?

Ask students to give examples of religious intolerance in the colonies.

Ask students why the Founders thought it was important to protect religious freedom.

You may wish to discuss some modern instances of religious persecution: the treatment of the Jews in Nazi Germany, the suppression of Tibetan religious institutions by the Chinese government, or the suppression of religion in the former Soviet Union.

Can government limit your right to freedom of belief?

Can government put limits on how you practice your beliefs?

Emphasize that the government has no power to interfere with our right to believe in a religion of our own choosing, or not to believe in any religion at all.

Make it clear that in some cases, religious practices can be limited. Practices that conflict with the common good, public morality, or the health and safety of others are regulated by government.

▶ *What rights does the establishment clause protect? Why?*

Most of the Founders were religious men and women. They did not want government to interfere with the right of the people to practice their religion. George Washington believed that people needed religion to develop good character. He did not believe in using taxes, however, to pay for teaching religion in public schools. The Founders' strong belief in religious freedom led them to protect it first and foremost in the First Amendment.

Can government limit your right to freedom of belief?

You may believe in any religion you wish or in no religion at all. This is stated in the free exercise clause. You have the right to **freedom of belief or conscience**. The government may not force you to swear to a belief you do not hold. You may not be forced by the government to pray in school or any other place.

Can government put limits on how you practice your beliefs?

The free exercise clause protects your right to practice your beliefs. But, this right may be limited. Not everyone agrees with all the limitations placed upon religious practices. You will often hear differences of opinion about this subject.

146

▶ *Why are some religious practices, such as the refusal to get vaccinations or the refusal to use road reflectors, not protected by the Constitution?*

What is the conflict about establishment of religion?

At the time the Constitution was written, almost every nation in Europe had one official religion. People who did not want to belong to that religion were often denied certain rights. They could not attend some schools or hold a government office. They were often discriminated against or persecuted just because they did not belong to the official religion of the government.

Your religious practices may only be limited if they are considered harmful to public health or the common good. Suppose your religion forbids vaccination. The public authorities may still require anyone who attends school to get a vaccination. Vaccination is required for the protection of the common good. Other religious practices, such as handling snakes, refusing to use modern reflectors required for road safety, and parents refusing medical care for their children, are all issues that have gone to the courts.

In our country, people have the right to hold different opinions. They have the right to try to get laws changed to protect their particular religious practices. They also have the right to argue their positions in our courts.

147

What is the conflict about establishment of religion?

Have students read the section aloud. Clarify any remaining questions about the conflict between the establishment and free exercise clauses. Ask students to speculate on the impact of prayer in public schools. Are such practices in conflict with the establishment clause?

IDEAS TO DISCUSS

How would you decide this case?

Have students read *Engle v. Vitale* (1962). Then divide the class into groups of three to five students. Each group should prepare answers to the four questions and select a spokesperson to report its findings to the rest of the class.

1. Suppose your teacher began each day by leading the class in saying a prayer. Would this violate your right to believe in any religion you wish or to believe in no religion at all? Why or why not?

   Students may answer that saying a prayer is a violation of their right to believe or not to believe. Attending school is compulsory and students are required to be in class at the time the prayer is being said. They may feel coerced into participating in a religious belief even though they may not wish to do. Another argument could be made that saying a prayer during school hours in a public school promotes one belief over another and assumes that all students in the class would benefit by saying the prayer.

2. Teachers in this school system were paid by tax money collected from the citizens of New York. Does this mean that the government was supporting religion? Why or why not?

   If teachers in the district were required to read the prayer with students each morning, it could be argued that the district would be supporting religion. There may be students in the classroom who do not believe in prayer, or who belong to a religion that does not use any prayers, or who say different prayers as part of their worship. The government would be favoring one type of religion over another.

When a government only supports one official religion, we say that it is the established religion of the government. The First Amendment does not allow our government to have an established religion or to favor one religion over others.

There are often conflicts, however, about what the establishment clause means. Most conflicts about the establishment clause have been about religion in public schools. Does the establishment clause mean that public schools may not have prayers in the classroom? Does it mean that government may not give money to religious schools to buy textbooks? These are not easy questions to answer. Many cases about religion and the public schools have gone to the United States Supreme Court.

▷ *Do you think public schools should be allowed to set aside time for prayer? Why or why not?*

Ideas to discuss

How would you decide this case?

Read about the court case *Engle v. Vitale*. Then, in small groups discuss the questions that follow it. Be prepared to share your ideas with the class.

Engle v. Vitale (1962)

In 1958, a Board of Education in New York gave the district's principals a prayer to be recited in their schools. Teachers were required to lead students in saying the prayer aloud every day. Students who did not want to say the prayer were permitted to sit quietly or leave the room.

The parents of ten students complained. They said the use of this prayer in public schools was against their religious beliefs. They said that praying was something people should do at home and in church. They also said that to have prayers in school put pressure on all students to say the prayer. Students who did not want to say the prayer might be criticized. The parents took the case to court.

1. Suppose your teacher began each day by leading the class in saying a prayer. Would this violate your right to believe in any religion you wish or to believe in no religion at all? Why or why not?

2. Teachers in this school system were paid by tax money collected from the citizens of New York. Does this mean that the government was supporting religion? Why or why not?

3. Do you think it is all right for the government to support religion if it helps all religions equally? Why or why not?

4. Do you think the Board of Education violated the Constitution? Why or why not?

3. Do you think it is all right for the government to support religion if it helps all religions equally? Why or why not?

Accept any reasonable answers.

4. Do you think the Board of Education violated the Constitution? Why or why not?

The establishment clause states that the government may not set up a religion or favor one religion over another. The First Amendment says that people have the right to believe in and practice the religion of their choice. It also implies that they may choose to not believe in or practice a religion. Saying a prayer during school time may violate some people's right to worship as they wish.

LESSON REVIEW

1. In what part of the Constitution will you find the right to freedom of religion?

   The right to freedom of religion is in the First Amendment.

2. What is the meaning of the establishment clause?

   Congress may not establish (set up) an official religion for our country or favor any one religion over others.

3. What is the meaning of the free exercise clause?

   Congress may not stop you from holding any religious beliefs you choose or to have no religious beliefs at all. The government may not unfairly or unreasonably limit your right to practice any religious beliefs you wish.

4. Freedom of belief is an absolute right. What does this mean?

   There are two parts to the right to freedom of religion: the freedom to believe and the freedom to practice your beliefs. The U.S. Supreme Court has said that people have an absolute right to freedom of belief. Absolute means without any limit. Government may not limit your freedom of belief.

5. Can you think of any situations when the government would have a duty to restrict religious practices?

   Accept reasonable answers that refer to practices that are harmful to public health or the common good.

ADDITIONAL INSTRUCTIONAL ACTIVITY

Suggested activities are intended to extend and apply learning outside the classroom.

Students might write individual reports on some of the early religious dissenters such as Roger and Mary Williams, Anne Hutchinson, or Thomas Hooker. Students might conduct a survey of their parents and adult community members to determine if prayers were said in public school classrooms when they were students—and, if so, under what circumstances. Students might also examine their own school experience to determine if there have been times when prayers have been said— and, if so, under what conditions.

Review the lesson

1. In what part of the Constitution will you find the right to freedom of religion?

2. What is the meaning of the establishment clause?

3. What is the meaning of the free exercise clause?

4. Freedom of belief is an absolute right. What does this mean?

5. Can you think of any situations when the government would have a duty to restrict religious practices?

Activities to do

1. What religious beliefs did American Indians in the colonies have? What religious beliefs did African Americans in the colonies have? What were their ideas about freedom of religion? Share what you learn in the form of a report, a poem, or a song.

2. Learn about different religious beliefs held in the colonies by European Americans: Baptists, Catholics, Jews, Puritans, or Quakers. What were their ideas about freedom of religion? Write a newspaper article about one or more of these groups to share with the class.

3. Thomas Jefferson and James Madison had strong opinions about the separation of church and state. Find out what they said about freedom of religion. Write a short story about what they would say about these issues today.

4. Draw a picture expressing your opinion of the *Engle v. Vitale* case.

Lesson 19

How does the Constitution protect your right to equal protection of the laws?

Purpose of the lesson

In this lesson, you will learn about the right of all people to be treated equally by government. You will learn the meaning of the term "equal protection of the laws." The equal protection clause is one part of the Fourteenth Amendment. This clause has been used to prevent states from being unfair to citizens because of their race or gender.

When you have finished this lesson, you should be able to explain the meaning of "equal protection of the laws." You should also be able to describe some important steps in history that were taken to prevent state governments from being unfair to people.

151

OVERVIEW

It was not until after the Civil War, when the Fourteenth Amendment had been passed, that the concept of equality gained a foothold in the Constitution. The equal protection clause finally incorporated into the Constitution the ideal that "all men are created equal"—the ideal first stated in the Declaration of Independence that inspired so many during the American Revolution.

In this lesson, students will first engage in a discussion activity that examines problems involving inequality of treatment under state and local laws. Then they will read and discuss sections explaining the Fourteenth Amendment's equal protection clause, its original interpretation by the Supreme Court in 1896—the "separate but equal" ruling—and the change in its interpretation by the Supreme Court in the famous case of *Brown v. Board of Education* in 1956. The lesson ends with an examination and discussion of the following issues: attempts to stop racial discrimination, the passage of the Civil Rights Act of 1964, and how the equal protection clause has helped other groups in America.

OBJECTIVES

At the conclusion of this lesson, students should be able to

- name and describe the three new Amendments passed shortly after the Civil War ended
- explain why the Fourteenth Amendment was needed
- describe the equal protection clause and the change in its interpretation in *Brown v. Board of Education* that helped ensure equal treatment by government to all citizens
- describe some attempts to stop racial discrimination

INTRODUCTORY ACTIVITY

Have students read the section and consider the objectives of the lesson.

Ask them to explain what they think the phrase "to be treated equally by government" means. Ask them if they can think of examples of unequal treatment by the government.

- boycott
- Civil Rights Act of 1964
- Civil War amendments
- equal protection clause
- equal protection of the laws
- segregate

LESSON 19

Write the "Terms to understand" on the board, or use a vocabulary-building activity of your choice. You may wish to have students look up the words in the glossary at the back of their text.

see next student page

IDEAS TO DISCUSS

Are these actions by government fair?

Organize the class into groups of three to five students. Each group should read and discuss the five situations. They should decide if the government was being fair in each situation. Each group should choose a spokesperson to explain their ideas and reasons to the class. Accept any reasonable responses.

1. A new law in your state says you must go to a certain school because of your race.

   The law is unfair. Students are being separated from others without a good or fair reason. They are being treated unequally.

2. Your town has a law that says you cannot live in a certain area because of your religion.

   This law is unfair. The people who practice the religion are being treated unequally.

3. Your city police department will not allow women on the police force.

   This regulation is unfair. Government agencies may not discriminate against someone because of their gender. Men and women are not being treated equally by a government agency.

Ideas to discuss

Are these actions by government fair?

Work in a group of three to five students. Discuss each of the imaginary situations below. Decide if the government was being fair in the situation. Be prepared to share the reasons for your decisions with the class.

1. A new law in your state says that you have to be 21 years old to get a driver's license.

2. Your town has a law that says that you cannot live in a certain area because of your religion.

3. Your city police department will not allow women on the police force.

4. Your state has a law that says you cannot marry someone of a different race.

5. A man and a woman work for the state government at the same jobs. The man is paid much more than the woman is paid.

▶ *When, if ever, might it be fair for your government to treat people unequally because of their age? their gender? their religion? their race?*

Terms to understand

boycott	equal protection clause
Civil Rights Act of 1964	equal protection of the laws
Civil War Amendments	segregate

Why was the Fourteenth Amendment needed?

After the Civil War, three amendments were added to the Constitution: the Thirteenth, Fourteenth, and Fifteenth Amendments. We call these the **Civil War Amendments**. They ended slavery and attempted to give former slaves the same rights as other people.

The Fourteenth Amendment was passed to stop state governments from unfairly discriminating against African Americans. To unfairly discriminate means to treat some people differently without having a good reason. The Fourteenth Amendment says, "No State shall…deny to any person…the equal protection of the laws. **Equal protection of the laws** means that state governments must not treat people differently unless there is a good and fair reason for doing so.

There are good and fair reasons why most states have laws that say you cannot drive a car until you are a certain age. The **equal protection clause** prohibits laws that unreasonably and unfairly favor some groups over others.

Just passing the Civil War Amendments in 1868 did not stop unfair treatment of African Americans. States still passed laws that allowed unfair discrimination. Some states passed laws that required African American children to go to schools separate from other children. Other laws required separate seats on trains and separate entrances. Some laws made it impossible for African Americans to vote or have the basic rights that other citizens had.

These state laws were unfair. People said they violated the Fourteenth Amendment. In 1896, the Supreme Court ruled that laws requiring

4. Your state has a law that says you cannot marry someone of a different race. The law is unfair.

   It unfairly discriminates against some couples.

5. A man and a woman work for the state government at the same jobs. The man is paid much more than the woman is paid.

   Unless there is a good and fair reason for treating two people who are doing the same work differently, this practice is unfair. Some students may suggest that perhaps the man had been working longer and that he receives more money based on his years of service.

Why was the Fourteenth Amendment needed?

Review the three Amendments, passed after the Civil War, known as the Civil War Amendments. Help students understand that even though the Fourteenth Amendment was passed in 1868, states in the South continued to discriminate against African Americans. To illustrate the extent of this discrimination, you may wish to have students extrapolate the examples from this section while you write them on the board or chart paper. Discuss students' reactions to the list.

LESSON 19

READING AND DISCUSSION

What is the importance of *Brown v. Board of Education*?

Have students read the section. Discuss the importance of the Court's change in interpreting the equal protection clause. Stress that separation or segregation in itself implies inequality and is unfair. You may wish to share some of the Court's decision with students simplifying the vocabulary as necessary. Also, remind students that the Brown case was decided in 1954, almost 100 years after the Fourteenth Amendment was passed.

Excerpts from the Supreme Court's decision in *Brown V. Board of Education.*

> Where a State has undertaken to provide an opportunity for an education in its public schools, such an opportunity is a right that must be made available to all on equal terms.

> Segregation of children in public schools solely because of race deprives children of the minority group of equal educational opportunities, even though the physical facilities and other "tangible" factors may be equal.

> The "separate but equal" doctrine adopted in *Plessy v. Ferguson*, 163 U.S. 537, has no place in the field of public education.

> To separate (children) from others of similar age and qualifications solely because of their race generates a feeling of inferiority as to their status in the community that may affect their hearts and minds in a way unlikely ever to be undone…. Any language in *Plessy v. Ferguson* contrary to this finding is rejected…. Separate educational facilities are inherently unequal…. (We) hold that the plaintiffs…(are) deprived of the equal protection of the laws guaranteed by the Fourteenth Amendment.

separation of the races were constitutional. The Court said it was legal for states to separate people by race if the public places for each group were equal. For example, separate schools should have the same quality of classrooms and teachers.

During the next half century, Americans' ideas about fairness and equality began to change. In 1954, the Supreme Court decided one of the most important legal cases in our country's history.

How did Thurgood Marshall help bring an end to segregation in our country?

What is the importance of Brown v. Board of Education?

Linda Brown was a seven-year old African American student. She lived in Topeka, Kansas. Her home was five blocks from an elementary school. The school close to Linda's home was for white students only. The school board required that Linda cross town to go to a school twenty-one blocks away. The school that was far away was for African American students.

Linda's parents sued the school board of Topeka. They said that the school system was treating Linda unfairly. They claimed that the school board had violated Linda's right to the equal protection of the laws.

One of the Brown's lawyers was Thurgood Marshall. Marshall later became the first African American justice of the Supreme Court. He argued that segregated schools could not be equal. To **segregate** means to set apart from others. The Supreme Court agreed. The Court said that segregated schools by their nature were not equal. The Court said that requiring separate schools denied students the equal protection of the laws.

▶ *Why was* Brown v. Board of Education *one of the most important legal cases in our country's history?*

How did people work to change the laws and end unfair discrimination?

The Brown case dealt only with public schools. It did not end other types of unfair discrimination. The Civil Rights Movement started in the 1950s. It was a time when many people of both races worked to end other kinds of unfair treatment. The people marched in the streets. They wrote letters to Congress asking for stronger laws. They held boycotts. A **boycott** is an act of protest. It means that, as a group, people avoid something like a store or company.

One of the earliest boycotts began in 1955. Rosa Parks was a working woman who lived in Alabama. On her way home one day, Parks refused to give her seat on the bus to a white person. Parks was arrested for violating a city law. The African American community boycotted the city buses

▶ *Why did Rosa Parks' refusal to give up her seat have such far-reaching effects?*

155

How did people work to change the laws and end unfair discrimination?

Stress that the Brown case only dealt with issues in public schools and that African Americans were not protected from other types of discrimination.

Ask students to read the examples of how people worked to end unfair discrimination. Have students work with a partner or in small groups to make a graphic design reflecting the different ways that people in the Civil Rights Movement worked to end discrimination.

LESSON 19

How has the equal protection clause helped other groups in America?

Finally, explain to students that many other groups in the United States have benefited from the equal protection clause.

▶ *How did Martin Luther King Jr. strengthen the civil rights movement?*

until the city changed the law. The boycott lasted more than a year.

In August of 1963, thousands of Americans marched in Washington, D.C. They wanted to show their support for the Civil Rights Movement. Dr. Martin Luther King Jr. was an important civil rights leader. It was here that King gave his famous "I Have a Dream" speech. King told the crowd, "I have a dream that my four little children will one day live in a nation where they will not be judged by the color of their skin, but by the content of their character."

In 1964, Congress passed a law called the Civil Rights Act.

The **Civil Rights Act of 1964** ended segregation in public places. Public places included restaurants, movie theaters, and hotels. The law also said that employers could not unfairly discriminate against people because of their race, national origin, religion, or gender.

How has the equal protection clause helped other groups in America?

As African Americans won the right to equal protection, other groups began to ask for the same right. Asians, Latinos, Native Americans, people with disabilities, the elderly, and other groups have worked to gain the right to equal protection. It is now against the law to unfairly discriminate because of a person's age, disability, or ethnic background.

Women are the largest group to benefit from these efforts. Many laws protect women from unfair discrimination where they work. The law prohibits discrimination in pay based on gender. Education programs that receive money from the federal government cannot discriminate based on gender.

▶ *What were the results of the Civil Rights Act of 1964?*

President Lyndon Baines Johnson signing Civil Rights Bill, April 11, 1968.

▶ *How were other groups of people affected by the civil rights movement?*

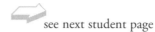 see next student page

LESSON REVIEW

The questions in the student book are intended to assess learning and to reinforce knowledge through discussion. The questions are directly related to the lesson objectives. You may wish to include additional questions developed by yourself or by students.

1. Why was the Fourteenth Amendment added to the Constitution?

   The Fourteenth Amendment was added to the Constitution to prevent states from discriminating against African Americans.

2. What does "equal protection of the laws" mean?

   Equal protection of the laws means that states may not treat people differently unless they have a good and fair reason for doing so.

3. Why did the Fourteenth Amendment not immediately end unfair treatment of African Americans?

   After the Civil War, many Southern states passed laws that limited the rights of African Americans. Many people thought these state laws were unfair. The Supreme Court said it was not unfair for states to separate people according to race. The states could do so if the public places for each group were equal. For example, separate schools should have near the same quality of classrooms and teachers.

4. Why was the *Brown v. Board of Education* legal case so important?

   The Brown v. Board of Education *decision, by determining that segregation of the races in public schools was not legal, ended such segregation. It put a stop to the "separate but equal" doctrine established in 1896.*

5. What was the Civil Rights Movement? Give some examples of how people of different races worked together to change unfair laws.

   The Civil Rights Movement, beginning in the 1950s, was a time when people worked together to change unfair laws. The people marched in the streets, wrote letters to Congress, held boycotts, and engaged in sit-ins.

6. Why was the Civil Rights Act of 1964 important?

The Civil Rights Act ended segregation in public places such as restaurants, hotels, and movie theaters. It also mandated that employers could not discriminate against their employees because of their race, national origin, religion, or gender.

ACTIVITIES

The suggested activities are intended to extend and apply learning outside the classroom. You may wish to have students complete one or more of the activities. Then, have them share the results with the class.

Review the lesson

1. Why was the Fourteenth Amendment added to the Constitution?

2. What does "equal protection of the laws" mean?

3. Why did the Fourteenth Amendment not immediately end unfair treatment of African Americans?

4. Why was the *Brown v. Board of Education* legal case so important?

5. What was the Civil Rights Movement? Give some examples of how people of different races worked together to change unfair laws.

6. Why was the Civil Rights Act of 1964 important?

Activities to do

1. Learn about important people in the Civil Rights Movement: Martin Luther King Jr., Rosa Parks, Linda Brown, and Medgar Evers. Share what you learned with your class.

2. Read Dr. Martin Luther King Jr.'s "I Have a Dream" speech. Draw a picture or a poster showing Dr. King's dream. Share your picture with the class.

3. Learn more about how one of the following groups struggled to achieve the right to equal protection of the law. Share what you learned with the class.

   - Chinese
   - Latinos
   - Native Americans
   - People with disabilities
   - Women

Lesson 20

How does the Constitution protect your right to due process of law?

Purpose of the lesson

In this lesson, you will learn another way the Constitution protects your right to be treated fairly by government. You will learn the meaning of the term "due process of law." You will learn how due process protects you from unfair and unreasonable acts by people in government.

When you have finished this lesson, you should be able to explain why your right to due process of law is so important.

159

OVERVIEW

One of the great fears of the Founders and Framers was the tendency of powerful governments to act unfairly and unreasonably. The due process clause in the Fifth Amendment was intended by the Framers to prevent such abuse on the part of the federal government.

The due process clause in the Fourteenth Amendment protects against state or local government abuse of power. This clause has been interpreted by the courts to extend most of the protections in the Bill of Rights, which originally applied only to the federal government, to also protect against unfair action by state and local governments.

Students first read about what due process means, then discuss ideas about the importance of due process in criminal proceedings and of other situations in which the right to due process applies. After studying what rights are guaranteed by due process, students engage in a problem-solving activity that raises questions about who should have the right to a lawyer in a criminal case. The lesson ends with other examples of due process rights.

OBJECTIVES

At the conclusion of this lesson, students should be able to

- state in general terms what due process means
- explain the importance of the due process clauses in the Fifth and Fourteenth Amendments
- identify situations in which due process rights are important, particularly the right to a lawyer in criminal proceedings

INTRODUCTORY ACTIVITY

Have students read the "Purpose of the lesson" section and consider the objectives of the lesson. Ask them if they can think of any examples of unfair and unreasonable acts by people in government.

Write the "Terms to understand" on the board, or use a vocabulary-building activity of your choice. You may wish to have students look up the words in the glossary at the back of their text.

- Fifth Amendment
- Fourteenth Amendment
- right to due process of law

READING AND DISCUSSION

What is the right to due process of law?

Why are due process rights important in your daily life?

Locate the Amendments to the Constitution in the student book Reference Section. Read the Fifth and Fourteenth Amendments. Explain the difference between the two due process clauses and the meaning of the phrase.

As an optional activity, you might ask students individually or in small groups to create an illustration of one or both Amendments; ask them to show what is similar and what is different in the Amendments.

Terms *to understand*

Fifth Amendment

Fourteenth Amendment

right to due process of law

What is the right to due process of law?

Due process means that members of government must use fair methods or procedures when doing their jobs. They must use fair procedures when they enforce the law. They must use fair procedures when they make decisions. They must use fair procedures when they gather information.

The **right to due process of law** is the right to be treated fairly by your government. You will find the term "due process of law" used in two places in the United States Constitution.

- **Fifth Amendment.** It says that no person shall be "...deprived of [have taken away] life, liberty, or property without due process of law." This amendment protects your right to be treated fairly by the *federal* government.

- **Fourteenth Amendment.** It says "...nor shall any State deprive any person of life, liberty, or property without due process of law." This amendment protects your right to be treated fairly by your *state* and *local* governments.

The Bill of Rights only protects you from unfair treatment by the federal government. The Fourteenth Amendment protects you from unfair treatment by state and local governments.

Why are due process rights important in your daily life?

You have the right to be treated fairly by all agencies of your government. The government must treat you fairly whenever it creates laws about your right to travel, raise a family, use your property, or receive government benefits. The right to due process means the right to be treated fairly in your dealings with all levels of government. Due process also requires that people in government follow the law.

Ideas to discuss

Why is due process important in criminal trials?

It is very important that you understand the meaning of fair procedures in enforcing the law. Read the following imaginary situations. Use the questions to help you explain what is wrong in each situation.

- The police suspect you of a crime. Suppose they use force to make you give them information to show that you might be guilty.

- You must appear in court. Suppose the judge listens to all the witnesses against you but does not allow you to present your side of the story.

- The leaders of the country make decisions about your life, liberty, and property. Suppose they make these decisions in secret. They do not allow you or anyone else to participate.

1. Do you believe that you would be treated fairly if you were accused of a crime? Why or why not?

2. Even if you have not broken the law or been arrested, would you want other people suspected of crimes treated in these ways? Why or why not?

3. Would you want decisions that affected your life, liberty, or property made in secret? Why or why not?

▶ *What might happen to people accused of crimes if there was no right to due process of law?*

IDEAS TO DISCUSS

Why is due process important in criminal trials?

Divide students into pairs, or in groups of three to five. After students read the section, discuss the three situations presented. Ask the groups to respond to the questions that follow the situations. Debrief the activity by asking the groups to suggest examples of rights that are important to schoolchildren. Have students share their ideas with the class.

1. Do you believe that you would be treated fairly if you were accused of a crime? Why or why not?
   You would not be treated fairly if due process rules were ignored.

2. Even if you have not broken the law or been arrested, would you want other people suspected of a crime treated in these ways? Why or why not?
   Every individual has to be treated fairly. Government cannot choose to treat some people fairly and not others.

3. Would you want decisions that affected your life, liberty, or property made in secret? Why or why not?
   Government might make these decisions for its own benefit and not for the benefit of all.

LESSON 20

When should you have the right to a lawyer?

Divide the class into groups of three to five and ask them to read the section and the summary of *Gideon v. Wainwright* (1963). Ask groups to discuss the situation of Clarence Gideon and answer the questions that follow. You may wish to have students write their answers on chart paper, then share their opinions with the class. Accept reasonable responses.

1. Should the judge have appointed a lawyer to help Gideon? Why or why not?

   Most students will agree that the judge should have appointed a lawyer for Gideon because he was uneducated and did not have the skill to serve as his own attorney, nor could he afford to hire an attorney.

2. Should the right to have a lawyer mean that government has to provide one for all people who do not have the money to hire one?

   Why or why not? Students will probably agree that any person who cannot afford to hire an attorney should be provided one by the government.

3. When should a person have a right to a lawyer?
   - *upon arrest?*
   - *before being questioned?*
   - *before the trial?*
   - *after the trial, if he or she thinks the trial*
   - *was unfair and wants another trial?*

   Students will probably agree that a person is entitled to a lawyer before he or she is questioned, before the trial, and during the trial. Most will agree that he or she should be entitled to a lawyer after the trial as well, if the accused thinks the trial was unfair and wants to appeal the outcome.

Problem to solve

When should you have the right to a lawyer?

The Bill of Rights says that if you are accused of a crime, you have the right to have a lawyer defend you. Suppose the government did not allow you to have a lawyer. The government would have violated your right to due process, which is guaranteed by the Constitution.

- What does the right to have a lawyer in a criminal case mean?

- Must the government pay a lawyer to defend you if you cannot afford to pay for one yourself?

In the famous case, *Gideon v. Wainwright*, the United States Supreme Court thought again about what the constitutional right to a lawyer means. In a small group, read the following story. Then answer the questions that follow it. Be prepared to share your responses with the class.

Gideon v. Wainwright (1963)

The police accused Clarence Gideon of breaking into a poolroom in Florida. They said he had stolen a pint of wine and taken some coins from a cigarette machine. Gideon was 50 years old. He was a poor, uneducated man who did not know much about the law.

▶ Do you think it is important to have a lawyer defend you in a court of law? Why?

In court, Gideon asked the judge to appoint a lawyer for him. Gideon said that he was too poor to hire one himself. The judge said no. He said that Gideon did not have the right to have the court pay for a lawyer. The court could only do so when the charge was murder.

Gideon was tried before a jury. He tried to be his own lawyer. He made an opening speech to the jury. He asked questions of the witnesses against him. Gideon called his own witnesses to tell his side of the story. Then he made his final speech to the jury.

The jury decided that Gideon was guilty of the charges. The judge sent Gideon to prison for five years.

While in prison, Gideon wrote a petition to the Supreme Court. He wrote it by hand and in pencil. Gideon argued that all citizens have a right to a lawyer in cases where they might be sent to prison. The Court agreed to hear the appeal.

1. Should the judge have appointed a lawyer to help Gideon? Why or why not?

2. Should the right to have a lawyer mean that government has to provide one for all people who do not have the money to hire one? Why or why not?

3. When should a person have a right to a lawyer?

- Upon arrest?

- Before being questioned?

- Before the trial?

- After the trial, if the person thinks the trial was unfair and wants another trial?

▶ What right did Gideon exercise while in prison? Why is this right important?

LESSON REVIEW

The review questions are intended to assess learning and reinforce knowledge through discussion with students. You may wish to include additional questions developed by yourself or students.

1. What does the right to due process mean?

   Due process means the right to be treated fairly by the government. The government must use fair procedures when gathering information and making decisions.

2. Why is the right to due process important?

   Without due process the government and its agencies might treat the people in arbitrary or even cruel ways. The people would not feel secure; they would not trust the government to ensure the common good.

3. Explain how due process protects your rights to life, liberty, and property from unfair and unreasonable acts by people in government.

   Due process protects these rights by ensuring that all people are treated according to fair and reasonable standards and that these standards are known and accessible to all the people. If government officials violate these rights, they can be prosecuted and removed from office.

4. How does the Fourteenth Amendment differ from the Fifth Amendment in what it says about due process?

   The Fourteenth Amendment protects due process rights from infringement by state governments. The Fifth Amendment protects due process rights from being infringed upon by the national government.

ACTIVITIES

The suggested activities are intended to extend and apply learning outside the classroom. You may wish to have students complete one or more of the activities. Then, have them share the results with the class.

Review the lesson

1. What does the right to due process mean?

2. Why is the right to due process important?

3. Explain how due process protects your right to life, liberty, and property from unfair and unreasonable acts by people in government.

4. How does the Fourteenth Amendment differ from the Fifth Amendment in what it says about due process?

Activities to do

1. Watch a television drama or movie that deals with law enforcement. Keep a journal of how due process rights are protected or violated. Share your observations with the class.

2. With your teacher's help, invite a police officer to your class. Ask the officer to discuss what the police have to do to protect due process rights when they suspect someone of a crime. Prepare questions to ask your guest before the visit.

3. Find a newspaper article that gives an example of a due process right. Share your article with the class.

4. Draw a picture or poster. Divide your poster into two parts. On one side, show a situation in which a due process right is being violated. On the other side, show the same situation but with the due process right being protected. Share your drawing with the class.

5. Interview your school principal or a school board member. Ask them about your school's due process rules when dealing with students. Share what you learn with your class.

Lesson 21

How does the Constitution protect your right to vote?

Purpose of the lesson

Today, citizens of the United States who are 18 years of age or older have the right to vote. It was not always this way. In this lesson, you will learn how people worked to gain the right to vote. You will learn the laws and amendments to the Constitution that give citizens this right.

When you have finished this lesson, you should be able to explain how people of different groups gained the right to vote.

OVERVIEW

This lesson focuses on the expansion of voting rights to groups who previously had been denied the right to vote. It discusses the elimination of voting barriers applied to African Americans, the achievement of woman suffrage, and the extension of the vote to Native Americans and eighteen-year-olds. It points out the failure of citizens between the ages of eighteen and twenty-one to use their right to vote.

Students are introduced to key amendments dealing with the right to vote as well as certain laws passed by many Southern states to prevent African Americans from voting.

OBJECTIVES

At the conclusion of this lesson, students should be able to

- describe steps taken to remove African American voting barriers, to gain voting rights for women, and to extend the vote to Native Americans and to citizens over eighteen years of age
- explain some laws passed by many Southern states to prevent voting by African Americans
- describe voting requirements that are still left to the prerogative of the individual states

INTRODUCTORY ACTIVITY

Have students read the "Purpose of the lesson" section and consider the objectives of the lesson.

Write the "Terms to understand" on the board, or use a vocabulary-building activity of your choice. Tell them to watch for these key words as they read and study the chapter.

- Civil Rights Movement
- grandfather clause
- literacy test
- Nineteenth Amendment
- poll tax
- Twenty-fourth Amendment
- Twenty-sixth Amendment
- Voting Rights Act

IDEAS TO DISCUSS

Should the right to vote be given to all people?

Divide the class into groups of three to five students and have them discuss and respond to the three questions. Members of each group should be prepared to give the group's opinion to the rest of the class. After each group reports, have the class vote on the ideas expressed about who should have the right to vote. You might experiment with allowing only the girls to vote, or only students with brown eyes, or those under (or over) a certain age.

Ideas to discuss

Should the right to vote be given to all people?

Work in a group of three to five students. Answer these questions. Be prepared to share your opinions with the class.

1. Why should people have the right to vote for or choose government officials in an election?

2. Who should have the right to vote for government officials?

3. Who should not have this right? Explain your reasons.

4. Should all the states have the same rules for allowing people to vote?

▶ *How is the right to vote related to the ideas of republican government and consent of the governed?*

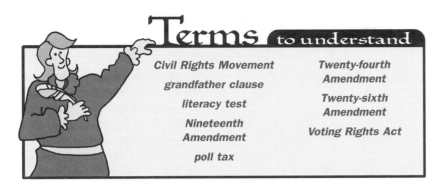

Terms to understand

Civil Rights Movement

grandfather clause

literacy test

Nineteenth Amendment

poll tax

Twenty-fourth Amendment

Twenty-sixth Amendment

Voting Rights Act

Why did the states limit the right to vote to white male property owners?

The Framers could not agree about who should have the right to vote.

▷ In 1776, why were only white men who owned property allowed to vote?

They left it up to the state governments to decide. Early in our nation's history, the state governments usually only allowed white men who owned property to vote. They believed that a white man with property could have a lot to lose if a bad government came to power. Therefore, he would be more careful with his vote. He would choose leaders who would respect his property.

During the 50 years after the adoption of the Constitution, the states gave the right to vote to all white men, not only those who owned property. African Americans, Native Americans, and women still could not vote. It took many years and much hard work before these groups gained the right to vote.

The right to vote in a democracy is very important. It is also a right that many citizens frequently ignore.

READING AND DISCUSSION

Why did the states limit the right to vote to white male property owners?

Engage the class in a discussion about why the Founders left this important aspect of democracy to the states, rather than mandating voting qualifications in the Constitution. Use the questions below as guidelines to the discussion.

1. Why was voting limited to men with property?
   What might have been the reason for excluding women?
   In eighteenth century England, it was the custom for men to obtain a formal education, to talk about and be involved in politics and government. Women were supposed to be only interested in things that related to the home, and perhaps reading and music. Most men thought it was not appropriate for women to participate in politics or make decisions that affected all citizens. Some students may suggest that because of this culturally pervasive belief and because men wrote the Constitution, they excluded women.

2. Would property owners be better voters than those who did not own property? Why or why not?
   Property holders might be more educated, more informed about the men running for office and about the state and local laws being proposed. It was thought that they had more to lose if a government came into power and abused that power. Therefore, they would be more responsible about voting. On the other hand, a man with property would generally vote for politicians and laws that favored the interests of men with property and not for politicians or laws favorable to non-property owners.

How did African American men gain the right to vote?

Ask students to read the section through the discussion of the Poll Tax. Emphasize the need for the three Civil War Amendments.

Because the South's defeat did not free the slaves, the Thirteenth Amendment was adopted. Because enslaved people were not citizens, the Fourteenth Amendment was adopted. Because enslaved people were not citizens, they did not have the right to vote. The Fifteenth Amendment says that states cannot deny the right to vote based on race, color, or former condition of servitude. Because Southern states said voting was not a right of United States citizenship, the Fifteenth Amendment was added. Review the laws that many Southern states passed to attempt to get around the Fifteenth Amendment.

Point out the distinction between a constitutional amendment that establishes a right of freedom that cannot be taken away, and a congressional law that establishes methods of enforcing that right. Explain that the Civil Rights Movement was what prompted the Twenty-fourth Amendment and the Voting Rights Act of 1965 to be passed.

How did African American men gain the right to vote?

More than 130 years ago, the Thirteenth Amendment ended slavery in America. You read about the Civil War Amendments in Lesson 19. They were intended to give the newly freed slaves the rights of citizens.

- The **Thirteenth Amendment** abolished slavery.

- The **Fourteenth Amendment** made the newly freed slaves citizens of the United States.

- The **Fifteenth Amendment** said that states could not deny the right to vote to anyone because of race or color, or because the person had once been a slave.

The Fifteenth Amendment gave African American men the right to vote. Many Southern states, however, passed laws that made it impossible for African Americans to vote. Here are some examples of these laws.

- **Literacy test.** This is a test to prove that a person is able to read and write. Some states required that African American men pass these tests to be able to vote. Most African American men had been denied an education. Often the people who gave the test were unfair. They made it impossible for even educated African American men to pass the test.

- **Grandfather clause.** Some states had voting laws with clauses that were called grandfather clauses. They said that a person had the right to vote if his grandfather had the right to vote. Few African American men could qualify because none of their grandfathers, who had been slaves, had the right to vote.

- **Poll tax.** This is a tax that a person must pay to be allowed to vote. Some states charged a poll tax. Since most former slaves were very poor, they could not pay the tax. Therefore, they could not vote.

People fought to get these laws changed. It took a long time. In 1915, the United States Supreme Court said that grandfather clauses in state laws were unconstitutional. Even so, some states used literacy tests and poll taxes to keep African Americans from voting until the 1960s.

In the 1950s, more and more people began to demand that the federal government protect the right of people to vote. People of all races worked together to change unfair state laws. The people gave speeches and marched in the streets. These actions became known as the **Civil Rights Movement.**

▶ *What rights were the people who participated in the Civil Rights Movement exercising?*
In 1963, people from all over the U.S. marched on Washington, D.C. for civil rights and jobs.

As a result of the Civil Rights Movement in 1964, the Twenty-fourth Amendment was added to the Constitution. The **Twenty-fourth Amendment** says that the right to vote in a national election shall not be denied because a person fails to pay a poll tax, or any other tax. Two years later, the Supreme Court said this right also applied to state elections.

In 1965, Congress passed a law called the Voting Rights Act. The **Voting Rights Act of 1965** further protected the right to vote for all United States citizens. It forced the states to obey the Constitution. It made it clear that the right to vote could not be denied because of a person's color or race.

169

How did women gain the right to vote?

How did American Indians gain the right to vote?

How did eighteen-year-olds gain the right to vote?

Form groups of three students each. Assign one student in each group to read one of the remaining sections—women, Native Americans, or eighteen-year-olds. Students should then prepare a brief report for the other members in the group.

Who is eligible to vote today?

Assign the last section for the class to read aloud. Discuss the following question.

Do you think our nation is more democratic today than it was in 1901? Why or why not?

see next student pages

LESSON REVIEW

The questions in the student book are intended to assess learning and to reinforce knowledge through discussion. The questions are directly related to the lesson objectives. You may wish to include additional questions developed by yourself or by students.

1. In the early years of our nation's history, why did the states give the right to vote only to white men who owned property?

   The Framers left the criteria for voting up to the states. The states had traditionally allowed only white men with property to vote; they continued that practice. They thought men who owned property would be more thoughtful about their votes.

2. Explain how African American men gained the right to vote. What laws had to be changed to make voting rights for African Americans fair?

   During the Civil Rights Movement, people of all races worked hard to make changes in unfair laws. They made speeches, engaged in boycotts, and marched in the streets. Their efforts resulted in the elimination of the following unfair laws:

   - *Literacy tests – required people to prove they could read and write. The people administering these difficult tests made it impossible for anyone that they did not want to vote to pass the test.*

   - *Grandfather clause – gave a person the right to vote if his grandfather had the right to vote. Most African Americans could not qualify because their grandfathers had been slaves and did not have the right to vote.*

   - *Poll tax – required a man to pay a tax in order to vote. Most former slaves were very poor and could not afford to pay the tax. Therefore, they could not vote.*

▶ *How did Lucretia Mott and Elizabeth Cady Stanton help women gain the right to vote?*
Elizabeth Cady Stanton

How did women gain the right to vote?

For most of our history, women did not have the right to vote. Women are the largest group ever denied the right to vote in our nation.

Women began the national fight to gain the right to vote at a convention held in New York in 1848. Women's rights leaders such as Lucretia Mott and Elizabeth Cady Stanton argued that women should have equal rights with men. They said women's rights could be protected only if women had the right to vote. After the Civil War, many women supported the Fifteenth Amendment that gave African American men the right to vote. They tried hard to win their own right to vote at the same time. In those days, in was common to believe that women should not participate in government. This belief hurt women's chances of winning the right to vote.

The struggle for women's right to vote was long and difficult. Women picketed the White House. They marched in parades in cities and towns. Some women went to the polls and insisted on voting. The most famous leader in the struggle for women's rights was Susan B. Anthony. Anthony was arrested and fined $100 for voting illegally in 1872. She refused to pay the fine and the judge did not force her to.

Women continued to fight and win support for their cause. Then, in 1920, the Nineteenth Amendment was added to the Constitution. The **Nineteenth Amendment** gave women the right to vote. More than 130 years after the Framers signed the Constitution, women finally won the right to vote in all elections in the U.S.

▶ *Why was the right to vote so important to women?*

How did American Indians gain the right to vote?

American Indian tribes governed themselves by their own laws, treaties with the United States, and by special laws passed by Congress. Most American Indians were not recognized as citizens of the United States. They did not have the right to vote.

A law passed in 1924 recognized American Indians as citizens of the United States. This law gave them the right to vote in both state and federal elections.

How did 18-year-olds gain the right to vote?

In 1970, only four states let citizens younger than 21 vote. In that year, thousands of young Americans were fighting a war in Vietnam. Many of them were under 21 years of age.

People argued that if 18-year-olds were old enough to fight, then they were old enough to vote. In March 1971, the Twenty-sixth Amendment was added to the Constitution. The **Twenty-sixth Amendment** gives citizens eighteen years of age or older the right to vote in all elections.

The people who fought for the young adults' right to vote believed they would use this right. Today

▶ How did Native Americans gain the right to vote?

however, fewer 18- to 24-year-olds vote than any other age group.

Who is eligible to vote today?

Today, state governments still make decisions about voting rights. All the states have passed laws saying that only citizens can vote. The states limit the right to vote to people who are residents of the state and to those who register to vote. Some states do not allow people who have been found guilty of serious crimes to vote.

The individual states decide what kinds of voting machines are acceptable. They also decide on the rules that make a vote valid.

3. Explain how women gained the right to vote. Why do you think women were not given the right to vote in the first place?

   At a convention in New York in 1848, women met to coordinate their fight to gain the right to vote. The struggle was long and hard. Women picketed the White House and marched in the streets. They gave speeches and argued for their right to vote. Some women went to the polls and demanded that they be allowed to vote. Women did not generally own property and traditionally had been viewed as having interests only related to the home. They were not considered able to deal with the complexities of politics and government or of making decisions that affected citizens.

4. Why did Native Americans not have the right to vote? How did this change?

   Native Americans governed themselves by their own laws, treaties with the United States, and by special laws passed by Congress. They were not considered to be citizens of the United States but of their own sovereign nations within the United States. In 1924, Congress passed a law that granted U.S. citizenship and thereby the right to vote to American Indians. [Over time, since the 1960s when it was introduced, the term Native American has been expanded to include all native peoples of the United States and its territories.]

5. Why was the right to vote given to eighteen-year-olds?

   During the 1960s and early 1970s, many young men were fighting in the Vietnam War. There was a movement of politically active young people who strongly opposed the war. People argued that if eighteen-year-olds were old enough to fight in a war, they were old enough to vote. In 1971, the Twenty-sixth Amendment was added to the Constitution. It gave citizens eighteen years old or older the right to vote.

ADDITIONAL INSTRUCTIONAL ACTIVITY

The suggested activities are intended to extend and apply learning outside the classroom. Students might role-play an African American man living in the South at the turn of the century, a Native American man, a woman, or an eighteen-year-old before these groups gained their right to vote. They could write a letter to a friend or family member, or put an entry in their diary expressing their feelings. The following prompts might be helpful:

- It is 1893 and you are an African-American living in the South. You went to register to vote, but were not allowed to register.
- It is 1900 and you are a woman with strong political convictions. You went to register to vote, but you were arrested for trying.
- It is 1920 and you are an American Indian and live on a reservation. You want to vote for the next governor of your state.
- It is 1952 and you are eighteen and soon to be drafted into the armed forces. You would like to vote for a senator who is against the Korean Conflict but you are too young to vote.

Answer the following questions about your group:

1. What group did you choose?
2. Describe any constitutional amendments that helped this group gain the right to vote.
3. Describe important events that happened or steps taken that helped this group gain the right to vote.
4. What dates or years are important to remember about the efforts of this group to gain the right to vote?
5. Explain your feelings about your situation and what you think should be done about it.
6. Do you think your constitutional rights were being violated?

Review the lesson

1. In the early years of our nation, why did the states only give the right to vote to white men who owned property?

2. Explain how African American men gained the right to vote. What laws had to be changed to make voting rights for African Americans fair?

3. Explain how women gained the right to vote. Why do you think women were not given the right to vote in the first place?

4. Why did Native Americans not have the right to vote? How did this change?

5. Why was the right to vote given to 18-year-olds?

Activities to do

1. With your teacher's help, invite someone from the League of Women Voters to come to your class to discuss elections in your state. Prepare questions to ask your guest before the visit.

2. Learn more about the women's struggle for the right to vote. Share what you learned with your class.

3. Make posters encouraging people to vote, especially 18- to 24-year-olds.

4. Find out how a citizen can register to vote in your state. Get a copy of a voter registration form. Share what you learned with your class.

5. Write a story with the title "Every Vote Counts." In the story, show how just one person's vote can make a difference. Read your story to the class.

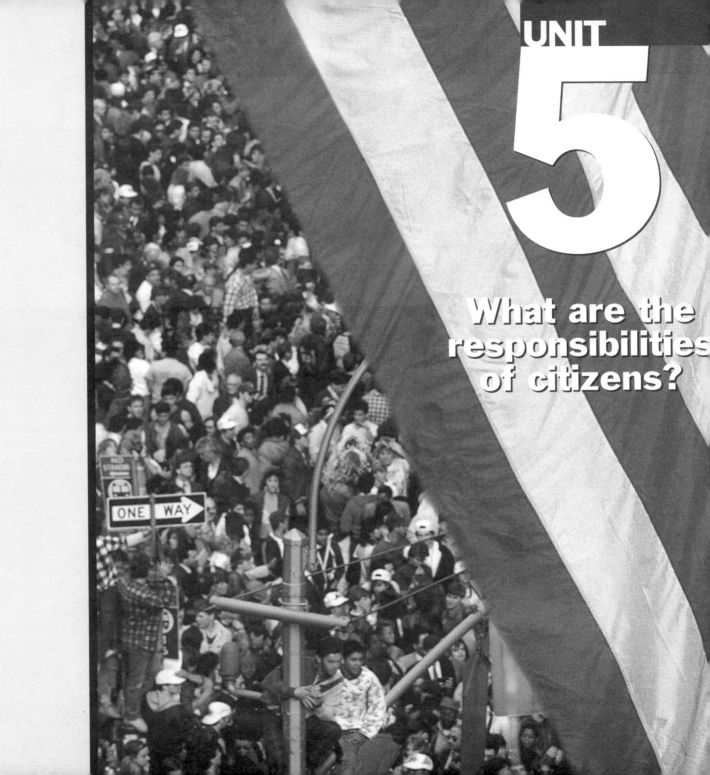

What are the
responsibilities
of citizens?

UNIT 5

OVERVIEW

This unit emphasizes the relationship between rights and responsibilities. We will examine the specific responsibilities associated with the five basic rights discussed in Unit Four.

The unit looks at the role of the United States in the world today. Students examine the influence the United States has had on other nations as well as the influences other nations have had on the United States.

Finally, the unit discusses the citizen's responsibility to work for the common good, and examines the problem of deciding what the common good might be in situations involving conflicting interests. The unit also addresses issues related to citizens of the future and what their responsibilities may include.

Various forms of age-appropriate participation are discussed, including studying about government, becoming informed about current events, expressing opinions, writing letters to government officials, volunteering, and taking part in school government. Students are reminded that the type and level of participation they engage in is a personal decision.

OBJECTIVES

At the conclusion of this unit, students should be able to

- identify responsibilities associated with certain basic rights of citizens and explain why they are important
- explain the importance of citizen participation
- explain ways in which nations interact with one another
- examine a problem concerning the common good, explain the responsibilities of citizens to understand and attempt to solve the problem, and take and defend a position on a possible solution to the problem

INTRODUCTION

Explain that the last unit deals with a question that concerns us all: "What are the responsibilities of citizens?" Read the introduction aloud with the class. The unit will raise a number of important questions that each student must answer for himself or herself.

Present the list of key topics. Post them on the board or chart paper. Instruct students to look for these topics as they read.

What are the responsibilities of citizens?

In this text, you have studied the principles and history of the United States Constitution. You learned why and how the Founders organized our government the way they did. You learned that the purpose of government is to protect our rights and to provide for the common good. You also learned that the power of our government comes from the people. The people delegate certain powers to the government.

It is important that our government does its job well. Government cannot do a good job if citizens do not participate. In this unit, you will learn about the United States and its place in world affairs. You will examine the responsibilities of citizens. You also will look at ways in which citizens can take part in government. You will discuss some important issues. For example, how might you balance your self-interest with the common good? What might you do when you think that a law is unfair?

It is very important for us to participate in our government. You should decide for yourself what you ought to do as a citizen of the United States.

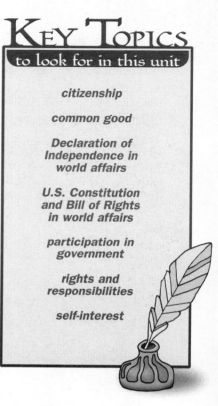

KEY TOPICS
to look for in this unit

citizenship

common good

Declaration of Independence in world affairs

U.S. Constitution and Bill of Rights in world affairs

participation in government

rights and responsibilities

self-interest

Lesson 22

What is the role of the United States in the world today?

Purpose of the lesson

Your studies would not be complete if you did not think about the role of the United States in the world today. In this lesson, you will learn some ways that countries interact with one another. You will also learn how some of the ideas about government in the Declaration of Independence and in the United States Constitution and Bill of Rights have influenced people in other countries.

OVERVIEW

Students will look at the powers that the Constitution gives to our government when dealing with other nations, and they will examine how the Declaration of Independence, the Constitution, and the Bill of Rights have influenced other nations. The lesson concludes by looking at the challenges that face the world today and how nations influence each other.

OBJECTIVES

At the conclusion of this lesson, students should be able to

- explain the ways in which nations interact
- identify ways in which the Declaration of Independence, the Constitution, and the Bill of Rights have influenced other nations
- explain what challenges we as U.S. citizens face in the world today and in the future

INTRODUCTORY ACTIVITY

Have students read the "Purpose of the lesson" section and consider the objectives of the lesson.

Write the "Terms to understand" on the board, or use a vocabulary-building activity of your choice. You may wish to have students look up the words in the glossary at the back of their text.

- diplomacy
- humanitarian
- United Nations

LESSON 22

READING AND DISCUSSION

How have other countries influenced the United States?

Have the class read the section. Upon completion of the reading, ask students to volunteer examples of how other countries influence the United States. Examples might include music, food, dress, dance, vehicles, space exploration programs, sports, and professional athletes. Students should give specific examples.

How do countries of the world interact?

Before reading the lesson, have students think of examples of nations interacting with one another. Examples might include trade between the U.S. and Mexico, space missions held jointly with other countries, collaboration on environmental issues, and nations assisting one another when a disaster strikes.

Then have students read the section. Upon completion of the reading go back to the ways in which nations interact with one another and write each category on the board or on chart paper. Ask students to explain in their own words each category. You might have students look for examples of each category on the internet or in newspapers. You might also have students interview adults and ask them to provide examples from each of the categories.

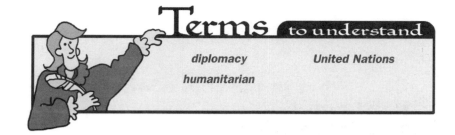

Terms to understand

diplomacy   United Nations

humanitarian

How have other countries influenced the United States?

Many of the ideals of government that you have studied started in other countries. A country consists of territory, people, government, and laws. The Founders learned about government from studying the histories of ancient Greece and Rome. From the Greeks and Romans, they learned about republican government, civic virtue, and the common good.

The European philosophers also had a great impact on the Founders. The theories of Baron de Montesquieu from France influenced their thinking about separation of powers. The writings of John Locke from Great Britain guided their thinking about natural rights.

The Founders had also enjoyed the rights of Englishmen. Among these were the right to trial by jury, the right to be secure in one's home, and the right to express one's

views about taxes through one's representative in government.

How do countries of the world interact?

Today, events in the United States influence many countries around the globe. What happens in other countries also affects the United States. It is important that we know how countries interact with one another and that we are informed about world events.

Here are some ways in which countries interact with one another.

- **Culture, science, and business exchanges.** People travel all over the world. People living in different countries share ideas. Doctors, scientists, and business people from many countries meet to share advances in their fields. Students and teachers live with families in other countries to learn about their culture. Artists show their work in the museums of other countries.

176

▶ *What types of treaties and agreements do countries make?*

Anwar Sadat (President of Egypt), President Jimmy Carter, and Menachem Begin (Prime Minister of Israel). Egypt-Israel Peace Agreement March 26, 1979.

They work to find ways to solve common problems in a peaceful manner.

- **Treaties and agreements.** Countries make treaties and agreements. They agree to promote trade among themselves. They agree to do certain things to protect the environment. Some agree to help each other in time of war.

- **Military force.** When two or more countries cannot solve their disagreements peacefully, they sometimes use military force. The disagreement might result in a war.

- **Humanitarian aid.** The term **humanitarian** means to show concern for the pain and suffering of others. During natural disasters such as floods and earthquakes, countries help the victims in other countries by giving humanitarian aid. Countries send medicine, food, and shelter to suffering people.

- **Trade.** Countries buy and sell factory and farm goods to one another in world markets.

- **Diplomacy.** The term **diplomacy** means to carry on a formal relationship with the governments of other countries. The official representatives of countries meet and discuss things important to both countries.

▶ *Why do countries trade goods?*

What powers does the U.S. Constitution give to the government to deal with other countries?

Have students work with a partner to list examples from current events that illustrate each of the powers mentioned in the text. You may want to distribute articles that illustrate each power. Choose articles that depict Congress, the president, and the U.S. Supreme Court exercising these powers. Examples might include Congress giving the president permission to send troops to an area of the world where conflict is taking place; the president meeting an ambassador from another nation; the U.S. Supreme Court making a decision about a case that involves another country.

There is no single organization in the world that has the power to force countries to settle conflicts peacefully. There are some organizations that help countries reach agreements without going to war. One such organization is the **United Nations**.

The United Nations was created in 1945. It was meant to be a general international organization to maintain peace and security for its members. The delegates of 50 nations drew up the United Nations Charter, which was adopted unanimously.

What powers does the U.S. Constitution give to the government to deal with other countries?

Each branch of government has certain powers. These powers come from the Constitution. The Constitution gives each branch the following powers to deal with other countries.

- **Congress**. Congress has the power to regulate commerce with other countries and with the Indian tribes. It can declare war, approve treaties, approve ambassadors, raise and support armies, punish piracies and crimes committed on the high seas.

▶ Why was the United Nations created? What power does the organization have?

178

- **President**. The president has the power to lead military forces as commander in chief, grant pardons, make treaties, and name ambassadors with the approval of Congress.

- **U.S. Supreme Court**. The Supreme Court has the power to hear all cases affecting ambassadors, cases in which the United States is a party, and cases involving a foreign state, its citizens or subjects.

How have the Declaration of Independence and the United States Constitution and Bill of Rights influenced other countries?

The United States has made many contributions to the world. Some of these include advanced medical and industrial technology and the personal computer. All the discoveries and inventions that we as a nation have contributed to the world are important. But they are not as valuable or long lasting as the democratic ideas expressed in the Declaration of Independence and the United States Constitution and Bill of Rights. Some of these ideas are listed here.

1. Power comes from the people, and the people are the ultimate source of the authority of their government.

▶ How have American ideas about government affected other countries?
Demonstration, Red Square, Moscow, Russia.

2. People in government are the servants of the people. They are not the masters of the people.

3. All people are political equals. No person's vote counts more than another's.

4. The people delegate their powers to their government. They consent to be governed only so long as those in power fulfill their responsibilities. They can take back those powers and change their government.

5. The purposes of government are to protect the people's rights to life, liberty, and property, and to promote the common good.

How have the Declaration of Independence and the United States Constitution and Bill of Rights influenced other countries?

After reading the section with the class, divide the class into groups of two or three. Write each of the numbered democratic ideas on slips of paper and have each group select one slip. Instruct the groups to demonstrate what the idea would look like. For example, if a group selects number three, the idea that "All people are political equals. No person's vote counts more than another's", the group might act out a scene in which they are walking to a voting booth and placing their ballots in a box. The group might then show the ballots being counted with all votes receiving the same value.

179

▶ *What countries have experienced democratic change in the last 200 years?*

6. A nation's constitution should be approved by the people and serve as a higher law that everyone must obey, including the people and those serving in their government.

7. A nation's constitution should include a list of the rights of the people.

During the nineteenth and twentieth centuries, the American ideal of self-government spread around the world. People from many countries read and studied the ideas in the Declaration of Independence and the Constitution and Bill of Rights. These documents influenced other countries to adopt similar ideas about government.

The American Revolution gave hope to many people in Europe and Latin America who wanted to promote democratic change in their own countries. The French Constitution of 1791 included many ideas from the United States. The Declaration of Independence and the U.S. Constitution and Bill of Rights also inspired Latin American leaders. Among these leaders were José de San Martín in Argentina, Simón Bolívar in Venezuela, and Miguel Hidalgo in Mexico.

Throughout our history, we have thought of citizenship only in terms of our country. The issues that citizens deal with today are becoming increasingly international.

Ideas to discuss

How do other countries influence each other?

Work with a partner. Discuss the following questions. Be prepared to share your ideas with the class.

1. What events in the United States today might have an effect on other people of the world?

2. What events in the world today might have an effect on citizens in the United States?

3. What do citizens in the United States gain from our relationships with other countries of the world? What do citizens in other countries gain?

4. Why is it important that countries be able to have a free exchange of ideas?

▶ Why might people in other parts of the world be interested in ideas such as natural rights, consent of the governed, and constitutional government?
Opening of the Berlin Wall, November 9, 1989, Germany.

IDEAS TO DISCUSS

How do other countries influence each other?

Have students work with a partner for this exercise. Go over each question to make sure students understand them. You might want to have newspapers or newsmagazines available for this exercise. The pairs could look for articles that relate to each question and present them with their discussion. The pairs should be prepared to share their ideas with the rest of the class. Possible responses are given but accept any reasonable examples.

1. What events in the United States today might have an effect on other people of the world?

   Examples cited might be the bombing of the World Trade Center in New York, trade agreements, human rights policies, or environmental laws.

2. What events in the world today might have an effect on citizens in the United States?

   Conflicts between nations, diseases such as AIDS, or laws passed in other nations that forbid the import of U.S. products.

3. What do citizens in the United States gain from our relationships with other countries of the world? What do citizens in other countries gain?

   Citizens in the United States might benefit from goods, services, or technology developed in other nations. Citizens in other nations might benefit from U.S. medical advances, humanitarian aid, or education for democracy.

4. Why is it important that countries be able to have a free exchange of ideas?

   The free exchange of ideas can promote solutions to cultural, economic, or environmental problems.

LESSON 22

LESSON REVIEW

The review questions are intended to assess learning and to reinforce knowledge through discussion. The questions are directly related to the lesson objectives. You may wish to include additional questions developed by yourself or by students.

1. List some things that countries do to carry out their relationships with other countries.

   Countries work together to establish and provide humanitarian aid, become involved in trade with other nations, develop and sign treaties and agreements with other nations, and provide military support when needed.

2. What powers does the U.S. Constitution give the national government to deal with other nations?

   The Constitution gives Congress the power to declare war, approve treaties, approve ambassadors, raise and support armies, and punish piracies and crimes committed at sea.

3. List some of the ideas in the Declaration of Independence and in the Constitution and Bill of Rights that have influenced government in other countries.

   Examples include: power comes from the people; all people are political equals; the people consent to be governed, the government is not the master of the people; the purpose of government is to protect the rights of the people; a country's constitution is the higher law and everyone must obey it; and a country's constitution should include a list of the rights of the people.

ACTIVITIES

The suggested activities are intended to extend and apply learning outside of the classroom. You may wish to have students complete one or more of the activities. Then, have them share the results with the class.

Review the lesson

1. List some things that countries do to carry out their relationships with other countries.

2. What powers does the U.S. Constitution give the national government to deal with other countries?

3. List some of the ideas in the Declaration of Independence and in the Constitution and Bill of Rights that have influenced government in other countries.

Activities to do

1. Learn more about the United Nations. Why and how was the United Nations established? What does the United Nations do? Share what you learned with your class.

2. Suppose you make a telephone call to a friend or relative in South Africa or in Jordan. Suppose you send a letter to China using a stamp from the United States. Learn about international agreements that make it possible for your telephone call or letter to reach its destination. Find information about the Universal Postal Union or the International Communications Union.

3. Select one of the leaders of the Latin American revolutions of the 1800s. Learn about the person's life. Learn about how the ideas in the Declaration of Independence and the U.S. Constitution and Bill of Rights influenced his thinking about government.

   - José de San Martín
   - Simón Bolívar
   - Miguel Hidalgo
   - Bernardo O'Higgins

4. Choose one of the following countries: China, Colombia, France, Israel, Panama, Russia, Saudi Arabia, or Vietnam. Learn about the country's relationship with the United States in the past and today. Share what you learned with the class.

Lesson 23

What are some important responsibilities of citizens?

Purpose of the lesson

Suppose your government does everything it can to protect your rights. Is this enough? Will your rights be protected? Do we have any responsibility to protect not only our own rights, but each other's as well? In this lesson, you will discuss some important questions about the responsibilities of citizens. You must develop your own answers to these questions. We hope this lesson helps you develop good answers.

When you have finished this lesson, you should be able to explain some of the responsibilities related to important rights. You should also be able to evaluate a situation in which the rights of individuals conflict with the common good, and take and defend a position on the issue.

OVERVIEW

This lesson looks at an important question students will face as citizens: What are some important responsibilities of citizens? The lesson begins by defining a citizen of the United States and discusses what kind of citizen is desired in a democratic society. The lesson leads the class into a discussion of the importance of fulfilling responsibilities necessary to protect rights. The class then engages in a problem-solving activity that examines specific responsibilities. The responsibilities should be connected to protecting the five basic rights studied in Unit Four. The activity then poses the question of what might happen if citizens did not fulfill these responsibilities.

OBJECTIVES

At the conclusion of this lesson, students should be able to

- explain the differences between a citizen and a resident alien and explain how one acquires citizenship in the United States
- explain the importance of the fulfillment of responsibilities by citizens so that everyone's rights are protected

INTRODUCTORY ACTIVITY

Have students read the "Purpose of the lesson" section and consider the objectives of the lesson.

Write the "Terms to understand" on the board, or use a vocabulary-building activity of your choice. You may wish to have students look up the words in the glossary at the back of their text.

- citizen
- naturalized citizens
- resident aliens

READING AND DISCUSSION

Who is a citizen of the United States?

Read this section aloud with the class. Make sure that students understand the different ways in which a person can become a citizen of the United States. Discuss the different rights that citizens have that resident aliens do not have.

As an optional activity, have students make up their own citizenship test.

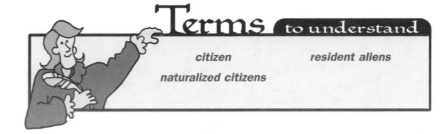

Terms to understand

citizen   resident aliens

naturalized citizens

Who is a citizen of the United States?

A **citizen** is a member of an official political body, such as a nation or a state. Citizens of the United States are those who are

▶ *What rights do resident aliens have? What rights don't they have?*

- born in the United States

- born to United States citizens living in another country

- born elsewhere, living legally in the United States, and have passed a test on the Constitution and history of the United States to become **naturalized citizens**

- children of naturalized citizens who were under the age of 18 when their parents became citizens

The national government protects the rights of all people who live in the United States. People who are not citizens, but who live legally in the United States, are called resident aliens. **Resident aliens** enjoy most of the rights of citizens. They have the same right to due process of law as citizens.

Resident aliens do not have the right to vote, serve on a jury, or run for public office. Like citizens, resident aliens have a responsibility to obey the law.

Is a good constitution enough to protect your rights?

The Framers planned our government carefully. They organized it so its powers were limited. They separated the powers of our government among three different branches. They balanced the powers among these branches. They provided ways each branch could check or limit the powers of the other branches. Finally, they added a Bill of Rights. The Bill of Rights now protects our rights from unfair treatment by our national, state, and local governments.

Some of the Framers believed they had organized the government very well. They believed the way they planned the government was enough to make sure our rights and the common good would be protected.

Other Framers did not agree. They believed that the government would only work well if there were good people running it. They also believed it would only succeed if the citizens were good citizens.

Today, most people agree that a well-written constitution is not enough to protect our rights. We need to elect leaders who will make and enforce laws that protect our rights and promote our welfare.

Even a good constitution and good leaders may not be enough. If we want to protect our rights and welfare, we, the people, have certain responsibilities to fulfill. Let's examine what some of these responsibilities might be.

▶ What might happen if people did not exercise their rights?

Is a good constitution enough to protect your rights?

Ask students to read the section quietly to themselves. When they have completed the reading, hold a whole-class discussion about the necessity of citizen participation in government to ensure protection of rights and promotion of the common good. Engage opposite points of view.

LESSON 23

What responsibilities go along with these rights?

Have students read the first paragraph of this section. Then divide the class into five groups. Assign each group one set of questions. If the groups have more than five students, subdivide them so that all students have a chance to discuss the questions. Each group is to answer its set of questions, write down the answers, and assign one or more members of the group to report the group's responses to the class. Allow time for discussion of each group's responses. You might develop a class consensus on what responsibilities should be associated with each of the basic rights. The groups should review Unit Four and the five basic rights presented in the unit.

In a debriefing class discussion, have students consider these questions:

- Do most people understand these responsibilities and the importance of fulfilling them?
- How do young children learn these responsibilities?
- Would they add any other responsibilities to the list?
- Which responsibilities do they think are the most difficult to fulfill?

Ideas to discuss

What responsibilities go along with these rights?

Let's examine some responsibilities that might go along with your basic rights. Work in small groups. Each group should answer the questions about one of the rights listed below. Then each group should share its ideas with the class.

▶ *Why might people have different ideas about new playground rules? How can we handle different opinions?*

Group 1   The right to freedom of expression

Suppose you attend a meeting of students in your school. The purpose of the meeting is to suggest rules for the playground. Every student has the right to speak and to make suggestions.

1. What should be your responsibilities for the way you speak and what you say?

2. What should be your responsibilities toward the right of others to speak?

3. What responsibilities should the other students have to you and your right to speak?

4. Government may not unfairly limit your right to express your ideas freely. What responsibilities should you have that might go along with this right?

5. Suppose no one fulfilled the responsibilities that you have discussed. What might happen to our right to freedom of expression?

▶ *What does it mean to practice religion responsibly?*

Group 2 **The right to freedom of religion**

Suppose you believe in a particular religion. You attend a church, meeting hall, mosque, or temple in your community.

1. What responsibilities should you have in the way you practice your religious beliefs?

2. What responsibilities should you have toward the right of other people to practice their religious beliefs?

3. What responsibilities should people who hold different religious beliefs have toward your right to practice your religious beliefs?

4. Government may not interfere with your right to believe as you wish. It may not unfairly limit your right to practice your religious beliefs. What responsibilities should you have that go along with these rights?

5. Suppose no one fulfilled the responsibilities that you have discussed. What might happen to our right to freedom of religion?

Ideas to discuss

Group 3 The right to the equal protection of the law

Suppose your city government officials are planning a picnic for the people who live in your community.

1. What responsibilities should officials have to you regardless of your age, gender, race, or religion?

2. If you volunteer to help plan the city's picnic, what responsibilities should you have to others?

3. Government is not permitted to favor some people over others because of their age, gender, race, or religion. What responsibilities should you have that go along with this right?

4. Suppose no one fulfilled the responsibilities that you have discussed. What might happen to our right to the equal protection of the law?

Group 4 The right to due process of law

Suppose someone accused you of doing something wrong in your school.

1. What responsibilities should the accuser have toward you?

2. If you were the one who accused another student of doing something wrong, what responsibilities should you have toward her or him?

3. Government must be fair to you when it is gathering information and making decisions. What responsibilities should you have that go along with this right?

4. Suppose no one fulfilled the responsibilities that you have discussed. What might happen to our right to due process of the law?

▶ *What ideas should people consider when deciding how to vote?*

Group 5 The right to vote and run for public office

Suppose you are about to vote in a school election. You must choose between two people running for class president.

1. What responsibilities should you have?

2. You have decided to vote for Bill. Your friends want to vote for John. What responsibilities should you have about their right to vote?

3. What responsibilities should they have about your right to vote?

4. When you are 18, you will have the right to vote in government elections. You will also have the right to run for some public offices. What responsibilities should go along with these rights?

5. Suppose that no one fulfilled the responsibilities that you have discussed. What might happen to our right to vote?

LESSON 23

LESSON REVIEW

The questions in the student books are intended to assess learning and to reinforce knowledge through discussion. The questions are directly related to the lesson objectives. You may wish to include additional questions developed by yourself or by students.

1. How does a person become a citizen of the United States?

    A person can be a citizen by being born in the United States, or by being born in another country to parents who are citizens of the United States. People not born in the United States can become citizens after living in the country for five years and passing a test. This is called becoming a naturalized citizen.

2. What are some responsibilities of citizens? Why is fulfilling these responsibilities important?

    Citizens have personal and civic responsibilities. They must know their rights and have the duty to fulfill the responsibilities that go with the rights. Fulfilling the responsibilities is necessary to a self-governing, free, and just society.

3. What are some responsibilities that go along with your right to free expression, freedom of religion, protection of the laws, due process of the laws, and the right to vote?

    The responsibilities that go along with these rights require that the rights of others be respected, that our democratic institutions be protected, that the dignity of all be considered, and that the common good should be acknowledged.

ADDITIONAL INSTRUCTIONAL ACTIVITIES

These activities are intended to extend and apply learning outside of the classroom.

Have students search the internet and look through newspapers or newsmagazines for evidence of individuals carrying out responsibilities as citizens. Based on their findings, compile a list of ways to participate in government.

Post this list on the board and tell students that they can add to it as they learn more about participation.

Review the lesson

1. How does a person become a citizen of the United States?

2. What are some responsibilities of citizens? Why is fulfilling these responsibilities important?

3. What are some responsibilities that go along with your right to free expression, freedom of religion, equal protection of the laws, due process of the laws, and the right to vote?

Activities to do

1. Find more information about how a person can become a naturalized citizen of the United States.

2. Do some research on a famous naturalized citizen. What contributions has that person made to the United States?

3. Create a poster that shows some rights of citizens and the responsibilities that those rights carry.

4. Write a story about what can happen in a community where people do not exercise their responsibility to be good citizens.

5. Interview someone who is a resident alien. In a report to the class, explain the person's opinion about whether he or she wants to be a citizen of the United States.

Lesson 24

How can citizens promote the common good?

Purpose of the lesson

In this lesson you will examine some responsibilities that we all have to promote the common good. We will also look at ways we can participate in making decisions about protecting our rights and the common good.

When you have finished this lesson, you should be able to explain the importance of promoting the common good. You should also be able to explain why it is so difficult to agree upon what is the common good. Finally, you should be able to explain why education is important in preparing citizens to participate in their government and the reasons why they should participate.

191

OVERVIEW

This lesson considers the reasons for participating in government, and suggests ways in which students of this age group can participate. The lesson concludes by raising the question of a citizen's participation in government, and how this affects the future of democracy. Students examine conflicts involved when citizens balance their self-interest with the common good.

OBJECTIVES

At the conclusion of this lesson, students should be able to

- give reasons why citizens participate in government
- explain how citizens participate in government to solve problems
- explain the difficulty of deciding between self-interest and the common good

MATERIALS

Handout Appendix D 3, "Reflecting on Your Experience"

INTRODUCTORY ACTIVITY

Have students read the "Purpose of the lesson" section and consider the objectives of the lesson.

READING AND DISCUSSION

How do we decide what is best for everyone?

Have students read the section. Call on individual students to explain the conflict, if any, between the principles of natural rights and those of republican government. Next, ask students to work with a partner to discuss the particular examples in the section and decide how to deal with potential differences of opinion about what is best for everyone.

How do we decide what is best for everyone?

When you studied the ideas of natural rights, you learned that the purpose of government is to protect our rights to life, liberty, and property. When we choose a government that promises to protect these rights, we protect our self-interest. We want to make sure that government fulfills its duties to us as individuals.

When you studied the ideas of republican government, you learned that the government and its citizens have a duty to serve the common good. Each citizen works cooperatively with the government and each other for the good of the whole community. In some situations, this might mean that we should put aside our own self-interest for the common good.

In some situations, the common good is quite clear. For example, it is good for all of us to live in a healthy environment. Our country needs to be protected by our armed forces. In other situations, citizens might disagree about the common good. For example, people disagree about whether it is good for everyone to begin each school day with a prayer.

Some people might also disagree about how to serve the common good. We know that protecting the environment serves the common good. But, some ways of protecting the environment might endanger people's jobs and violate property rights. Sometimes it is difficult to decide between our self-interest and the common good.

▶ How does recycling our household waste serve the common good?

192

Problem to solve

What decision would you make?

Work in small groups. Read the following situation and answer the questions that follow. Then, each group should share its answers with the class.

Problems in Smalltown, U.S.A.

Imagine that you live in a small community. Most of the people in Smalltown work in one large factory. The smoke from the factory pollutes the air and is a danger to everyone's health. The smoke also pollutes the air of communities nearby.

It would be very expensive to stop the pollution. The owners of the factory say they cannot afford to buy the machinery needed. They would lose money and might not be able to stay in business. If the factory closed, many people would lose their jobs. There are no other good jobs available nearby, and people might have to move to another town.

1. What might be some self-interests of the people who live in your community?

▶ *Why is pollution such an important problem to solve?*

2. What might be the common good for your community?

3. What are some different ways to solve the problem?

4. What are the advantages and disadvantages of each solution you have suggested?

5. What do you think is the best solution? Give the reasons for your choice.

PROBLEM TO SOLVE

What decision would you make?

Have students work in small groups to discuss the environmental problems in Smalltown. Ask each group to use the questions that follow the scenario as guidelines when responding to the problem. Have students choose a spokesperson to share their views with the class.

READING AND DISCUSSION

How can you participate in your government?

Have students read the section. It should be made clear to students that the level of civic participation they choose is up to them and is not mandated by government.

▶ *What are some ways that you can participate in our government?*

How can you participate in your government?

Our government is a government of the people, by the people, and for the people. You are a part of the people. We, the people, run our government. We elect people to work for us in our government.

We need to be sure they do a good job. If they do, we will vote for them again. If they do not, we may want to vote for others to take their place. We participate in government to protect our rights and our welfare.

You cannot vote until you are eighteen. However, you can still participate in our government. One of the most important things you can do is something you have already started to do. You can learn something about our government. You can learn what it is supposed to do. You can learn how it works. You can learn what rights you have. Finally, you can think about what responsibilities you should carry out.

Thomas Jefferson and other important Founders thought that all people should have an opportunity to get an education. They thought the main purpose of education should be to prepare you to become a thoughtful and responsible citizen. They knew our government could only work well if the people are well educated. Jefferson said, "If a nation expects to be ignorant and free, it expects what never was and what never will be."

You can also participate by keeping informed about what your government is doing. You can keep informed by reading newspapers, magazines, and responsible sites on the internet. You can listen to the news on radio and television. You can discuss the actions of government with your parents and friends. You can protect your rights and the rights of others. If there is a law or problem you feel strongly about, you can express your opinion.

You can tell your friends, and you can write to members of your government.

You can participate by volunteering to help people in your community. You can participate by taking part in the government of your classroom and your school. You can start now to be an informed and effective citizen.

What responsibilities will you fulfill?

You have learned a great deal about our nation's government. You have learned about the government's responsibilities and your rights. You have also discussed some of the responsibilities of citizens.

You have inherited a free society. It is your society. You are free to make many choices. You are free to choose what kind of citizen you want to be. You can help keep your society free. You can help make sure all people's rights are protected. You can help promote our common good. We hope that this book helps you make wise decisions about what kind of citizen you want to be.

▶ *What are some rights and responsibilities of citizens in a free society?*

What responsibilities will you fulfill?

Have students read and discuss their responsibilities as citizens of their communities and country. Distribute Handout D 3, "Reflecting on your Experience." Ask students to complete the form and consider the level of participation the program required.

Prepare the class for the culminating simulated congressional hearing activity.

LESSON 24

LESSON REVIEW

The questions in the student book are intended to assess learning and to reinforce knowledge through discussion. The questions are directly related to the lesson objectives. You may wish to include additional questions developed by yourself or by students.

1. How can schools help students become good citizens?
   They can educate them in the principles of democracy, give them the opportunity to participate in student government, and inform them about current events in their community, state, country, and the world.

2. What are some ways you can participate in government now?
   Accept any reasonable responses.

3. Does a good citizen have a responsibility to try to improve the lives of people who need help? Why or why not?
   Accept any reasonable responses.

4. What responsibilities should a citizen take to protect or promote the welfare of people in other countries? Explain your position.
   Students should incorporate the ideas that our country and other countries of the world have relationships that affect the quality of life for citizens of all countries.

5. Why is it necessary that a citizen balance his or her self-interest with the common good?
   It is necessary because our form of government is based on the balance of these ideas. You cannot have the common good infringe on individual freedoms and you cannot have self-interest overwhelm the needs of the whole and still maintain a stable democratic government.

Review the lesson

1. How can schools help students become good citizens?

2. What are some ways you can participate in your government now?

3. Does a good citizen have a responsibility to try to improve the lives of people who need help? Why or why not?

4. What responsibilities should a citizen take to protect or promote the welfare of people in other countries? Explain your position.

5. Why is it necessary that a citizen balance his or her self-interest with the common good?

Activities to do

1. Make a list of things that you can do for your community. Put these things in two columns. At the top of one column write Political Actions, and at the top of the other write Social Actions. Explain to your class the difference between these two kinds of community responsibilities.

2. Go to your library or use the internet to research the life of someone from your city, state, or tribal reservation who put the common good before his or her own self-interest. Write a short report to present to your class.

3. Make a poster that shows how students in your grade, but in another state or country, are engaged in good citizenship.

REFERENCE

R

Declaration of Independence

In Congress, July 4, 1776.
A Declaration by the
Representatives of the
United States of America, in
General Congress Assembled

WHEN in the Course of human Events, it becomes necessary for one People to dissolve the Political Bands which have connected them with another, and to assume among the Powers of the Earth, the separate and equal Station to which the Laws of Nature and of Nature's God entitle them, a decent Respect to the Opinions of Mankind requires that they should declare the causes which impel them to the Separation.

We hold these Truths to be self-evident, that all Men are created equal, that they are endowed by their Creator with certain unalienable Rights, that among these are Life, Liberty, and the Pursuit of Happiness—That to secure these Rights, Governments are instituted among Men, deriving their just Powers from the Consent of the Governed, that whenever any Form of Government becomes destructive of these Ends it is the Right of the People to alter or to abolish it, and to institute new Government, laying its Foundation on such Principles, and

organizing its Powers in such Form, as to them shall seem most likely to effect their Safety and Happiness. Prudence, indeed, will dictate that Governments long established should not be changed for light and transient Causes; and accordingly all Experience hath shewn, that Mankind are more disposed to suffer, while Evils are sufferable, than to right themselves by abolishing the Forms to which they are accustomed. But when a long Train of Abuses and Usurpations, pursuing invariably the same Object, evinces a Design to reduce them under absolute Despotism, it is their Right, it is their Duty, to throw off such Government, and to provide new Guards for their future Security. Such has been the patient Sufferance of these Colonies; and such is now the Necessity which constrains them to alter their former Systems of Government. The History of the present King of Great-Britain is a History of repeated Injuries and Usurpations, all having in direct Object the Establishment of an absolute Tyranny over these States. To prove this, let Facts be submitted to a candid World.

He has refused his Assent to Laws, the most wholesome and necessary for the public Good.

He has forbidden his Governors to pass Laws of immediate and pressing

Importance, unless suspended in their Operation till his Assent should be obtained; and when so suspended, he has utterly neglected to attend to them.

He has refused to pass other Laws for the Accommodation of large Districts of People, unless those People would relinquish the Right of Representation in the Legislature, a Right inestimable to them, and formidable to Tyrants only.

He has called together Legislative Bodies at Places unusual, uncomfortable, and distant from the Depository of their public Records, for the sole Purpose of fatiguing them into Compliance with his Measures.

He has dissolved Representative Houses repeatedly, for opposing with manly Firmness his Invasions on the Rights of the People.

He has refused for a long Time, after such Dissolutions, to cause others to be elected; whereby the Legislative Powers, incapable of Annihilation, have returned to the People at large for their exercise; the State remaining in the mean time exposed to all the Dangers of Invasions from without, and Convulsions within.

He has endeavored to prevent the Population of these States; for that Purpose obstructing the Laws for Naturalization of Foreigners; refusing to pass others to encourage their Migrations hither, and raising the Conditions of new Appropriations of Lands.

He has obstructed the Administration of Justice, by refusing his Assent to Laws for establishing Judiciary Powers.

He has made Judges dependent on his Will alone, for the Tenure of their Offices, and the Amount and Payment of their Salaries.

He has erected a Multitude of new Offices, and sent hither Swarms of Officers to harass our People and eat out their Substance.

He has kept among us, in Times of Peace, Standing Armies, without the consent of our Legislatures.

He has affected to render the Military independent of and superior to the Civil Power.

He has combined with others to subject us to a Jurisdiction foreign to our Constitution, and unacknowledged by our Laws; giving his Assent to their Acts of pretended Legislation:

For quartering large Bodies of Armed Troops among us:

For protecting them, by a mock Trial, from Punishment for any Murders which they should commit on the Inhabitants of these States:

For cutting off our Trade with all Parts of the World:

For imposing Taxes on us without our Consent:

For depriving us, in many Cases, of the Benefits of Trial by Jury:

For transporting us beyond Seas to be tried for pretended Offenses:

For abolishing the free System of English Laws in a neighbouring Province, establishing therein an Arbitrary Government, and enlarging its Boundaries, so as to render it at once an Example and fit Instrument for introducing the same absolute Rule into these Colonies:

For taking away our Charters, abolishing our most valuable Laws, and altering fundamentally the Forms of our Governments:

For suspending our own Legislatures, and declaring themselves invested with Power to legislate for us in all Cases whatsoever.

He has abdicated Government here, by declaring us out of his Protection and waging War against us.

He has plundered our Seas, ravaged our Coasts, burnt our Towns, and destroyed the Lives of our People.

He is, at this Time, transporting large Armies of foreign Mercenaries to compleat the Works of Death, Desolation, and Tyranny, already begun with circumstances of Cruelty and Perfidy, scarcely paralleled in the most barbarous Ages, and totally unworthy the Head of a civilized Nation.

He has constrained our fellow Citizens taken Captive on the high Seas to bear Arms against their Country, to become the Executioners of their Friends and Brethren, or to fall themselves by their Hands.

He has excited domestic Insurrections amongst us, and has endeavoured to bring on the Inhabitants of our Frontiers, the merciless Indian Savages, whose known Rule of Warfare, is an undistinguished Destruction, of all Ages, Sexes and Conditions.

In every stage of these Oppressions we have Petitioned for Redress in the most humble Terms: Our repeated Petitions have been answered only by repeated Injury. A Prince, whose Character is thus marked by every act which may define a Tyrant, is unfit to be the Ruler of a free People.

Nor have we been wanting in Attentions to our British Brethren. We have warned them from Time to Time of Attempts by their Legislature to extend an unwarrantable Jurisdiction over us. We have reminded them of the Circumstances of our Emigration and Settlement here. We have appealed to their native Justice and Magnanimity, and we have conjured them by the Ties of our common Kindred to disavow these Usurpations, which, would inevitably interrupt our Connections and Correspondence. They too have been deaf to the

Voice of Justice and of Consanguinity. We must, therefore, acquiesce in the Necessity, which denounces our Separation, and hold them, as we hold the rest of Mankind, Enemies in War, in Peace, Friends.

We, therefore, the Representatives of the UNITED STATES OF AMERICA, in GENERAL CONGRESS, Assembled, appealing to the Supreme Judge of the World for the Rectitude of our Intentions, do, in the Name, and by Authority of the good People of these Colonies, solemnly Publish and Declare, That these United Colonies are, and of Right ought to be, FREE AND INDEPENDENT STATES; that they are absolved from all Allegiance to the British Crown, and that all political Connection between them and the State of Great Britain, is and ought to be totally dissolved; and that as FREE AND INDEPENDENT STATES, they have full Power to levy War, conclude Peace, contract Alliances, establish Commerce, and to do all other Acts and Things which INDEPENDENT STATES may of right do. And for the support of this Declaration, with a firm Reliance on the Protection of divine Providence, we mutually pledge to each other our Lives, our Fortunes, and our sacred Honor.

Signed by ORDER and in BEHALF of the CONGRESS,

JOHN HANCOCK, PRESIDENT.

Signers of the Declaration of Independence

New-Hampshire

Josiah Bartlett,
Wm. Whipple,
Matthew Thornton.

Massachusetts-Bay

Saml. Adams,
John Adams,
Robt. Treat Paine,
Elbridge Gerry.

Rhode-Island and
Providence, &c.

Step. Hopkins,
William Ellery.

Connecticut

Roger Sherman,
Saml. Huntington,
Wm. Williams,
Oliver Wolcott.

New-York

Wm. Floyd,
Phil. Livingston,
Frans. Lewis,
Lewis Morris.

New-Jersey

Richd. Stockton,
Jno. Witherspoon,
Fras. Hopkinson,
John Hart,
Abra. Clark.

Pennsylvania

Robt. Morris,
Benjamin Rush,
Benja. Franklin,
John Morton,
Geo. Clymer,
Jas. Smith,
Geo. Taylor,
James Wilson,
Geo. Ross.

Delaware

Casar Rodney,
Geo. Read,
(Tho M:Kean.)

Maryland

Samuel Chase,
Wm. Paca,
Thos. Stone,
Charles Carroll, of
Carrollton.

Virginia

George Wythe,
Richard Henry Lee,
Ths. Jefferson,
Benja. Harrison,
Thos. Nelson, jr.,
Francis Lightfoot Lee,
Carter Braxton.

North-Carolina

Wm. Hooper,
Joseph Hewes,
John Penn.

South-Carolina

Edward Rutledge,
Thos. Heyward, junr.,
Thomas Lynch, junr.,
Arthur Middleton.

Georgia

Button Gwinnett,
Lyman Hall,
Geo. Walton.

The Constitution of the United States

Preamble

We the People of the United States, in Order to form a more perfect Union, establish Justice, insure domestic tranquility, provide for the common defence, promote the general Welfare, and secure the Blessings of Liberty to ourselves and our Posterity, do ordain and establish this Constitution for the United States of America.

Article I
The Legislative Branch

Section 1

All legislative Powers herein granted shall be vested in a Congress of the United States, which shall consist of a Senate and House of Representatives.

Section 2
House of Representatives: Organization and Power of Impeachment

1. The House of Representatives shall be composed of Members chosen every second Year by the People of the several States, and the Electors in each State shall have the Qualifications requisite for Electors of the most numerous Branch of the State Legislature.

2. No Person shall be a Representative who shall not have attained to the Age of twenty five Years, and been seven Years a Citizen of the United States, and who shall not, when elected, be an Inhabitant of that State in which he shall be chosen.

3. [Representatives and direct Taxes shall be apportioned among the several States which may be included within this Union, according to their respective Numbers, which shall be determined by adding to the whole Number of free Persons, including those bound to Service for a Term of Years, and excluding Indians not taxed, three fifths of all other Persons.]* The actual Enumeration shall be made within three Years after the first Meeting of the Congress of the United States, and within every subsequent Term of ten Years, in such Manner as they shall by Law direct. The number of Representatives shall not exceed one for every thirty Thousand, but each State shall have at Least one Representative; and until such enumeration shall be made, the State of New Hampshire shall be entitled to choose three, Massachusetts eight, Rhode Island and Providence Plantations one, Connecticut five, New York six, New Jersey four, Pennsylvania eight, Delaware one, Maryland six, Virginia ten, North Carolina five, South Carolina five, and Georgia three.

*Changed by Section 2 of the Fourteenth Amendment

4. When vacancies happen in the Representation from any State, the Executive Authority thereof shall issue Writs of Election to fill such Vacancies.

5. The House of Representatives shall choose their Speaker and other Officers; and shall have the sole Power of Impeachment.

Section 3
The Senate, Organization and Powers to Try Cases of Impeachment

1. The Senate of the United States shall be composed of two Senators from each State, [chosen by the Legislature thereof,]* for six Years; and each Senator shall have one Vote.

2. Immediately after they shall be assembled in Consequence of the first Election, they shall be divided as equally as may be into three Classes. The seats of the Senators of the first Class shall be vacated at the Expiration of the second Year, of the second Class at the Expiration of the fourth Year, and of the third Class at the Expiration of the sixth Year, so that one third may be chosen every second Year; [and if Vacancies happen by Resignation, or otherwise, during the Recess of the Legislature of any State, the Executive thereof may make temporary Appointments until the next Meeting of the Legislature, which shall then fill such Vacancies.]†

3. No Person shall be a Senator who shall not have attained to the Age of thirty Years, and been nine Years a Citizen of the United States, and who shall not, when elected, be an Inhabitant of that State for which he shall be chosen.

4. The Vice President of the United States shall be President of the Senate, but shall have no Vote, unless they be equally divided.

5. The Senate shall choose their other officers, and also a President pro tempore, in the Absence of the Vice President, or when he shall exercise the Office of President of the United States.

6. The Senate shall have the sole Power to try all Impeachments. When sitting for that Purpose, they shall be on Oath or Affirmation. When the President of the United States is tried, the Chief Justice shall preside; And no person shall be convicted without the Concurrence of two thirds of the Members present.

7. Judgment in Cases of Impeachment shall not extend further than to removal from Office, and disqualification to hold and enjoy any Office of honor, Trust or Profit under the United States; but the Party convicted shall nevertheless be liable and subject to Indictment, Trial, Judgment and Punishment, according to Law.

Section 4
Elections and Meeting of Congress

1. The Times, Places and Manner of holding Elections for Senators and Representatives shall be prescribed in each State by the Legislature thereof;

*Changed by the Seventeenth Amendment
†Changed by the Seventeenth Amendment

but the Congress may at any time by Law make or alter such Regulations, except as to the Places of choosing Senators.

2. The Congress shall assemble at least once in every Year, and such Meeting shall be [on the first Monday in December,]* unless they shall by Law appoint a different Day.

Section 5
Congress's Rules of Procedure, Powers, Quorum, Journals, Meetings, Adjournments

1. Each House shall be the Judge of the Elections, Returns and Qualifications of its own Members, and a Majority of each shall constitute a Quorum to do Business; but a smaller Number may adjourn from day to day, and may be authorized to compel the Attendance of absent Members, in such Manner, and under such Penalties as each House may provide.

2. Each House may determine the Rules of its Proceedings, punish its members for disorderly Behavior, and, with the Concurrence of two thirds, expel a Member.

3. Each House shall keep a Journal of its Proceedings, and from time to time publish the same, excepting such Parts as may in their Judgment require Secrecy; and the Yeas and Nays of the Members of either House on any question shall, at the Desire of one fifth of those Present, be entered on the Journal.

*Changed by Section 2 of the Twentieth Amendment

4. Neither House, during the Session of Congress, shall, without the Consent of the other, adjourn for more than three days, nor to any other Place than that in which the two Houses shall be sitting.

Section 6
Pay, Privileges, Limitations

1. The Senators and Representatives shall receive a Compensation for their Services, to be ascertained by Law, and paid out of the Treasury of the United States. They shall in all cases, except Treason, Felony and Breach of the Peace, be privileged from Arrest during their Attendance at the Session of their respective Houses, and in going to and returning from the same; and for any Speech or Debate in either House, they shall not be questioned in any other Place.

2. No Senator or Representative shall, during the Time for which he was elected, be appointed to any civil Office under the Authority of the United States, which shall have been created, or the Emoluments whereof shall have been increased during such time; and no Person holding any Office under the United States, shall be a Member of either House during his Continuance in Office.

Section 7
Procedure in Passing Bills, President's Veto Power

1. All Bills for raising Revenue shall originate in the House of Representatives;

but the Senate may propose or concur with Amendments as on other Bills.

2. Every Bill which shall have passed the House of Representatives and the Senate, shall, before it becomes a Law, be presented to the President of the United States; if he approves he shall sign it, but if not he shall return it, with his Objections, to that House in which it shall have originated, who shall enter the Objections at large on their Journal, and proceed to reconsider it. If after such Reconsideration two thirds of that House shall agree to pass the Bill, it shall be sent, together with the Objections, to the other House, by which it shall likewise be reconsidered, and if approved by two thirds of that House, it shall become a Law. But in all such Cases the Votes of both Houses shall be determined by yeas and nays, and the Names of the Persons voting for and against the Bill shall be entered on the Journal of each House respectively. If any Bill shall not be returned by the President within ten Days (Sundays excepted) after it shall have been presented to him, the Same shall be a Law, in like Manner as if he had signed it, unless the Congress by their Adjournment prevent its Return, in which Case it shall not be a Law.

3. Every Order, Resolution, or Vote to which the Concurrence of the Senate and House of Representatives may be necessary (except on a question of Adjournment) shall be presented to the President of the United States; and

before the Same shall take Effect, shall be approved by him, or being disapproved by him, shall be repassed by two thirds of the Senate and House of Representatives, according to the Rules and Limitations prescribed in the Case of a Bill.

Section 8
Powers Delegated to Congress

The Congress shall have Power

1. To lay and collect Taxes, Duties, Imposts and Excises, to pay the Debts and provide for the common Defence and general Welfare of the United States; but all Duties, Imposts and Excises shall be uniform throughout the United States;

2. To borrow Money on the credit of the United States;

3. To regulate Commerce with foreign Nations, and among the several States, and with the Indian Tribes;

4. To establish a uniform Rule of Naturalization, and uniform Laws on the subject of Bankruptcies throughout the United States;

5. To coin Money, regulate the Value thereof, and of foreign Coin, and fix the Standard of Weights and Measures;

6. To provide for the Punishment of counterfeiting the Securities and current Coin of the United States;

7. To establish Post Offices and post Roads;

8. To promote the Progress of Science and useful Arts, by securing for limited Times to Authors and Inventors the exclusive Right to their respective Writings and Discoveries;

9. To constitute Tribunals inferior to the Supreme Court;

10. To define and punish Piracies and Felonies committed on the high Seas, and Offenses against the Law of Nations;

11. To declare War, grant Letters of Marque and Reprisal, and make Rules concerning Captures on Land and Water;

12. To raise and support Armies, but no Appropriation of Money to that Use shall be for a longer Term than two Years;

13. To provide and maintain a Navy;

14. To make Rules for the Government and Regulation of the land and naval Forces;

15. To provide for calling forth the Militia to execute the Laws of the Union, suppress Insurrections and repel Invasions;

16. To provide for organizing, arming, and disciplining the Militia, and for governing such Part of them as may be employed in the Service of the United States, reserving to the States respectively, the Appointment of the Officers, and the Authority of training the Militia according to the discipline prescribed by Congress;

17. To exercise exclusive Legislation in all Cases whatsoever, over such District (not exceeding ten Miles square) as may,

by Session of particular States, and the Acceptance of Congress, become the Seat of the Government of the United States, and to exercise like Authority over all Places purchased by the Consent of the Legislature of the State in which the Same shall be, for the Erection of Forts, Magazines, Arsenals, dock-Yards and other needful Buildings;—and

18. To make all Laws which shall be necessary and proper for carrying into Execution the foregoing Powers, and all other Powers vested by this Constitution in the Government of the United States, or in any Department or Officer thereof.

Section 9
Powers Denied to Congress

1. The Migration or Importation of such Persons as any of the States now existing shall think proper to admit, shall not be prohibited by the Congress prior to the Year one thousand eight hundred and eight, but a Tax or duty may be imposed on such Importation, not exceeding ten dollars for each Person.

2. The Privilege of the Writ of Habeas Corpus shall not be suspended, unless when in Cases of Rebellion or Invasion the public Safety may require it.

3. No Bill of Attainder or ex post facto Law shall be passed.

4. [No Capitation, or other direct, Tax shall be laid, unless in Proportion to the Census or Enumeration herein before directed to be taken.]*

*Changed by the Sixteenth Amendment

207

5. No Tax or Duty shall be laid on Articles exported from any State.

6. No Preference shall be given by any Regulation of Commerce or Revenue to the Ports of one State over those of another; nor shall Vessels bound to, or from, one State, be obliged to enter, clear, or pay Duties in another.

7. No Money shall be drawn from the Treasury, but in Consequence of Appropriations made by Law; and a regular Statement and Account of the Receipts and Expenditures of all public Money shall be published from time to time.

8. No Title of Nobility shall be granted by the United States: And no Person holding any Office of Profit or Trust under them, shall, without the Consent of the Congress, accept of any present, Emolument, Office, or Title, of any kind whatever, from any King Prince, or foreign State.

Section 10
Restrictions on States' Powers

1. No State shall enter into any Treaty, Alliance, or Confederation; grant Letters of Marque and Reprisal; coin Money; emit Bills of Credit; make any Thing but gold and silver Coin a Tender in Payment of Debts; pass any Bill of Attainder, ex post facto Law, or Law impairing the Obligation of Contracts, or grant any Title of Nobility.

2. No State shall, without the Consent of the Congress, lay any Imposts or Duties on Imports or Exports, except what may be absolutely necessary for executing its inspection Laws: and the net Produce of all Duties and Imposts, laid by any State on Imports or Exports, shall be for the Use of the Treasury of the United States; and all such Laws shall be subject to the Revision and Control of the Congress.

3. No State shall, without the Consent of Congress, lay any Duty of Tonnage, keep Troops, or Ships of War in time of Peace, enter into any Agreement or Compact with another State, or with a foreign Power, or engage in War, unless actually invaded, or in such imminent Danger as will not admit of delay.

ARTICLE II
The Executive Branch
Section 1

President and Vice President: Election, Qualifications, and Oath

1. The executive Power shall be vested in a President of the United States of America. He shall hold his Office during the term of four Years, and, together with the Vice President, chosen for the same Term, be elected, as follows.

2. Each State shall appoint, in such Manner as the Legislature thereof may direct, a Number of Electors, equal to the whole Number of Senators and Representatives to which the State may be entitled in the Congress: but no Senator or Representative, or Person holding an Office of Trust or Profit under

the United States, shall be appointed an Elector.

3. [The Electors shall meet in their respective states, and vote by Ballot for two Persons, of whom one at least shall not be an Inhabitant of the same State with themselves. And they shall make a List of all the Persons voted for, and of the Number of Votes for each; which List they shall sign and certify, and transmit sealed to the Seat of the Government of the United States, directed to the President of the Senate. The President of the Senate shall, in the Presence of the Senate and House of Representatives, open all the Certificates, and the Votes shall then be counted. The Person having the greatest Number of Votes shall be the President, if such Number be a Majority of the whole Number of Electors appointed; and if there be more than one who have such Majority, and have an equal Number of Votes, then the House of Representatives shall immediately choose by Ballot one of them for President; and if no Person have a Majority, then from the five highest on the List the said House shall in like manner choose the President. But in choosing the President, the Votes shall be taken by States, the Representation from each State having one Vote; A quorum for this Purpose shall consist of a Member or Members from two thirds of the States, and a Majority of all the States shall be necessary to a Choice. In every Case, after the Choice of the President, the Person having the greatest Number of Votes of the Electors shall be the Vice

President. But if there should remain two or more who have equal Votes, the Senate shall choose from them by Ballot the Vice President.]*

4. The Congress may determine the Time of choosing the Electors, and the day on which they shall give their Votes; which Day shall be the same throughout the United States.

5. No Person except a natural born Citizen, or a Citizen of the United States at the time of the Adoption of this Constitution, shall be eligible to the Office of the President; neither shall any person be eligible to that Office who shall not have attained to the Age of thirty five Years, and been fourteen Years a Resident within the United States.

6. [In Case of the Removal of the President from Office, or of his Death, Resignation, or Inability to discharge the Powers and Duties of the said Office, the Same shall devolve on the Vice President, and the Congress may by Law provide for the Case of Removal Death, Resignation or Inability, both of the President and Vice President, declaring what Officer shall then act as President, and such Officer shall act accordingly, until the Disability be removed, or a President shall be elected.]†

7. The President shall, at stated Times, receive for his Services, a Compensation, which shall neither be increased nor diminished during the Period for which he shall have been elected, and he shall

*Changed by the Twelfth Amendment
†Changed by the Twenty-fifth Amendment

not receive within that Period any other Emolument from the United States, or any of them.

8. Before he enter the Execution of his Office, he shall take the following Oath or Affirmation:—"I do solemnly swear (or affirm) that I will faithfully execute the Office of President of the United States, and will to the best of my Ability, preserve, protect, and defend the Constitution of the United States."

Section 2
Powers of the President

1. The President shall be Commander in Chief of the Army and Navy of the United States, and of the Militia of the several States, when called into the actual Service of the United States; he may require the Opinion, in writing, of the principal Officer in each of the executive Departments, upon any Subject relating to the Duties of their respective Offices, and he shall have Power to grant Reprieves and Pardons for Offenses against the United States, except in Cases of Impeachment.

2. He shall have Power, by and with the Advice and Consent of the Senate, to make Treaties, provided two thirds of the Senators present concur; and he shall nominate, and by and with the Advice and Consent of the Senate, shall appoint Ambassadors, other public Ministers and Consuls, Judges of the supreme Court, and all other Officers of the United States, whose Appointments are not

herein otherwise provided for, and which shall be established by Law: but the Congress may by Law vest the Appointment of such inferior Officers, as they think proper, in the President alone, in the Courts of Law, or in the Heads of Departments.

3. The President shall have Power to fill up all Vacancies that may happen during the Recess of the Senate, by granting Commissions which shall expire at the End of their next Session.

Section 3
Duties of the President

He shall from time to time give to the Congress Information of the State of the Union, and recommend to their Consideration such Measures as he shall judge necessary and expedient; he may, on extraordinary Occasions, convene both Houses, or either of them, and in Case of Disagreement between them, with Respect to the Time of Adjournment, he may adjourn them to such Time as he shall think proper; he shall receive Ambassadors and other public Ministers; he shall take Care that the Laws be faithfully executed, and shall Commission all the Officers of the United States.

Section 4
Impeachment and Removal from Office for Crimes

The President, Vice President and all civil Officers of the United States, shall be removed from Office on Impeachment for, and Conviction of, Treason, Bribery, or other high Crimes and Misdemeanors.

ARTICLE III
The Judicial Branch
Section 1

Federal Courts, Tenure of Office

The judicial Power of the United States, shall be vested in one supreme Court, and in such inferior Courts as the Congress may from time to time ordain and establish. The Judges, both of the supreme and inferior Courts, shall hold their Offices during good Behavior, and shall, at stated Times, receive for their Services a Compensation, which shall not be diminished during their Continuance in Office.

Section 2
Jurisdiction of Federal Courts

1. The judicial Power shall extend to all Cases, in Law and Equity, arising under this Constitution, the Laws of the United States, and Treaties made, or which shall be made, under their Authority;—to all Cases affecting Ambassadors, other public Ministers and Consuls;—to all Cases of admiralty and maritime Jurisdiction;— to Controversies to which the United States shall be a Party;—to Controversies between two or more States; [between a State and Citizens of another State;]* between Citizens of different States;— between Citizens of the same State

claiming Lands under Grants of different States;—[and between a State, or the Citizens thereof, and foreign States, Citizens or Subjects.]*

2. In all Cases affecting Ambassadors, other public Ministers and Consuls, and those in which a State shall be Party, the supreme Court shall have original Jurisdiction. In all the other Cases before mentioned, the supreme Court shall have appellate Jurisdiction, both as to Law and Fact, with such Exceptions, and under such Regulations as the Congress shall make.

3. The Trial of all Crimes, except in Cases of Impeachment, shall be by Jury; and such Trial shall be held in the State where said Crimes shall have been committed; but when not committed within any State, the Trial shall be at such Place or Places as the Congress may by Law have directed.

Section 3
Treason: Conviction Of and Punishment For

1. Treason against the United States shall consist only in levying War against them, or in adhering to their Enemies, giving them Aid and Comfort. No Person shall be convicted of Treason unless on the Testimony of two Witnesses to the same overt Act, or on Confession in open Court.

2. The Congress shall have Power to declare the Punishment of Treason, but

*Changed by the Eleventh Amendment

*Changed by the Eleventh Amendment

no Attainder of Treason shall work Corruption of Blood, or Forfeiture except during the Life of the Person attainted.

ARTICLE IV
Relations Among the States
Section 1
Full Faith and Credit

Full Faith and Credit shall be given in each State to the public Acts, Records, and judicial Proceedings of every other State; And the Congress may by general Laws prescribe the manner in which such Acts, Records and Proceedings shall be proved, and the Effect thereof.

Section 2
Rights of State Citizens;
Right of Extradition

1. The Citizens of each State shall be entitled to all Privileges and Immunities of Citizens in the several States.

2. A Person charged in any State with Treason, Felony, or other Crime, who shall flee from Justice, and be found in another State, shall on Demand of the executive Authority of the State from which he fled, be delivered up, to be removed to the State having Jurisdiction of the Crime.

3. [No person held to Service or Labour in one State, under the Laws thereof, escaping into another, shall, in Consequence of any Law or Regulation therein, be discharged from such Service or Labour, but shall be delivered up on Claim of the Party to whom such Service or Labour may be due.]*

Section 3
Admission of New States

1. New States may be admitted by the Congress into this Union; but no new State shall be formed or erected within the Jurisdiction of any other State; nor any State be formed by the Junction of two or more States, or parts of States, without the Consent of the Legislatures of the States concerned as well as of the Congress.

2. The Congress shall have Power to dispose of and make all needful Rules and Regulations respecting the territory or other Property belonging to the United States; and nothing in this Constitution shall be so construed as to Prejudice any Claims of the United States, or of any particular State.

Section 4
Republican Government
Guaranteed

The United States shall guarantee to every State in this Union a Republican Form of Government, and shall protect each of them against Invasion; and on Application of the Legislature, or of the Executive (when the Legislature cannot be convened) against domestic Violence.

*Changed by the Thirteenth Amendment

ARTICLE V
Amendment Procedures

The Congress, whenever two thirds of both Houses shall deem it necessary, shall propose Amendments to this Constitution, or, on the Application of the Legislatures of two thirds of the several States, shall call a Convention for proposing Amendments, which, in either Case, shall be valid to all Intents and Purposes, as Part of this Constitution, when ratified by the Legislatures of three fourths of the several States, or by Conventions in three fourths thereof, as the one or the other Mode of Ratification may be proposed by the Congress; Provided that no Amendment which may be made prior to the Year One thousand eight hundred and eight shall in any Manner affect the first and fourth Clauses in the Ninth Section of the first Article; and that no State, without its Consent, shall be deprived of its equal Suffrage in the Senate.

ARTICLE VI
Supremacy of the Constitution and Federal Laws

1. All debts contracted and Engagements entered into, before the Adoption of this Constitution, shall be as valid against the United States under this Constitution, as under the Confederation.

2. This Constitution, and the Laws of the United States which shall be made in Pursuance thereof; and all Treaties made, or which shall be made, under the Authority of the United States, shall be the supreme Law of the Land; and the Judges in every State shall be bound thereby, any Thing in the Constitution or Laws of any State to the Contrary notwithstanding.

3. The Senators and Representatives before mentioned, and the Members of the several State Legislatures, and all executive and judicial Officers, both of the United States and of the several States, shall be bound by Oath or Affirmation, to support this Constitution; but no religious Test shall ever be required as a Qualification to any Office or public Trust under the United States.

ARTICLE VII
Ratification

The Ratification of the Conventions of nine States, shall be sufficient for the Establishment of this Constitution between the States so ratifying the Same.

Done in Convention by the unanimous consent of the States present the seventeenth day of September in the year of our Lord one thousand seven hundred and eighty seven and of the Independence of the United States of America the Twelfth. In witness whereof we have hereunto subscribed our Names,

213

George Washington –
President and deputy
from Virginia

This constitution was adopted on
September 17, 1787,
by the Constitutional Convention,
and was declared ratified
on July 2, 1788.

Signers of the Constitution

New-Hampshire

John Langdon
Nicholas Gilman

Massachusetts

Nathaniel Gorham
Rufus King

Connecticut

William Samuel Johnson
Roger Sherman

New York

Alexander Hamilton

New Jersey

William Livingston
David Brearley
William Paterson
Jonathan Dayton

Pennsylvania

Benjamin Franklin
Thomas Mifflin
Robert Morris
George Clymer
Thomas Fitzsimons
Jared Ingersoll
James Wilson
Gouverneur Morris

Delaware

George Read
Gunning Bedford, Jr.
John Dickinson
Richard Bassett
Jacob Broom

Maryland

James McHenry
Daniel of St. Tho. Jenifer
Daniel Carroll

Virginia

John Blair
James Madison, Jr.

North Carolina

William Blount
Richard Dobbs Spaight
Hugh Williamson

South Carolina

John Rutledge
Charles Cotesworth Pinckney
Charles Pinckney
Pierce Butler

Georgia

William Few
Abraham Baldwin

Attest:

William Jackson,
Secretary

Amendments to the Constitution

Articles in Addition to, and Amendment of, the Constitution of the United States of America, Proposed by Congress, and Ratified by the Several States, Pursuant to the Fifth Article of the Original Constitution.

Amendment I

Congress shall make no law respecting an establishment of religion, or prohibiting the free exercise thereof; or abridging the freedom of speech, or of the press; or the right of the people peaceably to assemble, and to petition the Government for a redress of grievances.

Amendment II

A well regulated Militia, being necessary to the security of a free State, the right of the people to keep and bear Arms, shall not be infringed.

Amendment III

No Soldier, in time of peace be quartered in any house, without the consent of the Owner, nor in time of war, but in a manner to be prescribed by law.

Amendment IV

The right of the people to be secure in their persons, houses, papers, and effects, against unreasonable searches and seizures, shall not be violated, and no Warrants shall issue, but upon probable cause, supported by oath or affirmation, and articularly describing the place to be searched, and the persons or things to be seized.

Amendment V

No Person shall be held to answer for a capital, or otherwise infamous crime, unless on a presentment or indictment of a Grand Jury, except in cases arising in the land or naval forces, or in the Militia, when in actual service in time of War or public danger; nor shall any person be subject for the same offence to be twice put in jeopardy of life or limb; nor shall be compelled in any criminal case to be a witness against himself, nor be deprived of life, liberty, or property, without due process of law; nor shall private property be taken for public use, without just compensation.

Amendment VI

In all criminal prosecutions, the accused shall enjoy the right to a speedy and public trial by an impartial jury of the State and district wherein the crime shall have been committed, which district shall have been previously ascertained by law, and to be informed of the nature and cause of the accusation; to be confronted with the witness against him; to have compulsory process for obtaining Witnesses in his favor, and to have the Assistance of Counsel for his defence.

Amendment VII

In Suits at common law, where the value in controversy shall exceed twenty dollars, the right of trial by jury shall be preserved, and no fact tried by a jury, shall be otherwise re-examined in any Court of the United States, than according to the rules of the common law.

Amendment VIII

Excessive bail shall not be required, nor excessive fines imposed, nor cruel and unusual punishments inflicted.

Amendment IX

The enumeration in the Constitution, of certain rights, shall not be construed to deny or disparage others retained by the people.

Amendment X

The powers not delegated to the United States by the Constitution, nor prohibited by it to the States, are reserved to the States respectively, or to the people. [The first ten amendments were ratified Dec. 15, 1791.]

Amendment XI

The Judicial power of the United States shall not be construed to extend to any suit in law or equity, commenced or prosecuted against one of the United States by Citizens of another State, or by Citizens or Subjects of any Foreign State. [Ratified February 1795]

Amendment XII

The Electors shall meet in their respective states and vote by ballot for President and Vice President, one of whom, at least, shall not be an inhabitant of the same state with themselves; they shall name in their ballots the person voted for as President, and in distinct ballots the person voted for as Vice President, and they shall make distinct lists of all persons voted for as President, and of all persons voted for as Vice President, and of the number of votes for each, which lists they shall sign and certify, and transmit sealed to the seat of the government of the United States, directed to the President of the Senate;—The President of the Senate shall, in the presence of the Senate and

House of Representatives, open all the certificates and the votes shall then be counted;— The person having the greatest number of votes for President, shall be the President, if such number be a majority of the whole number of Electors appointed; and if no person have such majority, then from the persons having the highest numbers not exceeding three on the list of those voted for as President, the House by ballot, the President. But in choosing the President, the votes shall be taken by states, the representation from each state having one vote; a quorum for this purpose shall consist of a member or members from two-thirds of the states, and a majority of all the states shall be necessary to a choice. And if the House of Representatives shall not choose a President whenever the right of choice shall devolve upon them, before the fourth day of March next following, then the Vice President shall act as President, as in the case of the death or other constitutional disability of the President—The person having the greatest number of votes as Vice President, shall be the Vice President, if such number be a majority of the whole number of Electors appointed, and if no person have a majority, then from the two highest numbers on the list, the Senate shall choose the Vice President; a quorum for the purpose shall consist of two-thirds of the whole number of Senators, and a majority of the whole number shall be necessary to a choice. But no person constitutionally ineligible to the office of President shall be eligible to that of Vice President of the United States. [Ratified June 1804]

Amendment XIII

Section 1 Neither slavery nor involuntary servitude, except as a punishment for crime whereof the party shall have been duly convicted, shall exist within the United States, or any place subject to their jurisdiction.

Section 2 Congress shall have power to enforce this article by appropriate legislation. [Ratified December 1865]

Amendment XIV

Section 1 All persons born or naturalized in the United States and subject to the jurisdiction thereof, are citizens of the United States and of the State wherein they reside. No State shall make or enforce any law which shall abridge the privileges or immunities of citizens of the United States; nor shall any State deprive any person of life, liberty, or property, without due process of law; nor deny any person within its jurisdiction the equal protection of the laws.

Section 2 Representatives shall be apportioned among the several States according to their respective numbers, counting the whole number of persons in each State, excluding Indians not taxed. But when the right to vote at any election for the choice of electors for President and Vice President of the United States, Representatives in Congress, the Executive and Judicial officers of a State, or the

217

members of the Legislature thereof, is denied to any of the male inhabitants of such State, being twenty-one years of age, and citizens of the United States, or in any way abridged, except for participation in rebellion, or other crime, the basis of representation therein shall be reduced in the proportion which the number of such male citizens shall bear to the whole number of male citizens twenty-one years of age in such State.

Section 3 No person shall be a Senator or Representative in Congress, or elector of President and Vice President, or hold any office, civil or military, under the United States, or under any State, who, having previously taken an oath, as a member of Congress, or as an officer of the United States, or as a member of any State legislature, or as an executive or judicial officer of any State, to support the Constitution of the United States, shall have engaged in insurrection or rebellion against the same, or given aid or comfort to the enemies thereof. But Congress may by a vote of two-thirds of each House, remove such disability.

Section 4 The validity of the public debt of the United States, authorized by law, including debts incurred for payment of pensions and bounties for services in suppressing insurrection or rebellion, shall not be questioned. But neither the United States nor any State shall assume or pay any debt or obligation incurred in aid of insurrection or rebellion against the United States, or any claim for the loss

or emancipation of any slave; but all such debts, obligations and claims shall be held illegal and void.

Section 5 The Congress shall have power to enforce by appropriate legislation, the provisions of this article. [Ratified July 1868]

Amendment XV

Section 1. The right of citizens of the United States to vote shall not be denied or abridged by the United States or by any State on account of race, color, or previous condition of servitude.

Section 2. The Congress shall have power to enforce this article by appropriate legislation. [Ratified February 1870]

Amendment XVI

The Congress shall have power to lay and collect taxes on incomes, from whatever source derived, without apportionment among the several States, and without regard to any census or enumeration. [Ratified February 1913]

Amendment XVII

The Senate of the United States shall be composed of two Senators from each State, elected by the people thereof, for six years; and each Senator shall have one vote. The electors in each State shall have the qualifications requisite for electors of the most numerous branch of the State legislatures. When vacancies happen in the representation of any State in the Senate, the executive authority of such State shall issue writs of election to fill such vacancies: Provided, That the legislature of any State may empower the executive thereof to make temporary appointments until the people fill the vacancies by election as the legislature may direct. This amendment shall not be so construed as to affect the election or term of any Senator chosen before it becomes valid as part of the Constitution. [Ratified April 1913]

Amendment XVIII

Section 1 After one year from the ratification of this article the manufacture, sale, or transportation of intoxicating liquors within, the importation thereof into, or the exportation thereof from the United States and all territory subject to the jurisdiction thereof for beverage purposes is hereby prohibited.

Section 2 The Congress and the several States shall have concurrent power to enforce this article by appropriate legislation.

Section 3 This article shall be inoperative unless it shall have been ratified as an amendment to the Constitution by the legislatures of the several States, as provided in the Constitution, within seven years from the date of the submission hereof to the States by the Congress. Ratified January 1919, Repealed by the Twenty-first Amendment 1933]

Amendment XIX

The right of citizens of the United States to vote shall not be denied or abridged by the United States or by any State on account of sex.Congress shall have power to enforce this article by appropriate legislation. [Ratified August 1920]

Amendment XX

Section 1 The terms of the President and Vice President shall end at noon on the 20th day of January, and the terms of Senators and Representatives at noon on the 3d day of January, of the years in which such terms would have ended if this article had not been ratified; and the terms of their successors shall then begin.

Section 2 The Congress shall assemble at least once in every year, and such meeting shall begin at noon on the 3d day of January, unless they shall by law appoint a different day.

Section 3 If, at the time fixed for the beginning of the term of the President, the President elect shall have died, the Vice President elect shall become President. If a President shall not have been chosen before the time fixed for the beginning of his term, or if the President elect shall have failed to qualify, then the Vice President elect shall act as President until a President shall have qualified; and the Congress may by law provide for the case wherein neither a President elect nor a Vice President elect shall have qualified, declaring who shall then act as President, or the manner in which one who is to act shall be selected, and such person shall act accordingly until a President or Vice President shall have qualified.

Section 4 The Congress may by law provide for the case of the death of any of the persons for whom the House of Representatives may choose a President whenever the right of choice shall have devolved upon them, and for the case of the death of any of the persons from whom the Senate may choose a Vice President whenever the right of choice shall have devolved upon them.

Section 5 Sections 1 and 2 shall take effect on the 15th day of October following the ratification of this article.

Section 6 This article shall be inoperative unless it shall have been ratified as an amendment to the Constitution by the legislatures of three-fourths of the several States within seven years from the date of its submission. [Ratified January 1933]

Amendment XXI

Section 1 The eighteenth article of amendment to the Constitution of the United States is hereby repealed.

Section 2 The transportation or importation into any State, Territory, or possession of the United States for delivery or use therein of intoxicating liquors, in violation of the laws thereof, is hereby prohibited.

Section 3 This article shall be inoperative unless it shall have been ratified as an amendment to the Constitution by conventions in the several States, as provided in the Constitution, within seven years from the date of the submission hereof to the States by the Congress. [Ratified December 1933]

Amendment XXII

Section 1 No person shall be elected to the office of the President more than twice, and no person who has held the office of President, or acted as President, for more than two years of a term to which some other person was elected President shall be elected to the office of the President more than once. But this Article shall not apply to any person holding the office of President when this Article was proposed by the Congress, and shall not prevent any person who may be holding the office of President, or acting as President, during the term within which this Article becomes operative from holding the office of President or acting as President during the remainder of such term.

Section 2 This article shall be inoperative unless it shall have been ratified as an amendment to the Constitution by the legislatures of three-fourths of the several States within seven years from the date of its submission to the States by the Congress. [Ratified February 1951]

Amendment XXIII

Section 1 The District constituting the seat of Government of the United States shall appoint in such manner as the Congress may direct: A number of electors of President and Vice President equal to the whole number of Senators and Representatives in Congress to which the District would be entitled if it were a State, but in no event more than the least populous State; they shall be in addition to those appointed by the States, but they shall be considered, for the purposes of the election of President and Vice President, to be electors appointed by a State; and they shall meet in the District and perform such duties as provided by the twelfth article of amendment.

Section 2 The Congress shall have power to enforce this article by appropriate legislation. [Ratified March 1961]

Amendment XXIV

Section 1 The right of citizens of the United States to vote in any primary or other election for President or Vice President, for electors for President or Vice President, or for Senator or Representative in Congress, shall not be denied or abridged by the United States or any State by reason of failure to pay any poll tax or other tax.

Section 2 The Congress shall have power to enforce this article by appropriate legislation. [Ratified January 1964]

Amendment XXV

Section 1 In case of the removal of the President from office or of his death or resignation, the Vice President shall become President.

Section 2 Whenever there is a vacancy in the office of the Vice President, the President shall nominate a Vice President who shall take office upon confirmation by a majority vote of both Houses of Congress.

Section 3 Whenever the President transmits to the President pro tempore of the Senate and the Speaker of the House of Representatives his written declaration that he is unable to discharge the powers and duties of his office, and until he transmits to them a written declaration to the contrary, such powers and duties shall be discharged by the Vice President as Acting President.

Section 4 Whenever the Vice President and a majority of either the principal officers of the executive departments or of such other body as Congress may by law provide, transmit to the President pro tempore of the Senate and the Speaker of the House of Representatives their written declaration that the President is unable to discharge the powers and duties of his office, the Vice President shall immediately assume the powers and duties of the office as Acting President.

Thereafter, when the President transmits to the President pro tempore of the Senate and the Speaker of the House of Representatives his written declaration that no inability exists, he shall resume the powers and duties of his office unless the Vice President and a majority of either the principal officers of the executive department or of such other body as Congress may by law provide, transmit within four days to the President pro tempore of the Senate and the Speaker of the House of Representatives their written declaration that the President is unable to discharge the powers and duties of his office. Thereupon Congress shall decide the issue, assembling within forty-eight hours for that purpose if not in session. If the Congress, within twenty-one days after receipt of the latter written declaration, or, if Congress is not in session, within twenty-one days after Congress is

required to assemble, determines by two-thirds vote of both Houses that the President is unable to discharge the powers and duties of his office, the Vice President shall continue to discharge the same as Acting President; otherwise, the President shall resume the powers and duties of his office. [Ratified February 1967]

Amendment XXVI

Section 1 The right of citizens of the United States, who are eighteen years of age or older, to vote shall not be denied or abridged by the United States or by any State on account of age.

Section 2 The Congress shall have power to enforce this article by appropriate legislation. [Ratified July 1971]

Amendment XXVII

No law varying the compensation for the services of the Senators or Representatives, shall take effect, until an election of Representatives shall have intervened. [Ratified May 1992]

Glossary

abolish To put an end to.

amendment A change in or addition to a document.

American Revolution The war fought by the American colonists to gain their independence from Great Britain. It took place from 1775 to 1781.

appeal The bringing of a court case from a lower court to a higher court to be heard again.

Article I The part of the Constitution that describes the legislative branch of the government.

Article II The part of the Constitution that describes the executive branch of the government.

Article III The part of the Constitution that describes the judicial branch of the government.

Articles of Confederation The first constitution of the United States. It was adopted in 1781 and replaced in 1788 by our present Constitution.

balancing powers Balancing the powers of government means that no one branch is given so much power that it can completely control the other branches.

basic rights Fundamental rights such as life, liberty, and property.

Bill of Rights The first ten amendments to the Constitution. It lists some basic rights of the people that the federal government may not interfere with and must protect.

bill A proposed law given to the legislature for approval.

boycott An act of protest such as when people get together as a group and refuse to buy from or deal with a store or company.

cabinet A group made up of the heads of the departments of the executive branch. They advise the president.

checking power Limiting power.

checks and balances The sharing and balancing of power among different branches of government so no one branch can completely control the others.

Chief Justice The head of a court. The Chief Justice of the United States is head of the Supreme Court of the United States.

citizen A person who is a member of a nation.

civic virtue Putting the common good above individual interests.

Civil Rights Act of 1964 This law ended segregation in public places including restaurants, movie theaters, and hotels. The law also said that employers could not unfairly discriminate against people because of their race, national origin, religion, or gender.

Civil Rights Movement In the U.S. during the 1950s and 1960s, people organized to demand that the federal government protect the rights of African Americans and other minorities. People worked together to change unfair laws. They gave speeches, marched in the streets, and participated in boycotts.

Civil War The war between the Northern and Southern states. It took place from 1861 to 1865 and ended slavery in the U.S.

Civil War Amendments The Thirteenth, Fourteenth, and Fifteenth Amendments to the Constitution passed after the Civil War. These amendments were intended to give former slaves the rights of citizens.

colony A settlement or territory ruled by another country.

commander in chief Highest leader of the military forces. In the U.S. it is the president.

common defense Protection of the people from enemies.

common good Good of the community as a whole.

compromise A way to settle differences by each side giving up some of its claims or demands.

confederation A form of political organization in which states combine for specified purposes, such as defense. The U.S. was a confederation from 1776 to 1788.

conflict A struggle among differing ideas.

Congress The national legislature of the U.S. Congress has two houses: the Senate and the House of Representatives.

consent of the governed The people agree to obey the laws and the government they create.

constitution A set of rules and laws that tells how a government is organized and run.

constitutional government A government in which the powers of the ruler or rulers are limited by a constitution. The rulers must obey the constitution.

Continental Congress The national legislature which governed the American colonies from 1774 until the adoption of the Articles of Confederation.

convention A formal assembly or meeting.

Declaration of Independence
Statement that listed the basic principles of democratic government and gave reasons why the colonists wanted to free themselves from British rule. It was signed by the members of Congress on July 4, 1776.

delegate Used as a verb, it means to entrust someone to represent your interests. As a noun, it means the person picked to act for you or represent you, usually at a convention or meeting.

democracy A form of government in which power is held by the people. The people exercise their power either directly or through elected representatives.

dictator A head of government who has unlimited power.

dictatorial government Government in which the rulers have unlimited power.

diplomacy The practice of managing relations between nations without use of warfare.

direct democracy This type of democracy means that the people themselves meet and make the laws that they decide are needed.

discrimination Unfair treatment of people because of such things as their race, religion, or gender.

diverse People of many different backgrounds.

domestic tranquility As used in the Preamble, this phrase means a peaceful situation within our country.

due process of law The requirement that procedures used by government in gathering information and making decisions be reasonable and fair.

enforce To make people obey the law.

equal protection clause The part of the Fourteenth Amendment that has been used to prevent states from being unfair to citizens because of their race or gender. It prohibits laws that unreasonably and unfairly favor some groups over others.

equal protection of the laws
Treating all individuals or groups of people equally under the law, unless there is a good and fair reason for not doing so.

establishment clause The part of the First Amendment that says the government cannot set up an official religion.

executive branch The branch of government that carries out the laws made by the legislative branch.

executive power The authority to carry out and enforce the law.

expression To make known your thoughts and feelings.

federal courts The courts of the national government. They deal with problems between states, with the Constitution, and with laws made by Congress.

federal government Another name for our national government.

federal system A form of government in which power is divided between a central government and state and local governments.

Fifth Amendment It states that no person shall have their life, liberty, or property taken away by the federal government without due process of law. This amendment protects your right to be treated fairly by the federal government.

Founders The people who were important in the establishment of the United States.

Fourteenth Amendment It states that no person shall have their life, liberty, or property taken away by state or local governments without due process of law. This amendment protects your right to be treated fairly by your state and local governments. It also defines a citizen as anyone born or naturalized in the United States. It was one of the Civil War amendments.

Framers The delegates to the Philadelphia Convention of 1787.

free exercise clause The part of the First Amendment that says the government shall not stop you from holding any religious beliefs you choose. The government may not unfairly or unreasonably limit your right to practice any religious beliefs you wish.

freedom of assembly The right to meet with others to discuss your beliefs, ideas, or feelings.

freedom of belief or conscience The government may not force you to believe in something if you do not wish to do so.

freedom of expression The right to make known such things as your beliefs and opinions by means that are protected by the First Amendment.

freedom to petition The right to ask your government to correct things that you think are wrong or to do things you believe are needed.

freedom of the press The right to read and write whatever you wish, as well as the right to publish your ideas without government interference.

freedom of religion The right to hold whatever religious beliefs you wish and the right to practice your beliefs without unfair or unreasonable interference from the government.

fugitive slave clause The part of the Constitution that stated that slaves who escaped must be returned to their owners.

general welfare The good of all the people.

government The organization through which political authority is exercised.

grandfather clause The law stated that a person could vote if his grandfather had been allowed to vote. It made it possible for white people who could not pass a literacy test to vote because their grandfathers had the right to vote. It also made it impossible for African Americans to vote because their grandfathers had not been allowed to vote.

Great Compromise The plan accepted at the Philadelphia Convention that called for Congress to have two houses. The Senate would have two senators from each state. The House of Representatives would have representatives from each state based on its population.

hearing A meeting in which citizens give their views to public officials.

higher law A set of laws that are superior to other laws. For example, the U.S. Constitution is a higher law than any federal or state law.

House of Representatives One house of Congress. The number of representatives from each state is based on its population.

humanitarian To have compassion and show concern for the pain and suffering of others.

immigrant A person who leaves his or her native land to settle in another country.

impeach To accuse a public official of committing a crime while he or she is in office.

indentured servant A person who agreed to work for someone for a set period of time in return for the cost of coming to America.

independence Self-rule; not ruled by another country.

interests Those things that are to your advantage or benefit.

interpret To explain the meaning of something.

judicial branch The branch of government that interprets and applies the laws and settles disputes.

judicial power The authority to settle disagreements about laws. This includes the power to say what the laws mean.

judicial review The power of the courts to say that the Constitution does not allow the government to do something.

Judiciary Act of 1789 The law that established the federal court system below the Supreme Court.

justices Members of the Supreme Court.

law A bill that has been passed by the legislature and signed by the executive or passed over an executive veto.

legislative branch The branch of government that makes the laws.

legislative power The authority to make laws and rules.

liberty, right to The right to be free. Some examples of liberties are the rights to believe what you wish, to read what you want, to speak freely, and to travel wherever you want to go.

life, right to The right to live without fear of being injured or killed by others.

limits Restrictions or boundaries.

literacy tests Tests given to people to prove they are able to read and write. These tests were used in the South to keep African Americans from voting.

Loyalists Americans who supported Great Britain during the Revolution.

majority More than half.

national government The organization having political authority in a nation.

natural rights Such basic rights as those to life, liberty, and property.

naturalized citizen Someone who is born elsewhere but who passes a citizenship test on the Constitution and the history of the United States.

Nineteenth Amendment Added to the Constitution in 1920, it gave women the right to vote.

Northwest Ordinance of 1787 An important law passed by Congress under the Articles of Confederation. The law provided for settling the western lands and organizing new states.

participation Taking part in or sharing in the activities of a group or organization.

Patriots Those Americans who supported the war for independence against Great Britain.

persecute To cause suffering to a person or group because of such things as their beliefs, gender, or race.

petition A formal, written request.

Philadelphia Convention The meeting held in Philadelphia in 1787 at which the U.S. Constitution was written.

plantation A large farm usually found in the Southern states.

politics A process by which people with different opinions and interests reach decisions without the use of violence.

poll tax A tax that voters in many states had to pay before they could vote.

population The number of people living in an area.

Preamble The introduction to the Constitution. It states that the people establish the government and lists the purposes of the government.

press Newspapers, magazines and other news media. Also, the reporters and people who produce them.

principle A rule or standard of behavior.

procedures The methods or steps taken to accomplish something.

property, right to The right to own things. Your labor or work is also your property.

ratification The formal approval of the Constitution by the states.

ratifying conventions Meetings held in the states to approve the Constitution.

represent To take the place of or to stand in for someone.

representatives People elected to act for others.

republic A country that has a government in which power is held by the people who elect representatives to manage the government for them.

republican government A government in which power is held by the people who elect representatives to run the government for the common good. The term does not refer to a political party.

resident alien A person who is not a citizen, but who lives legally in the United States. Resident aliens enjoy most of the rights of citizens. They have the same right to due process of law as citizens.

responsibility Duty or obligation.

secretaries The heads of the departments in the executive branch who act as advisers to the president.

segregate To separate people in schools and other public places according to things such as their race.

self-sufficient Able to provide most of one's own needs.

Senate One house of Congress. Each state has two members in the Senate.

separation of powers The division of powers among the different branches of government. In the United States, powers are divided among the legislative, executive, and judicial branches.

slave A person whose human rights are denied and who is forced to work for another person.

slave trade The business of taking people from their homes in Africa and selling them in the colonies.

social contract An agreement among the people to set up a government and obey its laws.

speech, freedom of The right to talk about your beliefs, ideas, or feelings

state of nature A situation in which there is no government, rules, or laws.

subject A person under the authority or rule of another.

supremacy clause The clause in the U.S. Constitution that explains that states cannot make laws that conflict with the U.S. Constitution or with the laws made by Congress.

Supreme Court The highest court in the United States.

testify Give information or evidence, as at a hearing or trial.

three-fifths clause
The Framers' compromise about slavery that became part of the Constitution. It counted each slave as three-fifths of a person to determine how many representatives a state would have in Congress.

tolerant To be willing to let other people be different from yourself in such areas as religion, lifestyle, and political opinion.

trade The buying and selling of goods.

treaty An official agreement between two or more governments or rulers.

Twenty-fourth Amendment It states that the right to vote in a national election shall not be denied because a person fails to pay a poll tax, or any other tax.

Twenty-sixth Amendment It gave citizens 18 years of age or older the right to vote in all elections.

unconstitutional Not allowed by the U.S. Constitution; illegal.

United Nations An international organization created in 1945 to maintain peace and security for its members.

veto The power of the president to refuse to approve a bill passed by Congress.

Voting Rights Act The Act passed in 1965 that further protected the right to vote for all U.S. citizens. It forced the states to obey the Constitution. It made it clear that the right to vote could not be denied because of a person's color or race.

witness A person who is called to give evidence before a court.

Index

Picture Credits

Courtesy Associated Press
15

Courtesy Corbis
56, 65, 89, 121, 128, 143, 171, 183, 185, 191

Courtesy Cleveland Museum of Art
18

Courtesy D.C. Public Library,
Washington Star Collection
Washington Post. Reprinted with permission.
155-1, 156

Courtesy Eyewire
85, 173

Courtesy Eric Futran /
Futran Photography
144

Courtesy Independence
National Historical Park
63

Courtesy Index Stock
1, 8, 9, 14, 19, 22, 24, 25, 30, 51, 64, 90,
91, 93, 94, 99, 102, 109, 111-2, 115, 117-1,
120, 126, 127-1, 127-2, 129, 131, 134, 136,
146, 147-1, 147-2, 152-1, 152-2, 157-2, 59,
161, 166, 175, 177-1, 177-2, 179, 180, 181,
184, 186, 187, 189, 192, 193, 194, 197.

Courtesy Library of Congress,
Prints and Photographs Division
vii, 3, 5, 6, 7, 11, 13, 16, 21, 32-1, 32-2, 39,
44, 53, 55, 58, 66-1, 66-2, 67, 68-1, 68-2,
68-3, 79, 81, 87, 133, 144, 148, 151, 154,
155-2, 157-1, 169, 170-1, 170-2

Courtesy Massachusetts
State Art Commission
29

Courtesy Michigan
Association of Broadcasters
135

Reuters News Service
Reuters News Picture Service
Photo by Mark Theiler 12/06/02
71
Photo by Hyungwon Kang 02/09/02
103
Photo by Kevin Lamarque 08/02/03
111
Photo by David Friedman of USA
North Miami 02/11/02
165

Courtesy NY Public Library,
Astor, Lennox and Tilden Foundation,
Phelps Stokes Collection, 1793
47

Courtesy Photodisc
88, 124

Collection, The Supreme Court
Historical Society
Photographed by Richard Strauss,
Smithsonian Institution
117-2

Note
Every effort has been made to accurately locate and credit copyright holders.
Please contact the Center for Civic Education if you are aware of any omissions or errors.

Adler, David A. *B. Franklin, Printer*. New York: Holiday House, 2001. 128pp. ISBN 0-8234-1675-5. Illustrated with prints and photographs. Chronologies of Franklin and the New World, Source Notes, Web Sites, Bibliography, Index.

Avi. *Night Journeys*. Avon Books: Reissue Edition, 2000. 160pp. ISBN 0-3807-3242-4.

Bober, Natalie S. *Countdown to Independence: A Revolution of Ideas in England and Her American Colonies: 1760-1776*. New York: Atheneum Books for Young Readers, 2001. 368pp. ISBN 0-6898-1329-5. Illustrated with prints and photographs. Author's Notes, Bibliography, Index, Reference Notes.

Baker, Garin. *Jump at the Sun: An African American Storybook Treasury*. Jump at the Sun, 2001. 205pp. ISBN 0-7868-0754-7. Dramatic illustrations by Bryan Collier. Author's Notes, Illustrator's Notes, Important Dates, Additional Books, Web Sites.

Burningham, John. *Mr. Gumpy's Outing*. New York: Henry Holt & Co., 2001. 14pp. ISBN 0-8050-6629-2. Board book edition.

Commager, Henry Steele. *The Great Constitution: A Book for Young Americans*. Indianapolis: Bobbs-Merrill, 1961. 128pp. ISBN 0-0272-4200-5.

Diouf, Sylviane A. *Growing Up in Slavery*. Illustrated with prints and photographs. Brookfield: Millbrook Press, 2001. 96pp. ISBN 0-7613-1763-5. Bibliography, Index.

Evans, Freddi Williams. *A Bus of Our Own*. Morton Grove: Albert Whitman & Company, 2001. 32pp. ISBN 0-8075-0970-1. Illustrated by Shawn Costello. Author's Notes.

Faber, Harold and Doris Faber. *We the People: The Story of the Constitution Since 1787*. New York: Scribner, 1987. 244 pp. ISBN 0-6841-8753-1. Bibliography, Index.

Freeman, Russell. *Give Me Liberty! The Story of the Declaration of Independence*. New York: Holiday House, 2002. 90pp. ISBN 0-8234-1753-0. Illustrated, Bibliographical References and Index.

Fritz, Jean. *Shh! We're Writing the Constitution*. New York: Putnam, 1987. 64 pp. ISBN 0-3992-1403-8. Illustrated by Tomi dePaola.

Fritz, Jean. *Why Don't You Get a Horse, Sam Adams?* Original Edition: New York: Putnam, 1974. 47pp. ISBN 0-3992-3401-2. Reissue: Scott Foresman (Pearson K-12), 1996. ISBN 0-6981-1416-7. Illustrated by Trina Schart Hyman.

Fritz, Jean. *Will You Sign Here, John Hancock?* Original Edition: New York: Coward McCann, 1976. 47pp. ISBN 0-3992-3306-7. Reprint Edition: Paper Star, 1997. 48pp. ISBN 0-6981-1144-0.

Gaustad, Edwin S. *Roger Williams: Prophet of Liberty*. Oxford University Press Childrens Books, 2001. 144pp. ISBN 0-1951-3000-6. Oxford Portraits. Illustrated with prints and photographs.

Greenfeld, Howard. *After the Holocaust*. New York: Greenwillow Books, 2001. 160pp. ISBN 0-6881-7752-2. Illustrated with photographs. Bibliography, Index.

Gündisch, Karin. *How I Became an American*. Cricket Books, 2001. 144pp. ISBN 0-8126-4875-7. Translated by James Skofield.

Haskins, James and Kathleen Benson. *Building a New Land: African Americans in Colonial America*. New York: HarperCollins Juvenile Books, 2001. 44pp. ISBN 0-6881-0266-2. Illustrated by James Ransome. Milestones of the Period, Bibliography, Index.

Hilton, Suzanne. *We the People: The Way We Were, 1783-1793*. Philadelphia: Westminster John Knox Press, 1981. ISBN 0-6643-2685-4.

Kendall, Martha E. *Failure Is Impossible: The History of American Women's Rights*. New York: Lerner Publications Company, 2003. 96pp. ISBN 0-8225-1744-2. Illustrated with prints and photographs. Author's Notes, Bibliography, Index, Timeline, Remarkable Women.

Levy, Elizabeth. *If You Were There When They Signed the Constitution*. Original Edition: New York: Scholastic Inc., 1987. Revised Edition: 1992. ISBN 0-5904-5159-6. Illustrated by Joan Holub and Richard Rosenblum.

Littlefield, Holly. *Children of the Indian Boarding Schools*. Minneapolis: Carolrhoda Books, Inc./Lerner, 2003. 48pp. ISBN 1-5750-5467-1. Illustrated with photographs. Index, Glossary.

Littlesugar, Amy. *Freedom School, Yes!* Philomel Books, 2001. 40pp. ISBN 0-3992-3006-8. Based on the 1964 Mississippi Freedom School Summer Project. Illustrated by Floyd Cooper. Author's Notes, Bibliography.

Maestro, Betsy. *A More Perfect Union: The Story of Our Constitution*. Boston: Lothrop, Lee & Shepard Books, 1987. Reprint Edition: Scott Foresman, 1990. 48 pp. ISBN 0-6881-0192-5. Illustrated by Guilio Maestro.

Masoff, Joy. *Colonial Times 1600-1700*. New York: Scholastic Reference, 2000. 48 pp. ISBN 043905107X. Illustrated, Includes Bibliography and Index.

McPhillipps, Martin. *The Constitutional Convention (Turning Points in American History)* Morristown: Silver Burdett Press, 1986. 64pp. ISBN 0-3820-6927-0.

Mead, Alice. *Girl of Kosovo*. Farrar, Straus and Giroux (Juv), 2001. 128pp. ISBN 0-3743-2620-7.

Meltzer, Milton. *There Comes a Time: The Struggle for Civil Rights*. Illustrated with photographs. New York: Landmark Books/Random House (Merchandising), 2001. 208pp. ISBN 0-3758-0407-2. Foreword, Chronology, Bibliography, Index.

Morris, Richard. *The Constitution*. Minneapolis: Lerner Publications Company, 1985. 69pp. ISBN 0-8225-1702-7. Revised Edition of: *The First Book of the Constitution*, 1958. Illustrated by Leonard Everett Fisher.

Naidoo, Beverley. *The Other Side of Truth*. New York: HarperCollins, 2000. 252 pp. ISBN 0-0602-9628-3. Reprint Edition: Harper Trophy, 2002. 272pp. ISBN 0-0644-1002-1. Winner of Britain's 2000 Carnegie Medal.

O'Dell, Scott. *Zia*. Boston: Houghton Mifflin & Co., 1976. Reissue Edition: Laureleaf, 1996. 192pp. ISBN 0-4402-1956-6.

Peterson, Helen Stone. *The Making of the United States Constitution*. Illinois: Garrard Publishing Company, 1974. (Out of print)

Prolman, Marilyn. *The Story of the Constitution*. Chicago: Children's Press, 1995. 36pp. ISBN 0-5160-6692-7.

Rappaport, Doreen. *Martin's Big Words: The Life of Dr. Martin Luther King, Jr.* New York: Jump at the Sun / Hyperion Books for Children, 2001. 40pp. ISBN 0-7868-0714-8, Dramatic illustrations by Bryan Collier. Author's Notes, Illustrator's Notes, Important Dates, Additional Books, Web Sites.

Robertson, Jr., James I. *Standing Like a Stone Wall: The Life of General Thomas J. Jackson*. New York: Simon & Schuster Children's, 2001. 192pp. ISBN 0-6898-2419-X. Illustrated with photographs and prints. Introduction, Epilogue, Notes, Sources, Index.

Seuss, Dr. *Yertle the Turtle*. New York: Random House. 74pp. ISBN 0-3948-0087-7, 1976. Dr. Seuss Classics Series.

Sigerman, Harriet. *Elizabeth Cady Stanton: The Right Is Ours*. Oxford University Press Childrens Books, 2001. 144pp. ISBN 0-1951-1969-X. Oxford Portraits Series. Illustrated with prints and photographs. Chronology, Further Reading, Museums and Historic Sites, Biographies of Other Women's Rights Leaders.

Spier, Peter. *We the People: The Story of the U.S. Constitution*. New York: Doubleday & Co, 1987. 48pp. ISBN 0-3852-3789-8,

St. George, Judith. *John And Abigail Adams: An American Love Story*. New Jersey: Holiday House, 2001. 192pp. ISBN 0-8234-1571-6. Illustrated with prints. Author's Notes, Bibliography, Index, Adams Family Chronology, Websites, Epilogue.

Taylor, Mildred D. *Song of the Trees*. Original Edition: New York: Bantam Books, 1984. Reissue Edition: Bantam Doubleday Dell Books for Young Readers, 1997. 52pp. ISBN 0-4404-1396-6. Illustrated by Jerry Pinkney. Yearling Book Series.

Turner, Ann Warren. *Nettie's Trip South*. Original Edition: New York: Simon & Schuster Children's, 1987. 32pp. Reprint Edition: Simon & Schuster Children's, 1995. 32pp. ISBN 0-6898-0117-3. Illustrated by Ronald Himler.

Uchida, Yoshiko. *Journey to Topaz*. Original Edition: New York: Charles Schribner's Sons. 1971. Reissue Edition: Creative Arts Book Company, 1986. 149pp. ISBN 0-9168-7085-5. Illustated by Donald Carrick.

Winn, Marie. *Shiver, Gobble and Snore: A Story About Why People Need Laws*. New York: Simon and Schuster, 1972. 44pp. ISBN 0-6716-5180-3. Illustrated by Whitney Darrow. Her Concept Storybooks.

Wooldridge, Connie Nordhielm. *When Esther Morris Headed West: Women, Wyoming and the Right to Vote*. New York: Holiday House, 2001. 32pp. ISBN 0-8234-1597-X. Illustrated by Jacqueline Rogers. Author's Notes, Bibliography.

SUGGESTED READING LIST FOR TEACHERS

Bahmueller, Charles. *Civitas: A Framework for Civic Education*. Calabasas: Center for Civic Education, 1991. 665pp. ISBN 0-8981-8124-0

Baker, Daniel B., ed. *Power Quotes: 4,000 Trenchant Soundbites on Leadership & Liberty, Treason & Triumph, Sacrifice & Scandal, Risk & Rebellion, Weakness & War, and Other Affaires Politiques*. Detroit: Visible Ink Press, 1991. 408pp. ISBN 0-8103-9416-2.

Bernstein, Richard B. *Are We To Be A Nation? The Making of the Constitution*. Cambridge: Harvard University Press, 1987. 342pp. ISBN 0-6740-4475-4.

Bowen, Catherine Drinker. *Miracle at Philadelphia*. Amereon Ltd., 2003. ISBN 0-8488-2565-9.

Center for Civic Education. *We the People: The Citizen and the Constitution*, Level II. Calabasas: Center for Civic Education, 1988. 168pp. ISBN 0-8981-8108-9.

Center for Civic Education. *We the People: The Citizen and the Constitution*, Level III. Calabasas: Center for Civic Education, 1995. 283pp. ISBN 0-8981-8177-1.

Collier, Christopher, and James Lincoln Collier. *Decision in Philadelphia: The Constitutional Convention of 1787*. Ballantine Books, 1987. 448pp. ISBN 0-3453-4652-1

Farrand, Max. *The Framing of the Constitution of the United States*. Beard Group, 2000. 296pp. ISBN 1-5879-8054-1.

Frantzich, Stephen E. *Citizen Democracy*. Totowa: Rowman & Littlefield, 1999. 248pp. ISBN 0-8476-9151-9.

Hall, Kermit L. *Major Problems in American Constitutional History, Volume I: The Colonial Era Through Reconstruction*. Lexington: D.C. Heath, 1991.

Hall, Kermit L. *Major Problems in American Constitutional History, Volume II: From 1870 to the Present*. Lexington: D.C. Heath, 1991.

Hand, Learned. *The Bill of Rights*. Cambridge: Harvard University Press, 1958. ISBN 0-6740-7300-2. Out of print.

Ketcham, Ralph, ed. *The Anti-Federalist Papers and the Constitutional Convention Debates*. Mentor Books: Reissue edition, 1996. 406pp. ISBN 0-4516-2525-0.

Johnson, Johanna. *They Led the Way: 14 American Women*. New York: Scholastic, Reissue edition, 1992. ISBN 0-5904-4431-X.

Kammen, Michael, ed. *The Origins of the American Constitution: A Documentary History*. New York: Penguin Books, 1986. 407pp. ISBN 0-1400-8744-3.

Kelly, Alfred Hinsey, Herman Belz, and Winifred A. Harbison. *The American Constitution: Its Origins and Development*. New York: W.W. Norton, 1997. 7th edition. Volume I: 922pp. ISBN 0-3939-6056-0. Volume II: 767pp. ISBN 0-3939-6119-2.

Kerber, Linda K. *Women of the Republic: Intellect and Ideology in Revolutionary America*. University of North Carolina: Reprint edition, 1997. 318pp. ISBN 0-8078-4632-5.

Ketcham, Ralph, ed. *The Anti-Federalist Papers and the Constitutional Convention Debates*. Mentor Books: Reissue edition, 1996. 406pp. ISBN 0-4516-2525-0.

Morris, Richard B. *Witnesses at the Creation: Hamilton, Madison, Jay, and the Constitution*. New American Library: Reprint edition, 1989. ISBN 0-4516-2686-9.

Murphy, Paul L. *The Constitution in the Twentieth Century*. Washington, D.C.: American Historical Association, 1986. 68pp. ISBN 0-8722-9036-0. Out of print.

Our Documents Teacher Sourcebook. National History Day, Inc., in cooperation with the National Archives. Free from info@nationalhistoryday.org

Patrick, John J. *The Bill of Rights: A History in Documents*. New York: Oxford University Press, 2003. 208pp. ISBN 0-1951-0354-8. Pages from History series.

Patrick, John J., ed. *The Supreme Court of the United States: A Student Companion*. New York: Oxford University Press, 2002. 400pp. ISBN 0-1951-5008-2. Oxford Student Companions to American Government Series.

Pious, Richard M. *The Presidency.* Pearson Education POD, 1995. 464pp. ISBN 0-0239-5792-1.

Ritchie, Donald. *The Congress of the United States Student Companion.* Oxford University Press, 2002. 248pp. ISBN 0-1951-5007-4. Oxford Student Companions to American Government series.

Rodell, Fred and Judith Schnell, ed. *55 Men, The Story of the Constitution: Based on the Day-By-Day Notes of James Madison.* Stackpole Books: Reprint edition, 1986. 281pp. ISBN 0-8117-2171-X. Out of Print.

Rossiter, Clinton, ed. *The Federalist Papers: Hamilton, Madison, Jay.* Mentor Books, 1999. 606pp. ISBN 0-4516-2881-0.

Schweizer, Steven L. *Wondering About Politics: Readings in Political Philosophy.* Greatunpublished, 2001. 478pp. ISBN 1-5889-8377-3.

Schultz, Charles. *This Is America, Charlie Brown: The Birth of the Constitution.* Los Angeles: Paramount Studios, 1995. ISBN 6-3034-5165-9. VHS videotape.

SUGGESTED BIBLIOGRAPHY ON AMERICAN INDIANS

Burt, Larry W. *Tribalism in Crisis, Federal Indian Policy 1953 -1961.* Albuquerque: University New Mexico Press, 1982. 180pp. ISBN 0-8263-0633-0.

Cook-Lynn, Elizabeth & Mario Gonzalez. *Politics of Hallowed Ground: Wounded Knee and the Struggle for Indian Sovereignty.* University of Illinois Press, 1998. 360pp. ISBN 0-2530-6669-3.

Deloria, Vine, Jr. *American Indian Policy in the Twentieth Century.* University of Oklahoma Press, Reprint: 1993. 272pp. ISBN 0-8061-2424-5.

Deloria, Vine, Jr. and Clifford M. Lytle. *The Nations Within. The Past and Future of American Indian Sovereignty.* University of Texas Press, Reprint: 1998. 296pp. ISBN 0-2927-1598-6.

Pommersheim, Frank and Anita Remerowski. *Reservation Street Law: A Handbook.* Sinte Gleska College Press, 1979. ISBN 9-9953-2920-X.

TEST MATERIALS ON THE CONSTITUTION AND THE BILL OF RIGHTS

CERTIFICATES

APPENDIX C

CONDUCTING A SIMULATED CONGRESSIONAL HEARING
GUIDELINES AND HANDOUTS

APPENDIX D

STUDENT HANDOUTS

MULTIPLE-CHOICE TEST – TEACHER'S INSTRUCTIONS FOR ADMINISTERING

1. This test is based on the *We the People: The Citizen and the Constitution* textbook and is designed as an integral part of the instructional program.

2. Teachers should instruct students to take the test without the aid of notes or their books and to select the best possible answer.

3. A reproducible answer sheet for students is included in the student handout section as Appendix D 4.

4. The teacher's answer guide for the test is in this section as Appendix A 3.

5. The total number of correct responses determines each student's test score. If students answer correctly at least 21 questions, their scores of 70 percent would be a favorable indication that they are prepared to participate in the authentic assessment activity at the end of the program. Information about the simulated congressional hearing culminating activity is available as Appendices C1-10.

6. Teachers who have not taught the entire curriculum should refer to the text-test correlation, Appendix A 4, to determine which questions pertain to lessons they have covered. They should instruct students to answer only the questions that were covered. In evaluating performance, a student's percentage should be calculated only on the questions used. Students may retake the test to achieve an acceptable score.

7. Certificates of Achievement may be awarded to students at the teacher's discretion. Certificates of Appreciation may be awarded to those individuals who contribute to the success of your program. Sample certificates are included as Appendix B. Additional free color certificates may be obtained from the Center toll-free at 800-350-4223; or email your request to wethepeople@civiced.org.

MULTIPLE-CHOICE TEST – TEACHER'S COPY

1. **How did living in the colonies influence the Americans' ideas about government?**
    a. The colonists took part in their own government
    b. In the colonies, the royalty made the laws
    c. The Founders believed that Great Britain would protect the rights of the colonists
    d. The colonists brought a single set of ideas about religion, government, and rights to the new land

2. **Which best describes what life might be like if there were no laws or government?**
    a. Nobody's rights would be protected
    b. Everyone's rights would be protected
    c. People would behave reasonably
    d. Strong people would have to help weak people

3. **A social contract is an agreement**
    a. Among people to get along with one another
    b. Among people that is not written
    c. Among the people to set up a government
    d. Between two governments

4. **The "common good" means that which is best for the**
    a. Government
    b. Largest number of people
    c. Rich
    d. Poor

5. **The term "civic virtue" means that the citizens**
    a. Put the common good ahead of their own interests
    b. Put their own interests ahead of the common good
    c. Rule themselves
    d. Limit the powers of government

6. **The best source of information about how a nation's government is organized is a**
    a. Dictionary
    b. Government report
    c. Constitution
    d. Speech by a government leader

7. **A government is a constitutional government when**
    a. It has a written constitution
    b. The people ratify the constitution
    c. Government protects the right to trial by jury
    d. There are limits on the power of government

8. **The Declaration of Independence expresses this idea**
    a. All people are created equal
    b. Government gets its power from the Supreme Court
    c. Government should protect the right to trial by jury
    d. The people never have the right to change their government

9. **In a republican government the**
    a. Leaders have all the power
    b. People elect members of government to represent them
    c. People make the laws
    d. Leaders are not responsible to anyone

10. **The Articles of Confederation had this serious problem**
    a. The state governments were too weak
    b. The national government was too weak
    c. There were no limits on the power of the national government
    d. No one had control over the army

11. **At the start of the Philadelphia Convention the delegates agreed to**
    a. Follow the instructions of Congress
    b. Improve the Articles of Confederation
    c. Give the state governments more power
    d. Write a new constitution

12. **The Great Compromise solved a conflict about**
    a. When slavery would be abolished
    b. How to collect taxes from the states
    c. How many representatives a state could send to Congress
    d. Which natural rights the government should protect

13. **One reason that the Framers were willing to compromise on the issues of slavery was because**
    a. Both the North and the South held large numbers of people as slaves
    b. Some Framers were from Southern states
    c. The Framers wanted the Southern states to join the new government
    d. The Framers agreed to pass a bill of rights

14. **The Preamble to Constitution begins with the words, "We the people... ." These words mean**
    a. Americans were one people
    b. The people approved of the new constitution
    c. The people wanted a better way of life
    d. It is the people who create government

15. **The Constitution separates the powers of government so that no branch can**
    a. Raise taxes
    b. Become too powerful
    c. Disagree with the other branches
    d. Protect the rights of the people

16. **The Constitution limits the power of the national government by**
    a. Denying the states certain powers
    b. A system of separation of powers and checks and balances
    c. Giving the president the power to veto bills
    d. Dividing Congress into two houses

17. **The legislative branch of government**
    a. Makes the laws
    b. Carries out and enforces the laws
    c. Settles disagreements about laws
    d. Declares laws unconstitutional

18. **The executive branch of government**
    a. Amends the Constitution
    b. Carries out and enforces the laws
    c. Settles disagreements about laws
    d. Makes the laws

19. **The judicial branch of government**
    a. Appoints the members of Congress
    b. Settles disagreements about laws
    c. Makes the laws
    d. Amends the Constitution

20. **The power of judicial review means that the Supreme Court can**
    a. Set up a system of lower courts
    b. Declare a law unconstitutional
    c. Approve treaties made by the president
    d. Decide when a justice may no longer serve on the Court

21. **The best description for a federal system of government is**
    a. One government has all the power
    b. The people do not have any power
    c. Power is divided between national and state governments
    d. Power is divided among the states

22. **The federal government is responsible for**
    a. Traffic laws and regulations
    b. Age requirements for school attendance
    c. Marriage and divorce laws
    d. A treaty in which nations agree to clean up the environment

23. **Freedom of expression gives people many benefits. One of the benefits is**
    a. It supports the need to make violent changes in government
    b. It allows the government to make strict requirements for voting
    c. It allows you to meet with others to discuss your beliefs, ideas, or feelings
    d. It makes sure that anything written for a newspaper praises the government

24. **The establishment and free exercise clauses are two parts of the First Amendment. They protect the right to**
    a. Due process
    b. Equal protection of the laws
    c. Freedom of religion
    d. Trial by jury

25. **The Fourteenth Amendment and the Civil Rights Act require state governments to treat people fairly without taking into account race, religion, national origin, or gender. This is called**
    a. Equal protection
    b. Disability protection
    c. A violation of the Constitution
    d. Discrimination

26. **The right to due process of law means that government cannot**
    a. Arrest you
    b. Make laws that you disagree with
    c. Send you to prison
    d. Treat you unfairly

27. **Women gained the right to vote**
    a. Because the Framers decided they deserved it
    b. After many decades of civil protest
    c. If their grandmothers had the right
    d. When they became landowners

28. **Some ways that countries of the world interact are**
    a. Restricting voting, travel, and the press
    b. Passing laws that prevent the sharing of culture and scientific discoveries
    c. Buying and selling goods only in their own national markets
    d. Giving humanitarian aid, making treaties, and engaging in trade

29. **Citizens of the United States are those who**
    a. Are born in countries that have treaties with the U.S.
    b. Work in the U.S. and pay taxes
    c. Have lived in the U.S. for at least twenty years
    d. Are born in the U.S. or are naturalized

30. **A good way for fifth- and sixth-graders to participate in our government is to**
    a. Vote in elections
    b. Write to a representative
    c. Run for public office
    d. Serve on a jury

1.	a	11.	d	21.	c
2.	a	12.	c	22.	d
3.	c	13.	c	23.	c
4.	b	14.	d	24.	c
5.	a	15.	b	25.	a
6.	c	16.	b	26.	d
7.	d	17.	a	27.	b
8.	a	18.	b	28.	d
9.	b	19.	b	29.	d
10.	b	20.	b	30.	b

Question 1.	**LESSON 1**	Question 11.	**LESSON 8**	Question 21.	**LESSON 16**
Question 2.	**LESSON 2**	Question 12.	**LESSON 9**	Question 22.	**LESSON 16**
Question 3.	**LESSON 2**	Question 13.	**LESSON 10**	Question 23.	**LESSON 17**
Question 4.	**LESSON 3**	Question 14.	**LESSON 11**	Question 24.	**LESSON 18**
Question 5.	**LESSON 3**	Question 15.	**LESSON 12**	Question 25.	**LESSON 19**
Question 6.	**LESSON 4**	Question 16.	**LESSON 12**	Question 26.	**LESSON 20**
Question 7.	**LESSON 4**	Question 17.	**LESSON 13**	Question 27.	**LESSON 21**
Question 8.	**LESSON 5**	Question 18.	**LESSON 14**	Question 28.	**LESSON 22**
Question 9.	**LESSON 6**	Question 19.	**LESSON 15**	Question 29.	**LESSON 23**
Question 10.	**LESSON 7**	Question 20.	**LESSON 15**	Question 30.	**LESSON 24**

CERTIFICATE OF ACHIEVEMENT

Certificates of Achievement may be awarded to students at the teacher's discretion. A sample certificate is provided.

Additional free color Certificates of Achievement and Certificates of Appreciation may be obtained from the Center by calling 800-350-4223; or email your request to wethepeople@civiced.org.

CERTIFICATE OF APPRECIATION

Certificates of Appreciation may be awarded those persons who contribute to the success of your program including the Simulated Congressional Hearing. A sample certificate is provided.

WE THE PEOPLE

THE CITIZEN & THE CONSTITUTION

For the study of the history and principles of the United States Constitution and Bill of Rights

PRESENTED TO

_____

PRESENTED BY

_____

Certificate of Achievement

A project of the Center for Civic Education funded by the U.S. Department of Education
under the Education for Democracy Act approved by the United States Congress

WE THE PEOPLE
THE CITIZEN & THE CONSTITUTION

Certificate
of
Appreciation

A project of the Center for Civic Education funded by the U.S. Department of Education under the Education for Democracy Act approved by the United States Congress

For outstanding contributions to civic education

PRESENTED TO

PRESENTED BY

SIMULATED CONGRESSIONAL HEARING – TEACHER INSTRUCTIONS

What is a simulated congressional hearing?

A simulated congressional hearing is the culminating activity for **We the People: The Citizen and the Constitution**. The simulated hearing is an authentic, performance-based assessment where students demonstrate their understanding of the United States Constitution and the Bill of Rights.

During the simulated hearing, students assume the role of constitutional experts. The students present prepared oral statements before a panel of judges, usually adults from the community. Following the formal presentations, students respond to follow–up questions from a panel of judges. The purpose of the follow-up questions is to give students the opportunity to demonstrate the depth of their understanding of the Constitution and Bill of Rights and to allow students time to clarify issues they may have raised in their formal statements.

This *Teacher's Edition* provides all the materials you need to prepare your class to participate in a simulated congressional hearing:

- A test on the Constitution and Bill of Rights

- Hearing questions for each of the five units in the student text

- Instructions for how to organize and prepare your students

- Instructions for the panel of judges

- Scoring sheets for the panel of judges

- Suggested follow-up questions for the panel of judges

- Certificates of achievement

- A list of suggestions from teachers who have participated in the program

What is a competitive hearing?

Each state has adopted a geographic organizational plan for the simulated congressional hearing. This is known as the Congressional District Level Hearing. Every congressional district has a district coordinator for the **We the People** program. The district coordinator is responsible for the organization of district hearings for elementary, middle, and high school students.

High school classes compete at the congressional district level. The winner of the district competition progresses to the state level, and the winner of the state competition progresses to the prestigious national competition in Washington, D.C. This is not the case at the elementary level. If an elementary class chooses to participate in their congressional district level hearings, they are measured against a standard of competence, and do not engage in competition. If all elementary teachers involved choose to participate in an actual competition, they may do so.

District level competitions are held under the supervision and authority of the district coordinators. They have the final word on all decisions regarding rules and logistics.

To inquire about participation in your congressional district hearing, contact your district coordinator. If you do not know who your coordinator is, contact your state coordinator from the list provided in the **We the People** brochure, or contact the Center for Civic Education at 800-350-4223.

Should a district coordinator be involved in my class's simulated hearing?

It is your decision whether to involve your district coordinator. You should notify the district coordinator about your hearing. You may want to ask your district coordinator for support, help in finding judges, or even to participate as a judge.

If your class participates in a hearing, please complete the form titled "Event Report Form," Appendix C 10. The form is also available on the Center's website at **www.civiced.org**, in the Teacher's Resource Section and the Program Coordinator's Resource Section.

How do students prepare for participating in a simulated congressional hearing?

Studying the *We the People* text is the best preparation for participating in the simulated congressional hearing. The instructional activities in each lesson require students to analyze, evaluate, take, and defend positions on a variety of constitutional issues. Each lesson is designed to help students acquire the knowledge, critical-thinking, and participation skills necessary to successfully take part in a hearing.

All students in the class must participate in the simulated congressional hearing. All students study the entire text. The teacher then divides the class into five equal groups (if possible) corresponding to the units of the text. Student preparation is based on topical questions. Each group assumes responsibility for preparing and presenting the question relating to their unit.

Students may use the text or any other reference materials to prepare a formal response to their question. Students are encouraged to investigate related topics in preparation for the follow-up questions that the panel of judges may ask during the actual hearing.

What criteria will the panel of judges use to evaluate student performance?

The panel of judges will score each group of students on six criteria:

- Understanding of constitutional principles
- Application of constitutional principles
- Reasoning
- Supporting evidence
- Responsiveness to questions from the panel of judges
- Cooperation and participation among the members of the group

At the conclusion of each presentation, the panel of judges provides feedback. Judges generally speak to the strengths of the presentation; they may offer suggestions for improvement. Judges give the teacher or scorekeeper the score sheets.

Who are the participants in a simulated congressional hearing and what should each do?

Students

The class is organized into groups, one group of students for each unit of the text. It is expected that every student in the class will participate in the activity. The number of students in each group should be as equal as possible, but each group should include at least three students.

Students should prepare a six-minute presentation responding to the question for their unit. Responses may be written on note cards and read aloud or memorized and recited. No other materials or references may be used.

Each group of students meets with the teacher to decide how responsibilities will be divided among the members of that group. Each group member should have a speaking role during the opening statement before the panel of judges. Each group member should also participate in the follow-up questioning period after the formal presentation. Evidence of cooperation and full participation by all members of the group is one criterion that will be evaluated.

After the six-minute opening statement, judges will ask suggested follow-up questions for four minutes (each hearing lasts a total of 10 minutes). Follow-up questions are provided for the panel of judges. Students should not be permitted to see the follow-up questions in advance of the hearing. The purpose of the follow-up questions is to probe the students' understanding of the material. It is also an opportunity for the judges to engage in discussion with the students. Follow-up questions should only encompass the material in the group's unit. Judges may decide to formulate their own questions; they are encouraged to do so.

Judges

Fifteen judges, three for each group of students, is ideal but not always practical. Minimally, three judges are needed to listen to and evaluate the presentations from all five groups.

People who serve as judges usually are recruited from the community. Suggestions for invitations include, but should not be limited to, the following:

- Your district social studies supervisor
- Professors from local colleges or universities
- Members of Congress or staffers from your congressional representative's local office
- Members of state legislatures or staffers
- Members of the city council or mayor's office
- Leaders of community groups or service organizations
- Lawyers
- Judges
- Social studies teachers
- **We the People** alumni

Once you have selected your panel of judges, provide each member of the panel with the following items:

- **We the People** text
- Hearing Questions for the Unit
- Suggested Follow-up Questions
- Judges Instructions
- Scoring Sheets
- Suggestions for Teacher

It is best to send the judges these materials a couple of weeks in advance of the event. You should also schedule a pre-event meeting with the judges. During the meeting review the procedures for the hearing and respond to questions that the judges may have. Remember that most of your judges have little or no classroom experience. You may want to share some of the characteristics of your class and tactfully remind the judges of your students' age and level of education. Also, emphasize the importance of comments to students at the end of each presentation. Judges should have a good experience interacting with your students.

Remind judges that at the conclusion of the hearing they have additional time to tabulate scores. Judges should consult with one another, but need not agree with one another, before completing their written comments and tabulating final scores. Judges must return their scoring sheets to the teacher before leaving the hearing site.

Timekeeper

Each hearing should have a timekeeper to officially keep and enforce time limits during each presentation. This person should be someone other than one of the judges.

The timekeeper should allot ten minutes for each group's presentation: six minutes for the formal statement and four minutes for follow-up questioning from the judges. Timing should start when students begin their opening statement. In the event that the full six minutes are not used for the opening statement, the remaining time should be allotted to the follow-up period. Judges may allow a student to speak beyond the time limit so that the student may finish a sentence or thought. Be mindful, however, that fairness is always an issue and exceptions to the rule should be applied judiciously.

The timekeeper should give notice when one minute remains for the opening statement. The timer may do this by holding up a card showing that one minute remains. At the end of the six minutes, the timekeeper calls "time." Repeat the process during the follow-up questioning period.

Audience

A simulated hearing is an excellent opportunity for your students to demonstrate to the community what they know and what they can do. Having an audience lends formality and excitement to the event. In addition, it helps to publicize the program both in your school and community.

Suggestions for those you might want to invite to the simulated congressional hearing:

- Parents
- Your **We the People** congressional district, regional, and state coordinators
- District superintendent
- Curriculum coordinators
- Building principal and staff
- Members of Congress or staffers from your congressional representative's local office
- State legislators
- City officials
- Journalists from both the print and electronic media
- Interested community organizations
- Other teachers in your school
- Other classes in your school

It is best to send invitations at least two weeks in advance of the event. The invitation should briefly describe the program and specify time and location. On the day of the hearing, someone should be available to greet guests and direct them to the site where the event will occur.

How can I recognize student achievement in the program?

You will likely want to hold an awards ceremony immediately after the simulated hearing. Certificates of Achievement may be given to the students and Certificates of Appreciation may be given to people who have supported the program in your school or district. You may want to invite a distinguished guest to present the awards, or to speak to the assembled group.

Often, a reception for students and guests follows the awards ceremony. The reception need not be elaborate. The important thing is to create an opportunity for your students and the adults to interact.

How can I organize a simulated congressional hearing?

To ensure a successful hearing and a good experience for your students, follow these steps (appropriate modifications should be made to suit individual situations):

Step 1. Prepare students

After students have studied the entire curriculum, administer and score the multiple-choice test.

Divide the class into five groups and assign each group to a unit. Explain to your students the purposes and procedures of a real congressional hearing. Explain the roles students will play and the procedures that will be followed.

Distribute the appropriate hearing question to each group. The students need to prepare a six-minute presentation addressing the issues raised in the question. Answers to the questions are in their *We the People* textbook. Encourage students to phrase answers in their own words and not to recite verbatim from the text. Questions may require students to gather additional information or form their own opinions.

Inform students about the following guidelines for the formal presentations:

- Students may use notes during their prepared presentations
- All students in each group should be prepared to speak during the formal presentation
- Students may not use visual aids such as posters, videos, computer presentations, pictures, or charts

Allow class time for groups to meet and prepare for the hearing. If desired, arrange for one or more outside experts to assist students in preparing their presentations. Subject matter experts, speech or debate specialists, attorneys, and other community representatives can be helpful and stimulating.

Students also should prepare for four minutes of spontaneous follow-up questioning from the judges. Inform students about the guidelines for responding to the follow-up questions:

- Students may not use notes during this period
- All students in the group should participate in responding to the judges' questions
- Students may assist each other during the response period
- Students may politely disagree with the responses of other members of the group

Note: These guidelines are intended to be flexible and may be modified to meet the needs of individual teachers and their classes.

Step 2. Determine the time and location for the hearing

Under the most favorable circumstances, the hearing would be conducted in an auditorium or other facility that can accommodate an audience. If it is not feasible to conduct the hearing in such a space, it may be conducted in a classroom with a smaller audience.

The simulated hearing may be held either during the school day or during evening hours when more parents are able to attend.

You may want to involve a cosponsoring organization to help in planning and running the hearing. Possible cosponsors might include local bar associations, judges' associations, historical societies, or community service groups. Cosponsors may help provide a site for the hearing, help students prepare for the hearing, donate refreshments, etc.

Each congressional district has a coordinator. You should attempt to involve your **We the People** congressional district coordinator in your program. This person is available to help you organize your simulated hearing. Please call your state coordinator or the Center for Civic Education at 800-350-4223, to identify your district coordinator.

Step 3. Select and invite judges

Step 4. Invite guests

Step 5: Invite a member of Congress to participate

The Center recommends that a member of Congress (or staff representative) in whose district the school is located be invited to participate by

- signing certificates
- visiting classes
- speaking to students and teachers
- observing or participating in simulated congressional hearings
- presenting certificates or speaking at awards ceremonies

Step 6. Prepare Certificates of Achievement and Certificates of Appreciation

Each student earns a Certificate of Achievement by passing the test on the principles and history of the Constitution and participating in the simulated congressional hearing. The Center for Civic Education will provide free Certificates of Achievement for each class set of materials used. The Center will provide Certificates of Appreciation for those who assist with the program.

You may order your certificates by calling the Center at 800-350-4223 or by sending an email request to wethepeople@civiced.org. You may also download certificates from the Center's website. Another choice may be to make photocopies of the sample certificate that is included with this set of materials.

Your member of the House of Representatives or someone on her or his staff should sign the certificates. An official of your school district also may sign the certificates.

Step 7. Organize your awards ceremony and reception

Step 8. Arrange the hearing room

If the hearing is held in a school auditorium or other large meeting room, arrange tables and chairs in a "V" shape at the front of the room. The open end of the "V" should face the audience. The panel of judges sits along one arm of the "V." Each group of students should be seated along the other arm when it is their turn to present their unit. If needed, provide microphones for both the panel of judges and the students.

Arrange an area of the room with seating for students waiting their turn to present.

If the hearing is to be held in a classroom, arrange the space so that a set of chairs faces the judges, in a "V" shape if possible. These chairs are for the students who will be presenting to the judges; other students will remain at their desks.

Arrange seating for the timekeeper in a location where he or she can be seen by both the students and the judges.

Step 9. Meet with the judges

Instruct the judges that student groups will have prepared statements to present. Each group of students will be prepared to respond to a hearing question for their assigned unit. During the follow-up question period, panel members may ask students to explain or expand upon their prepared statement. Follow-up questions should not raise topics with which students are not familiar. Rather, they should help the students demonstrate their knowledge and understanding of the basic constitutional principles they have studied.

Judges may ask follow-up questions that allow students to apply historical or contemporary events to their unit topic. Judges should address the entire group when asking a specific question.

Review the procedures for conducting the simulated hearing with the panels of judges. Be prepared to respond to the judges' questions and concerns.

Step 10. Conduct the hearing

What procedures should be followed during the simulated hearing?

1. Start the session by giving a brief overview of the **We the People** curriculum and a rationale for studying the Constitution and Bill of Rights. You may want to share some examples of student work and offer some anecdotes related to what students did during their study of the curriculum.

2. Introduce any dignitaries who are present in the audience. If you have cosponsoring organizations, people from those groups should also be introduced.

3. Introduce the judges. The initial introduction should identify the simulated congressional committee members by their actual professions. After the introductions, however, students may address the judges as "congressman" or "congresswoman." The moderator of the panel may be addressed as the chair of the committee.

4. You may call upon designated judges to make some brief opening remarks.

5. Call the first student group forward. The students sit in the chairs facing the judges.

6. The chairperson on the panel of judges should ask the students to introduce themselves. Name cards for the students and the judges are helpful.

7. The chairperson should read aloud the unit question in its entirety.

8. The students then present their prepared statement in response to the designated question for their unit. Timekeeping begins at this moment.

9. At the conclusion of the prepared statement, the judges begin their follow-up questions.

10. After each group's presentation and the follow-up period, each judge on the panel should offer brief feedback to the students on their performance. The judges may use their scoring sheet as a guide. This evaluation period is not timed.

11. At the conclusion of the evaluation feedback, the students return to the audience and you may call the next group forward.

SIMULATED CONGRESSIONAL HEARING – SUGGESTIONS FROM TEACHERS

Introducing the simulated congressional hearing

Talk to students about the simulated hearing at the beginning of their study. This will generate excitement for the project. This discussion will also allow students to focus on planning their presentations.

Show a video of a class participating in a simulated congressional hearing; videos are available from your district coordinator.

Involve parents in the process as early as possible

Send home a letter explaining the program; talk about the program at "Back to School Night"; have students write discussion reviews from their classes for the parent newsletter.

As homework, suggest that students discuss a related issue with their parents and older siblings. Require a signed note from parents saying the discussion took place. The more you stimulate discussion at home, the more your students will experience reinforcement of the concepts being studied.

Invite parents to come to the class and join in the discussions and activities.

Four to five weeks preceding the simulated congressional hearing

Divide the class into unit groups.

Present the simulated congressional hearing questions to each group. It is helpful to get an adult volunteer for each unit. Consider parents, community members, librarians, high school or college students, local attorneys, and alumni.

Gather reference materials for the classroom from the library or other sources. Make the materials available to all students.

After organized readings of related materials, help students begin a "web" or "concept map" of their responses to the questions. They can then easily see which concepts need more information. The webs may be used later for paragraph development.

Review and make suggestions to students about their presentations. Check accuracy of information and clarity of expression. Confer with the writers to discuss needed revision. Students should do all the writing themselves. You and other adults are free to give suggestions, but it is the students' choice whether to heed your advice. Please do not deny students the valuable experience of writing and revising thoughts by making changes for them. This could and should be a rather lengthy process, and it will force students to think through their responses again and again. This is where real learning occurs. Students must make the final decisions about their essays.

Listen to the students' ideas and testimony and do not be judgmental. Give positive suggestions.

Be sure that each presentation stays within the prearranged time limits: ten minutes for the presentation and follow-up questions. Division of the time between prepared and spontaneous questions has some flexibility for elementary students.

If you are holding a classroom hearing, you should determine date, time, and place for the event. Obtain a commitment from community resource people to judge the hearings. Consider asking attorneys, local judges, law enforcement personnel, university professors, ministers, administrators, city politicians, or similar resource people. Aim for high profile people to act as judges. Students will take themselves and the program more seriously if judges are widely respected in the community.

SIMULATED CONGRESSIONAL HEARING – SUGGESTIONS FROM TEACHERS

Two weeks preceding the simulated congressional hearing

If you can make arrangements for local attorneys or qualified community members to work directly with students, begin regular study sessions with them. A good arrangement is for each unit to have a community or attorney partner. Ask the partner to work with the oral delivery of the presentations, and to practice possible follow-up questions. If you cannot secure enough partners, you might use parents or other adults, or share partners among units. In addition to preparation, this is the time to invite parents, school officials, community members, and other interested parties to attend your classroom hearing.

The students will be more willing and attentive to detail if they feel that the guests and hearing judges for the evening are important people. Take risks with invitations. Many people in the community will be supportive of a program like this. Of course, include invitations to parents, grandparents, other classes, and school staff as well. Consider having students prepare the invitations.

Consider contacting local media or have a parent make the contact with information about the program and your hearing date and time.

Parents will be excited about the program and anxious to see the classroom hearing. You might ask some of them to provide refreshments for the event. Food creates a feeling of celebration, and the students will be ready to celebrate the enormous amount of work they put into their program! A classroom hearing with refreshments can be a great send off to classes that are preparing for district-sponsored hearings.

One week preceding the simulated hearing

Practice, practice, practice.

This is the time to polish public speaking skills. Urge students to speak audibly, slowly, and with an interesting expression. Work on eye contact, posture, and minimizing movement (e.g. swinging feet, happy fingers, etc.)

All prepared presentation material must be on note cards. Students may not use notes or prepared statements during the follow-up questioning.

Practice will make the students more comfortable with the material they have prepared and with the spontaneous thinking needed for follow-up questions. Classmates may ask follow-up questions to each unit. Often, this questioning is the more challenging part of the hearing.

Consider assigning the practice of presentations as homework, every evening this week. Have a parent sign the note cards verifying that the student practiced his or her speech.

Determine the appropriate attire for your students at the hearing. Most students will want to dress professionally. Discuss the dress standards as a class.

If you are using programs for the classroom hearing, they should be prepared during this time.

Consult your district coordinator for help throughout the **We the People** program and especially for your simulated congressional hearing.

UNIT 1

WHAT BASIC IDEAS ABOUT GOVERNMENT DID THE FOUNDERS HAVE?

Congress has formed a congressional committee. This committee will examine the United States Constitution and the purposes of government. The members of your group are expert witnesses who will appear before the committee. You will be asked to testify on the following questions.

- According to the Founders, what are the basic purposes of government?

- Why did the Framers think a constitution was necessary to achieve these purposes?

- Which did the Founders think was more important, the common good or individual rights?

- Does our government still serve the purposes that the Framers intended?

Suggested follow-up questions for judges

1. Have there been times when individual rights and the common good were in conflict? Can you give an example?

2. How did the way the people lived in the 1770s influence our government today?

3. How is government different today than it was in the 1770s?

4. Why did so many Europeans want to come to the colonies?

5. How can each one of us serve the common good?

6. In your opinion, what is more important, individual rights or the common good? Why?

7. Where did the Founders get their ideas about good government?

8. What is a constitution?

9. What is the difference between a constitution and a constitutional government?

10. What basic ideas were included in the Declaration of Independence? Why was this document written?

11. What is civic virtue? Give examples of people who practice civic virtue in your school and community

UNIT 2

HOW DID THE FRAMERS WRITE OUR CONSTITUTION?

Congress has formed a congressional committee to gather information on the United States Constitution and Bill of Rights. It is also looking at the compromises that were made at the Philadelphia Convention. As expert witnesses, you will be asked to testify on the following questions.

- What major conflicts required the Framers at the Philadelphia Convention to make compromises?

- Why was it so difficult for the Framers to reach agreement about how to resolve their conflicts?

- How did the compromise of later adding a Bill of Rights affect our Constitution?

- Do you agree with the Framers decision to keep the proceedings of the Philadelphia Convention secret? Why or why not?

- Was the group that assembled at the Philadelphia Convention a fair representation of the people? Why or why not?

Suggested follow-up questions for judges

1. Why did the Framers not abolish slavery at the time they wrote the Constitution?

2. Could the proceedings of a constitutional convention be kept secret today? Why or why not?

3. In your own words, what is the "common good?" Give some examples.

4. Do you believe that government should promote the common good? How?

5. People sometimes disagree about what is best for all in the community. Describe a situation where this might happen. How do you think such disagreements should be settled?

6. What can you learn about a country's government by studying its constitution?

7. How does our government ensure domestic tranquility? Do you think that the United States has domestic tranquility? Why or why not?

8. Fifty-five men attended the Philadelphia Convention. Do you think the Constitution would be different if the representatives had been women? How might it be different?

UNIT 3

HOW DOES THE CONSTITUTION ORGANIZE OUR GOVERNMENT?

Congress has formed a congressional committee to look at how power is divided among the three branches of our national government. As expert witnesses, you will be asked to testify on the following questions.

- How did the Framers use separation of powers and checks and balances to limit the powers of government?

- Give examples of checks and balances at work today.

- Give examples of the use of federalism to limit power.

- Do you think the Congress should have the power to pass a bill over the president's veto? Why or why not?

- Do you think the Supreme Court should have the power to declare a law passed by Congress unconstitutional? Why or why not?

Suggested follow-up questions for judges

1. Give an example of checks and balance and explain how the system works.

2. What are some powers of the president? Which power do you think is most important? Why?

3. What keeps the president from becoming too powerful?

4. What is judicial review? Is the power of judicial review given to the Supreme Court in the Constitution? Explain your answer.

5. How do cases get to the Supreme Court?

6. Should the Supreme Court be allowed to refuse to review a case?

7. Give an example of the Supreme Court exercising its power of judicial review. Explain how the decision made by the court affects your life.

8. Does judicial review give nine justices too much power? Why or why not?

9. Do you think Supreme Court justices should be appointed for life? Why or why not?

10. Should Supreme Court justices be elected instead of appointed? Why or why not?

11. Should the president be allowed to serve more than two terms? Why or why not?

12. Since the president can only serve two terms, should the same restriction be placed on Senators and Representatives?

UNIT 4

HOW DOES THE CONSTITUTION PROTECT OUR BASIC RIGHTS?

Congress has formed a congressional committee to examine the people's rights. They want to know how well they are being protected and what more might be done. As expert witnesses, you will be asked to testify on the following questions.

- What is freedom of expression, and why is it important to our democracy?

- How does the Constitution protect freedom of expression?

- Are there times when freedom of expression should be limited? Why or why not? Give examples.

- How is freedom of religion protected in the Constitution?

- When is it acceptable for government to limit the practice of people's religious beliefs?

- How has the idea of "equal protection of the laws" been used to protect people's rights? Give examples.

Suggested follow-up questions for judges

1. The Bill of Rights did not guarantee rights for all the people, for example women and African Americans. How was this corrected?

2. What are the benefits of freedom of expression?

3. Suppose a small group of people in an audience get angry with a speaker and try to stop the person from speaking. Whose rights should the police protect? Explain.

4. Do you think there should be prayer in the public schools? Why or why not?

5. Are there times when disabled people are discriminated against? Explain.

6. Is it constitutional for a group of people to stage a protest on the front lawn of your home without your permission? Why or why not?

7. Is it constitutional for someone to place a sign on their own property saying, "All politicians are crooks?" Why or why not?

8. Do you think there are times when your school principal can limit your freedom of expression? Explain.

9. Do you think schools should have the right to require that students wear uniforms to school? Is requiring students to wear uniforms a violation of their freedom of expression?

10. Do you think that government should regulate the internet? Why or why not?

UNIT 5

WHAT ARE THE RESPONSIBILITIES OF CITIZENS?

Congress has formed a congressional committee to examine the responsibilities of citizens in our constitutional democracy. As expert witnesses, you will be asked to testify on the following questions.

- What responsibilities go along with the rights of citizens?

- Do you think every citizen should be required to participate in his/her government? How?

- How does a responsible citizen promote the common good?

- Why do so many young people not fulfill their responsibility to vote?

- As citizens of a democracy, do we have responsibilities to other nations of the world?

Suggested follow-up questions for judges

1. What are the most important responsibilities of citizens in our democracy?

2. What can citizens do to change a law that they think is unfair?

3. Aside from the **We the People** program, are schools doing enough to educate voters? What more could be done?

4. If you had a brother or sister between the ages of 18 and 25, how would you convince them to become voters?

5. Some candidates choose to use negative campaigning. What are your feelings about negative campaigning? Explain.

6. Do political parties have responsibilities to the voters? What are those responsibilities?

7. What do you suggest that candidates do to encourage citizens to vote?

8. Some people have suggested that in the future citizens would be allowed to vote from their home computers. What are your opinions about this idea?

9. Do you think the current voting age is appropriate? Should the age be raised or lowered? Why?

10. Should citizens be allowed to vote if they have served time in prison for a serious crime? Explain.

11. What are some responsibilities of citizenship? What do you think is the most important responsibility? Why?

12. Some people have said that the electoral college is outdated. Do you believe that our constitution should be amended to allow our president to be elected by popular vote?

INSTRUCTIONS

As you know from studying your *We the People: The Citizen and the Constitution* textbook, members of Congress make laws. These laws should protect our rights and promote our welfare. To make good decisions about which laws they want to pass, members of Congress need to gather information. This information will help them understand how to address our nation's problems and pass good laws.

One way that members of Congress get the information they need is by holding congressional hearings. At these hearings, they ask experts to answer questions about important issues that affect proposed laws.

For this activity, you will role-play an expert who has been asked to speak at a congressional hearing. Each Unit Group will act as a team of experts on one of the five units in your text.

You will need a good understanding of your unit. You will also have to prepare answers to the questions assigned to your unit. At the hearing, committee members might ask you other questions about the information you have presented.

Your Unit Group should meet before the congressional hearing to prepare answers to your assigned questions. Most of the information you need for preparing good answers is in your text. In some cases, you might want to ask parents, teachers, and friends for their ideas about government in the United States today. Each member of your group should contribute to the presentation and speak at the hearing.

tHe VINEDRESSER'S NOTEBOOK

spiritual lessons in pruning, waiting, harvesting & abundance

judith sutera
illustrated by paul soupiset

Abingdon Press
Nashville

THE VINEDRESSER'S NOTEBOOK
SPIRITUAL LESSONS IN PRUNING, WAITING, HARVESTING, AND ABUNDANCE

Copyright © 2014 by Judith Sutera, OSB,
on behalf of Mount St. Scholastica, Inc.

Library of Congress Cataloging-in-Publication Data

Sutera, Judith.
    The vinedresser's notebook : spiritual lessons in pruning, waiting, harvesting, and abundance / Judith Sutera, OSB.
        pages   cm
    ISBN 978-1-4267-7383-9 (binding: trade paper with french flaps and deckled-edge paper : alk. paper)   1. Spiritual life—Catholic Church.   2. Vineyards—Miscellanea.   I. Title.
    BX2350.3.S855 2014
    242—dc23

                                                            2013041435

Scripture quotations—John 15:5; Matthew 7:16; Ecclesiastes 3:1—are from the World English Bible.

14 15 16 17 18 19 20 21 22 23—10 9 8 7 6 5 4 3 2 1

Introduction

WHEN I CAME TO THE BENEDICTINE MONASTERY of Mount St. Scholastica in Atchison, Kansas, many years ago, it was decided that the best way to channel my energy, short attention span, and love of the outdoors would be to assign me to the garden. I loved it, a much better fit than making infirmary beds or helping the sacristan, but I had no idea how enormous a role it would play in my religious formation.

My mentor was Sister Jeannette Obrist, well into her seventies at the time, who seemed to know everything about plants. That would be logical since she was doing this as a postretirement appointment after having been a botany professor in the monastery's college for decades.

"People think that just anyone can farm," she would say, "but you have to be very smart to do what we do. Don't let anyone downplay your work." This advice would become crucial when I later chose to serve an extended period in the maintenance department and frequently heard about how I was wasting myself and my talents.

There is a saying that everything one needs to know about life is learned in kindergarten. For me, much of what I need to know about life I can learn from the earth. Human beings operate on the same general principles as other creatures. We come from a seed, grow, develop complexity, age, and die. We are affected by many environmental factors and by the unique nature we have.

The grapevines have become one of my best guides. I have been with them now for forty years. They were here before me, and I like to believe they will be here after me. Scores of sisters, students, and retreatants have helped me, and I have tried to make the work more of a life lesson than a task for each of them. Some have been bored by the preaching, some have been energized, some have carried the lessons into situations in their own lives, and some have contributed their own realizations to what I teach.

Some years ago, during a retreat, I took a small notebook and began writing and sketching what I knew, both for myself and for those who would work with me. I did it because, on that day, I needed to summarize my learning, and I had no intention of it becoming a book. Many years later, I showed it to one of my vineyard helpers, author Judith Valente, who was writing a book about our community called *Atchison Blue*. My notebook consisted only of the sketched pages, and I didn't really want to add explanations or intellectual reflection. It was merely a picture book of practical advice that I wanted to let speak for itself and speak to its readers at whatever level it might touch them. In fact, if you don't want all that extra intellectualization, I won't be at all offended if you choose to tape the commentary pages together and let this book be just a picture story. Yet here it is in a more developed form, and perhaps it will help others to love a plant, love the miracles of life, love themselves and others.

This book is not an overtly religious book because I believe its insights apply to anyone. Nevertheless, those who come from a Judeo-Christian background will immediately recognize an additional level of significance. Old and New Testaments have numerous references to vineyards and vinedressers. At various times, the people are referred to as a vineyard or as vines. God and Jesus both identify themselves as vinedressers. Jesus takes it another step and says, "I am the vine. You are the branches."

To the agrarian peoples of those times, the meanings would have been obvious and rich. Today, many of us are far removed from such activities and thus cannot comprehend the message. Perhaps, in reading this book and understanding how the vines work and what the role of the vinedresser is, some readers can explore more deeply what this means for their spiritual development as well as their human development.

I went to visit
the Vinedresser
to learn to teND
the grapes.

She was old and bent,
but her smile was soft and bright.

Her hands were gnarled,
but they held everything with
great tenderness in their strength.

Throughout that year, we walked the morning-wet
fields between rows of vines. She told me everything
I needed to know about the secret world of the vines.

This, I am now passing on to you,
in case you ever tend a vine of your own.

To be a beginner is humbling. Everything seems so overwhelming and confusing. If there are others already doing it, it can be even more threatening as we compare ourselves to them and fear their judgment or ridicule. We feel watched, awkward, helpless, afraid, stupid—and any number of other feelings.

Sometimes we're asked, or told, to do things we've never done before. It may not be something we would have wanted to do or imagined doing or believed we could be good at doing. We never want to appear ignorant or incompetent—but if we act from our fear of seeming ignorant, we will never begin anything new.

When I first started vinedressing I was given some things to read. I read the extension bulletins and some gardening books and learned some general things about pruning and possible problems and such. Of course, books are useful companions when one embarks on something new (and in the spiritual life, they are useful companions all the way through). But as I read my way into vinedressing, I began to realize how much had to come from hands-on work and a good flesh-and-blood teacher. I really came to appreciate being with someone who had more experience and knowledge. Even more important than what is learned is making the deep connection with a person who actually cares about you, listens to you, and answers your questions.

In the spiritual realm, it seems to be especially important not to trust ourselves—to seek the insights of another who might be more experienced than we and who might look at us with both love and distance. Whether we call them spiritual directors, gurus, confessors, masters, or whatever, there are wise and holy people in all faith traditions to whom others are drawn. They draw others not as much by their preaching as by the sanctity of their own lives, the goodness that comes through them and by which others are touched and transformed.

When many early Christian people went to the desert to seek holiness, the tradition was that every person would find an *abba* or *amma* (spiritual father or mother) who would help him or her find the path for his or her life. In many faith traditions, one seeks wisdom from the word given by a person believed to have greater wisdom and insight than that which the seeker currently possesses. The Zen master, the *amma*, the rabbi, or whoever, often tells a story rather than gives a lecture. These stories take us beyond gathering mere information and show us how to live. They shape our experience into a quiet teaching.

Because of the way my mentor saw everything as a metaphor and all life as reflective of the same truths, I learned to see the plants the way she did. We were never just looking at vines. When she spoke about them, she sounded as if they were friends, and she cared for them that way. That alertness and caring taught me to pay attention to more than the basic techniques I got from the books and helped me to turn the techniques into something personal and instinctive. I started really looking at them and listening to what they were trying to tell me. When I saw something I didn't understand or hadn't seen before, she was always there to pass on what she knew from her many years with them (or suspected from a broader base of reference). Everyone needs a teacher, someone who knows the landscape and can take him or her into the vineyard at first.

THe BaSe OF each VINE iS LiKe a LiTTle **TREE**, OLD aND **THICK** aND gnaRLeD.

"Vines live a very long time," she said, "always sending out new shoots. Each plant is unique," she continued.

"Pay attention to what it tells you."

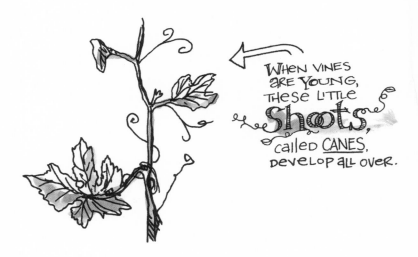

WHEN VINES ARE YOUNG, THESE LITTLE **Shoots**, called <u>CANES</u>, DEVELOP ALL OVER.

Your responsibility is to establish each young plant, helping it to thrive.

IT TAKES A LONG TIME TO GET OLD AND thick and gnarled. In the process, many things happen and each event leaves its mark. Some of what we see is a result of growth; some is damage. This external appearance is only part of the story that the plant or the person carries. With trees, there are growth rings that can only be seen when the plant is laid open and examined in cross section. The growth rings make up a living record of each year's ups and downs: cold, heat, drought, injury. In some way, the new shoots carry those effects as well. If there have been too many dry years or wet years or hard-weather years, it will affect the growth for years to come. Damage to an area may mean no shoots there for a long time or perhaps ever.

Like trees, people are marked by the formative events in their lives too. When we meet someone, we encounter what that person has become as a result of all that has come before. We can't see the growth rings inside, see how they mark the rich and the lean years, or know what each season did to him or her.

Sometimes with people, as with a vine, we can see the scars where something has been cut off, where there has been a pruning. All we can see, however, is the scar. We don't know how they were damaged or what the missing parts looked like or why they had to be cut away. Fears and insecurities, losses and pain, and the behaviors that do not serve us well—all of these are signs of our past wounds.

Such wounds become permanent parts of us, and they may become the most obvious things about us. The plants in our vineyard are old and thus have very weathered trunks with many stumps. I cannot know what nourished them, how many shoots they've had, or how much fruit has gone forth. I see them only as they are at this time, and thus I have a very incomplete picture. Some plants, perhaps, were once vigorous and productive but have diminished. Other plants may look strong, but I have no idea whether they have actually borne much fruit. Some may have weathered extraordinary difficulties.

As a Benedictine, I am instructed by St. Benedict's rule to "welcome everyone as Christ." Since we see such a limited view of a person, that can be a very tall order. Appearances can be quite deceiving, so I have to assume that there is much more to a person than meets the eye. I have to assume, too, that the parts of you that I do not see have value and goodness and potential.

We had a sister who was a very demanding teacher, a stern personality rarely satisfied with others. Hers was not a warm personality; consequently, most people knew her only from their superficial interactions with her, and those were often strained. When she died, another sister made some remark that she would not grieve or miss her much. I asked her if she was aware of the sister's background.

For whatever reasons, in her later years, that usually reserved sister had opened up to me, telling me stories about her childhood that were filled with pain. She had been harshly treated by the relatives who raised her after the loss of her own parents. Her aunt and uncle were demanding and punishing; nothing she did was ever good enough. As I told this story, the angry sister fell silent, then thanked me. On the day of the funeral there was bad weather, so only the sisters who were pallbearers or had other official functions went to the grave. I looked up to see the deceased's "enemy" coming slowly down the cemetery road huddled under an umbrella.

"I'm so glad you could come," I said.

Her reply: "I realized it's never too late for a little conversion and forgiveness."

We can never know how others got to be the way they are. We can only try to believe that they are doing the best they can with what they have. This is the filter that will enable us to see the glimmer of goodness and purity within them and treat them accordingly.

that New PLANT LooKS gooD WITH all THAT gRowTH...

...BUT THERE'S A PROBLEM.

The vine has only enough energy to nourish a few canes well. Let all of them grow, and none will flourish.

You have to make the decision to cut perfectly good canes in order to concentrate the vine's energy.

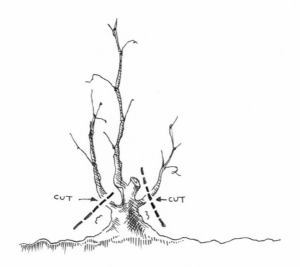

"How do I know which ones to cut?"
I asked the old Vinedresser.
"There's no one perfect answer," she replied.

"just seek to make the Vine Well-Balanced."

THE NEWBORN IS A MYSTERIOUS AND exciting bundle of potential. Some of what is going to be a part of this person's life is obvious from the beginning, such as a unique and distinctive combination of physical traits. Emotional tendencies, natural talents, and other attributes may also be manifest almost immediately. In our early years of life, we usually have a variety of experiences that help us grow in various ways. We get an early education that introduces us to multiple branches of learning. We participate in physical and social activities of many kinds.

A healthy life requires a balance of self-expression and discipline. No one benefits from never being denied anything or experiencing the consequences of negative behavior. During a period of frenzy over a particular high-demand toy, there was a story about a man who traveled to another country to get it for his child. When asked why he had gone to this extreme, he said that it broke his heart to see his daughter cry and he didn't want to disappoint her. God help anyone who has to deal with her as an adult after being raised in that atmosphere.

This kind of indulgence is one end of the spectrum of discipline. On the opposite end is the stunting that comes from too much discipline. There are many other ways that someone becomes misshapen in his or her formative years. A child may be ridiculed for something he or she enjoys. There may be clear messages that something about that activity is abnormal or unacceptable, as when a boy wants to dance ballet or a girl is too assertive. They may be forced into directions that are not compatible with their own talents or desires. I have met more than one young person who is suffering conflict over the expectation to take up a certain career because of a parent's attraction to it and not his or her own. An adult may tell a child to stop dreaming and accept the harsh reality of life rather than offer encouragement to think big. An abusive, deprived, or emotionally unbalanced environment can lead to lifelong struggles against the negative messages one has learned.

The failure to give a healthy balance of criticism and praise leaves one unprepared for the real world. Each person must face the way the past has affected the adult he or she has become. You can't choose where you came from, only where you end up.

"For those first few years, you determine the shape,"
the Vinedresser told me. "Every year little canes
appear and every year you cut most of them away.
In that way the trunk gains in size and strength."

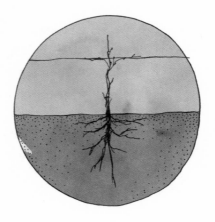

"At the same time, remember
to feed the roots as well."

No Matter How
Big AND Old AND Strong
a Plant APPears,
It Still Has LiMiTED
RESOURCES.

To grow a vine, to establish a vineyard,
you always have to keep making strategic choices.

THE FIRST YEARS ARE THE ROOTS THAT form the foundation for one's life. A person, like a plant, develops throughout life both above and below the surface. I have seen plants that appear strong and vigorous. Their foliage is impressive and they may even bear fruit. Yet, because of lack of water or some other problem, their roots are shallow. The roots trail along close to the surface and become thin. They provide a modicum of nourishment for the plant but don't have enough nourishment to develop a strong root system. A storm or strong wind can knock the plant down. Sometimes the roots are almost completely dead before the plant above them withers.

Our parents, our teachers, and other influential adults root us. Without much other information with which to compare it, we believe much of what they say and respond accordingly. A child who is reinforced for self-centered behavior may become more demanding. A child constantly derided or ignored may become more invisible. A child who feels loved and valued may face the world with growing confidence and security.

The challenges we face, the losses we experience, and the values we try to practice can seem like injuries or deprivations on the surface. Yet, as when a vine loses some of its branches, its vital energy is gathered in a deeper place. Some kinds of plants are nourished by dense networks of tiny hair-like roots. Their strength comes from the way these mat together and intertwine. Although each root by itself is frail, they are able to support one another. These kinds of plants are usually small and thick, like grasses.

The strongest root systems for larger plants involve thick, deep root systems. The grapevines reach deep below, harden along the surface, and branch out year after year. The more roots there are and the more sturdy and branched they are, the better the plant can search out what it needs from the soil to live. Such a system also gives the plant a broad and firm base so that it can get taller and stronger and still have a solid footing to keep it stable.

Many kinds of plants have a taproot, a very long and powerful root that runs straight down deep into the earth in addition to the regular system of roots. As it grows larger and deeper, it is able to bring hidden resources to the plant. Some desert plants have taproots that are more than a hundred feet deep, allowing them to get to a water

source deep below the surface in an area that appears
to be completely without moisture. These plants survive
despite their environment because they have been able to
grow down as well as up.

Every person needs a taproot, something that reaches
from within to find the deepest source of nourishment
that it can. We all need to be fed from sources other than
ourselves, sources that connect us to the broader web of
creation or to a reserve of refreshment for arid times or
essential elements that we cannot produce independently.
We have to be always reaching and searching, pushing
energy down as well as up. If not, when the surface
conditions are not sufficient to sustain us, we will quickly
starve.

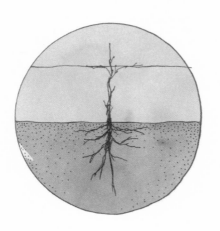

REMEMBER,
You **prune** for **now**
and for the future.

**Leave some large canes on top,
ready to bear fruit.**

**Leave some shorter canes
to grow stronger for next year's fruit.**

**Leave some new growth at the bottom,
allowing future canes to develop.**

And always consider and plan for an overall shape.

You're cutting for this
year's fruit, the vinedresser
said, but also in the hope
of many years to come.

ANYTHING OF VALUE IN OUR LIVES probably requires some advanced planning and some sense of both short-term action steps and long-term goals. Of course, there do have to be some small pleasures and achievements along the way if we are not to become disheartened. At the same time, these small pleasures need to be in service to a broader plan and not mere random moments. It's a tricky balance. If I'm always denying myself any satisfaction in the moment, I'll be pretty miserable when, and if, I get to the long-range goal. If I flit about with small goals only, I might know momentary joy but end up aimless and unsatisfied.

I can remember the careful storage of all that change I accumulated as a child and the growing stack of single dollar bills from birthday cards or extra chores that would slowly lead to enough for the big-ticket item I dreamed about. I can also remember the reluctance to let go of that "here and now" treat and the even greater reluctance to put some of my hard-earned savings into the basket at church or the collection at school for the poor.

Appreciating the value of planning ahead is tough but necessary.

Just as we put money in the bank for a rainy day, we have to think about what we are storing within ourselves for the hard times or the long-term benefit. A little bit of self-control or spiritual discipline will add up in the reserve that prepares me for life's challenges. Small efforts to be more kind or generous build up until I have a storehouse of patience and love from which I can draw. Doing the next right thing moves me in the direction of a peaceful life. If one has a faith tradition that stresses an eternal reward, there is the added hope of the most important goal toward which one moves. Faith traditions teach us also that each small act is important in moving either nearer or farther from that reward.

A vine that has only top growth will eventually use up all of the potential for fruit-bearing that those branches can provide. Something has to be deep at the source and continuing to push out from that reserve. If there are no new buds to take the place of those that have been spent, there will be nothing left but a woody trunk that will play itself out and die. If we do not have a vision of a future we really desire, there is not much incentive to forego any pleasure or ego gratification. We need a long-term goal for life. Otherwise, one may have it all, and have it now, but then what?

When old canes get thick, they stop bearing fruit.
Even so, new canes can grow from old ones.

Once there's new growth,
then the thick old canes get cut.

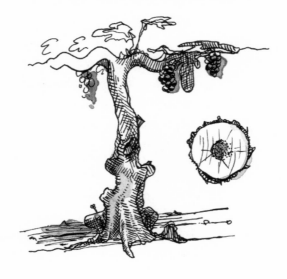

That's why the trunks have so many
bumps and turns, knotholes and stubs.

Pared down, it will grow new life.

"Look at the vine's natural shape and
decide how to focus and aid it."

The Vinedresser put pruning shears
in my hand and narrowed her eyes.

she commanded.

"You can't put shoots back on
once they are cut off."

GENERATIVITY IS THE GIFT OF BEING ABLE to bring something to birth. One does not have to have physically produced children to be generative; you can be generative simply by loving. Love is one thing that has no age limit. Love is generative even when our bodies cease to be.

The grapevine puts out many new shoots each year. At a certain stage of their growth they produce grapes, but that is only during a short part of their life span. The rest of the time they are playing some other role. There have to be old vines in order for new vines to grow. The biggest and best old ones become the trunk. Strong ones from them become main branches and pass the life energy on to the new ones that grow out of them and so on.

Whatever stage of life we are in, there are times when we question whether what we are doing is generative. Things just don't feel fruitful in some relationship, in a job or social group, even in spiritual practices. It's very hard to know when to stay the course and when to make the cut. We always have to think before we cut and then make peace with the result. Whether we prune or not, that experience, that person, that time in our lives has been part of the process of growth. It moved me from one place to the next; it caused me to face some truths about myself; it challenged me to a strengthened sense of purpose or appreciation.

St. Benedict speaks of keeping death daily before one's eyes. This is not meant to be a morbid preoccupation with mortality but a realistic expectation about it, the kind of realism that asks: "If I died today, what would my legacy be?" "Who would care and why?" "Have I done something today that brings good, that is loving, and that makes me productive, not in the world's sense but in the broader sense?"

In our lives, as with the vine, there comes a time when what has been fruitful is no longer there. Then it is time to move not to despair but to something else that will be equally, or more, meaningful. What is gone cannot be reattached. Those who keep death daily before their eyes eventually come to view death simply as the inevitable end that all humans face. They may eventually cease to even ask questions about their legacies. The questions become irrelevant because they come to realize that they cannot, in the end, remain attached to anything. They will keep death daily before their eyes by keeping their appreciation for each day in clear sight. Such an attitude is neither gloomy nor debilitating but liberating and enriching.

Being life-giving is more than just being a single branch producing an occasional bunch of colorful fruit. Most of what we produce is simple, ordinary, and even imperceptible, like the nutrients flowing through the rest of the vine that make the fruit happen.

It's easy to cut dead or misshapen branches but very hard to sacrifice the perfectly healthy for the sake of the whole.

However, if you aren't decisive about what to cut, you'll end up with a tangled mess.

KEEP TRIMMING

OR THE VINE KEEPS TRAILING AND LEAFING OUT.

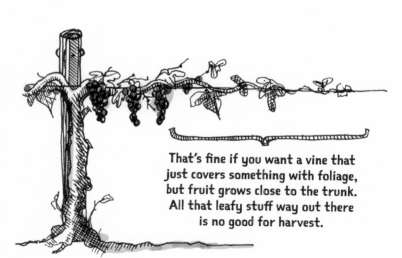

That's fine if you want a vine that just covers something with foliage, but fruit grows close to the trunk. All that leafy stuff way out there is no good for harvest.

"THE WORLD IS SO FULL OF A NUMBER OF things, I'm sure we should all be as happy as kings," says the Robert Louis Stevenson nursery rhyme. My version sometimes seems to go more like, "The world is so full of a number of things that I can't make up my mind or get focused."

We literally have the world at our fingertips. An evening's home entertainment is no longer a choice of three TV channels but hundreds, which have been joined by movies, video games, and all the world's knowledge on the Internet. If I don't find a book on the shelf, e-books are there for me. Shopping is no longer confined to what's in the local store but can expand to all the inventory of all the world's e-stores, and our friends can be chosen from all the world's special interest sites, chat rooms, and dating services.

How great is that? Well, it's great until I have to make choices. One of my special joys in the vineyard is when a young woman newly arrived at the monastery is sent to help me as I was sent so many years ago. These are people who have just recently made a huge leap of faith. They have decided to set aside all the other possibilities open to them in this unlimited buffet of modern life and to settle on one thing to which to devote their entire lives. It's frightening, it's daunting, and it's exciting all at the same time as all life commitments are.

When we make a major life choice, we cut off all kinds of other potentially great branches. What if I had married Joe instead of Bill? What if I had become a doctor instead of a musician? What if I hadn't come to this college and met these people who changed my life path? Life is full of what-ifs. Indeed, if other things had happened, I wouldn't be here . . . but I am and that is the life I live. I can go with that and put all my efforts into making it the best choice there is, or I can entertain fantasies and regrets that pull me in any number of fruitless directions. Leaving myself open for the next "better offer" means never being fully open to what is right here now.

One of the former novices, now past her silver jubilee, still reminds me of my challenge to her when she pruned with me. She wanted to leave extra canes just in case, and I kept prodding her to not be afraid to cut. What we always have to remember when making choices is that the fruit does grow close to the trunk. We can't get too distracted and begin to trail in various directions. Focusing on who we are rather than what we do will put life in a clearer perspective. Focusing on a few close relationships will deepen them. Focusing on our spiritual growth will bring us to greater self-knowledge and connectedness to the sacred. We are to be about the harvest and not the foliage.

that's why you need a Vinedresser:

to choose the ground,

to build the trellises,

to select the plants,

and to prepare the soil.

GOOD GROWTH TAKES ATTENTION, DEDICATION, AND TIME.

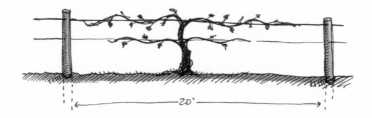

The Vinedresser took me to survey the vineyard,
to see that each vine had support and direction.
You don't need much support at first,
just enough so the vines don't fall over.

ATRELLIS RESTRICTS THE FREEDOM OF the vine. In every vineyard you pass along the highway, there is a distinct pattern that tells you it's a vineyard. The vines are always in neat, straight rows and growing along rigid lines of wire. These lines carefully control the growth of the vines. Without them, the vines could not grow upward because they need something they can trail along. The weight of the fruit could not be adequately supported, and it would pull the vine to the ground where the fruit would not mature well or would rot.

Freedom is an important value in our society, one of the pillars of the American way of life, but true freedom involves some judicious constraints, some supports. Freedom is not the right to do anything we please. I don't decide to drive on the wrong side of the road and run every stop sign just to assert personal freedom. Such freedom would likely be very short-lived. I may be free to say hurtful things or free to take advantage of another person, but I forego that kind of freedom if I care about that person and want his or her good.

I was once visiting a colleague to do some serious academic work, and we were constantly interrupted by her children. One needed to be taken to a music lesson; another couldn't find his shoe. A cry from one who had fallen off a bicycle sent us running. When one was told he could not have permission to do something, he complained, "I'll be glad when I'm grown up and I can do whatever I want." My uncensored response was "If grown-ups always did what they wanted, this paper would be finished and you would be staying with a babysitter while we were on a beach in Cancun!"

Yet, on the other hand, we *were* doing what we wanted because we wanted to take care of those children more than we wanted to do something for our own pleasure. Loving people replace "total" freedom with freely chosen obedience. The Latin root of *obedience* is *audire*, which means "to listen." Whether it is to God, to authority, or to others, our obedience is an act of listening. A parent runs to attend to a crying infant not because that tiny creature of only a few pounds can exercise any physical threat or exert any power but because of love. The child eventually learns that the support is there and that, though it sometimes limits behavior, it makes for a solid foundation.

Love and responsibility are the trellises that hold us up and move us in the right direction. The only person who can claim to be free of all obligations and who never needs to make hard choices is the one who loves no one and whom no one loves, and that would be a very sad freedom.

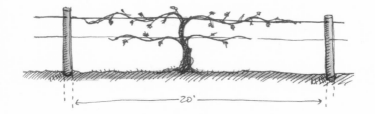

20'

New branches are creative—they grow every which way. They reach out with little fingerlike tendrils. They'll grab the ground, another branch, or a trellis. It's all the same to them.

Since a vine will cling to whatever is available, always remember to provide helpful support structures.

As soon as they touch an object, branches begin to curl. In the beauty lies the difficulty: once branches dry with the curl, they are VERY difficult to uncurl.

Timing and shaping are key. Time your vinedressing right by coming when the shoots are tender and malleable, giving a gentle push in the right direction so they can find grip.

GROWTH NECESSITATES REACHING OUT. As infants, we have to reach out for everything we need. We reach out for support to sit up or walk. As we grow, we reach out to other people to provide for us, to affirm our identity, and to teach us new things. Throughout our lives we reach out to others to lovingly hold our hands until, in our old age, we may come full circle and again need the physical support of someone to steady our gait.

The tiny tendrils of a grapevine function by being very sensitive to contact. They are naturally curved and as soon as something touches them, they begin to coil around it. So it really matters what is within their reach. When several branches are growing close together, they end up grasping one another and become tangled. When strong ones grow upward, the others attached to them are pulled along. When some move outward or fall off the trellis, others are pulled along in that direction as well. If a branch is curving downward and attaches itself to something below, it will be caught in that grasp and soon is unable to let go and continue upward.

The wires or slats placed by a caretaker provide something strong that is designed to encourage the vines to head in the right direction. As the branch takes hold and growth continues, the newly growing end will grasp the framework ahead and move in the desired direction. Nature has provided the tendrils so that the shoots, which are by nature quite spindly and flexible, will be able to use the strength of other things around them to pull themselves off the ground and to support the weight of fruit that will become much heavier than the vine alone can bear.

We are like those vine tendrils, sensitive and prone to curl ourselves around whatever we come near. If we inch along the ground of insecurity and failure, we are tempted to grasp that place and eventually may be unable to extricate ourselves and grow upward. If we find good companions or good social structures, we use them to climb upward and gain support.

Our relationships are an essential part of our humanity. We need other people and desire their support. Good companions reinforce our best behavior. They challenge us by their actions or their inspiring conversation. We can learn about things like forgiveness and charity only by experiencing them in real human situations.

Anyone trying to end an addiction or to stop a bad behavior knows that it is important to find other people who will reinforce the good and offer positive alternatives. If that is true for addictions, it also holds true in other, less serious circumstances. I love being with people who can share simple joys, helping me to grow in gratitude and awareness of all the wonders around me. I am grateful for the people who see the humor in life and not just the irritations, who find things to praise more often than things to complain about. They move me in a direction that faces upward and outward. They won't let me turn in on myself or drag me down. As we grow together, they are always there to hang on to and help to bear the weight.

A little untangling, a little nudge toward the frame, is all it needs to guide it.

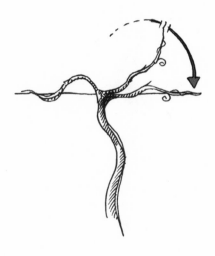

What was once so flexible BECOMES HARD AND TENACIOUS.

The canes turn woody and can't be rebent without significant effort, if at all.

Once you decide to rebend the hardened cane, work toward slight but important changes. Remember, even making the slightest change requires you to throw all your weight into the process.

BECAUSE THE TENDRILS ARE SO SENSITIVE, shaping the vine's direction can be a very easy process. The good vinedresser has to be there at just the right time. Since the vines can't reorient themselves, the person tending them keeps an eye on which ones are headed where. If some are starting to stray, the vinedresser simply picks them up and places them gently where they ought to be. As soon as the wandering cane feels the wires with those little tendrils, the tendrils begin to wrap and nature takes over. Sometimes I can almost imagine the cane's gratitude and relief as it is put back where it belongs and feels the support.

This is a good image for how discipline should be achieved. What do you think of when you hear the sentence "She was disciplined"? Do you imagine someone being scolded and punished for an offense, similar to the discipline one gets in the principal's office, or do you imagine someone with great focus and attention to self-determined practices, similar to one who is a careful and diligent practitioner of a skill? The same words can have two very different meanings and implications depending on our point of view. The origin of the word *discipline* is in a Latin word that means "a way of life," like when we speak of one studying in a particular academic discipline. Thus, to be disciplined is to have everything be consistent with that way of life. We can achieve that consistency with actions from within or from outside ourselves.

We recognize, however, that it's almost impossible to lead a completely consistent and disciplined life. I want to eat more healthy meals and lose some weight, but there are so many temptations. I want to be more faithful to my prayer, but there are so many distractions. I know I waste a lot of time on irrelevant diversions, but there are so many possible excuses. Discipline is the work of a lifetime, and change begins with very small actions. The person who wants to learn a musical instrument does not sit down and try to learn a concerto. First, there are those boring scales and simple tunes. The couch lover who has barely walked from the house to the car doesn't open the front door and charge out to run a marathon. One has to start by trying to make it to the end of the block. When that becomes fairly painless, the route can increase to two blocks, and so on. Body muscle builds gradually, and emotional and spiritual muscles do too.

The gradual course is the most gentle and ultimately achievable. We must pay attention to the incremental changes because we, like plants, will grow in the direction in which we are bent. We get set in our ways, and to truly change requires tremendous focus and effort. We all know that old negative habits are hard to break. We may not realize an action is becoming a habit until it is so ingrained that it feels as if we cannot live any other way. We have to throw our whole selves into that change.

Likewise, even the slightest effort toward a right choice means that it will be easier next time. As I achieve more happiness from the results of my exercise or practice or prayer, and get into the habit of doing it consistently, I will find it hard to imagine living any other way. When we nudge ourselves in the direction of the good that we seek, then that is the direction toward which we will be looking and toward which we will bend.

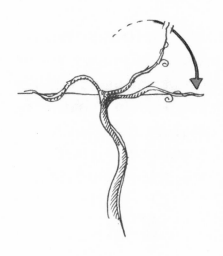

The Vinedresser showed
me how to shape the vine
so that the plant and the
trellis remain in harmony.
Nature and labor help
each other create
something wonderful.

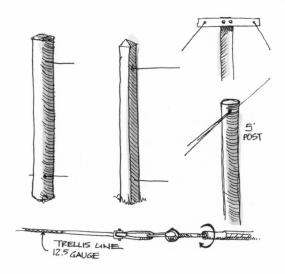

A good frame helps bear the weight of the
fruit and avoids breaks in branches. A strong
frame provides plants stable growth.

THE FRAMEWORK OR TRELLIS FOR THE vines is not something that distorts but something that enhances the potential. The vines are not twisted into unnatural positions; they are merely guided in a direction that is beneficial. They will certainly grow without anyone else around, but they will probably not have such successful fruit.

We have frameworks too. Every human body has a skeleton. We don't think much about it unless something goes wrong, but it is necessary to our shape and function and movement. Whether we are conscious of it or not, we have another skeleton as well. Something has to be holding us up internally to protect and move our emotional and moral components. There is always some narrative we have developed in order to hold us together when it comes to our worldview and our values.

All human beings seem to have an innate desire to know why they exist, where they came from and where they go when they die, why bad things happen, and other such deep and unanswerable questions. It seems that even the most basic human groupings try to address these questions with some common myth that will provide a framework for their lives. I do not know of any primitive culture where one person believes in a volcano spirit, the next person a corn mother, the next a heavenly deity, and so on. Their common myth binds their rituals and their behaviors. In primitive societies, the framework is usually pretty strong and universal.

We, on the other hand, do not live in that kind of centralized world. Our families have come from all over the globe and all over the spiritual map as well. We have access to all kinds of spiritual and moral systems. We can shop around until we find something that "suits" us, or we can simply decide to commit to no structure at all.

If we set our own rules for all of life, they aren't really rules at all because we get to decide what is an exception, what applies to what degree, what sanctions we will impose. Sometimes when speaking to those preparing for Lent, I pose a challenge. What if, instead of deciding for ourselves what would be a good discipline or picking some simple practice that inflicts only modest sacrifice, we were to ask our closest friends and family to choose our practices for us? Reactions range from smiles to groans.

A community that shares our values and concerns does matter. We know that it will generally bring us to greater growth and more courage to face life's challenges than if we go it alone. I am convinced that a monastic community is not for the strong but for the weak. I am absolutely sure that I would not get up as early as I do every morning and spend as much time in prayer if there were not all those other people expecting it of me and all those structures in place to help me make it happen. I know I would not be as good at practicing virtue if there weren't so many people lovingly challenging me to it.

There is probably still more of the primitive need for community as a framework for life than we may imagine. There are those who say that they don't need a worship community because they don't want to have to do certain things at certain times when they can be with God anywhere.

Maybe, but picture some of these same people who have a very special appointment every Sunday that they would not dare break. They put on special clothing, assemble in a certain place that is more stately and inspiring than their normal surroundings, perform actions and chants in unison with the assembled group, celebrate a common belief in the power and hope that they feel. Does a football game fulfill a primal need for communal worship?

Good vines require cutting and more cutting.
A mile of runners won't give you one more grape,
so get rid of branches that do not bear fruit.

Do you want to keep everything?

Then expect nothing.

Cut.

and then cut some more.

"These vines sure need a good dose of attention," I observed.

"That's because they're domestic grapes," was the Vinedresser's patient reply. "They weren't meant to fruit on their own. We are responsible to help form and shape their growth."

ALL THE CUTTING THAT SEEMS TO GO ON in life is hard enough when it happens because of external circumstances. It's even harder to decide that I should cut some more because of the ultimate benefit, as when I prune good branches so the energy of the vine can be concentrated. That's the same idea that is behind spiritual disciplines. We practice sacrifice so that our spiritual lives can be more fruitful.

Many years ago, a sister who was a real spiritual master pointed me to a book by an evangelical theologian who was proposing more fasting and other spiritual practices for people outside the faiths where these practices were a traditional part of their spirituality. In his book *The Spirit of the Disciplines*, Dallas Willard wants to educate his readers about these habits and the motivation behind them. Even though I was a member of a monastic community, I could still see myself in his challenge. He said that we are tempted to treat Jesus the way a child might treat a baseball star. The child wants to wear the same shoes, eat the same cereal, hold the bat the same way, and imitate other mannerisms, believing that this will make him or her great like the hero. What the child

does not see is that these are not the things that make
the hero great. The child cannot understand the years of
endless practice, of painful physical effort and injury, of
single-minded attention and desire, of the rigorous diet
and exercise, of the other pleasures or relationships that
the athlete sacrifices in order to become extraordinary.

Willard suggests that we can do the same with Jesus. We
want to do what he did—speak out for justice, preach the
word of God, take care of the needy—but we don't think
as much about the fact that his deeds were possible only
because of his internal life and the unseen discipline that
sustained him. The sacrifice of his own will, his intense
prayer and struggle with temptations, and all the unseen
preparation he had to do in his own soul were what gave
him the strength and faith to act.

The world will not become peaceful for us; we have to
find our interior peace within the world. The irony is that
this peace comes not from having things go more our
way but from cutting away at what is disturbing from
inside us. The athlete experiences pain and sacrifice
not because of self-hatred but because of desire for
a greater good. We might choose a prayer method,
sacred reading, a physical practice like yoga, service to

others, or self-awareness techniques. All of these ask us to take time, cut away distraction, and focus. These exercises gradually shape our spirits and cut away self-centeredness in the same way we would shape our bodies by cutting away calories. We will not wake up someday and find everyone around us lovable, but we can prune away our impatience and intolerance, our bad habits and behaviors, and practice the discipline of love.

We are what we think about. If we let go of what is not spiritual, we will be slowly but surely transformed. When an elderly sister was asked the secret of her apparent calm and happiness, she replied, "It started when I realized I didn't have to have an opinion about everything."

The Vinedresser pointed to some wild grapes—
mostly vine, with tiny, sour fruit.

Some things might happen naturally, but
other things require tending, made better and
more fruitful with a vinedresser's hand.

Wild grapes have their own beauty. But if you want big
sweet fruit, then you need domestic, cultivated vines.

you can grow WILD or you can grow grapes.

WILD GRAPES AND ALL THE REST OF THE plants and animals that have developed without human intervention are a wonder, and each has developed to have its own place in nature and its own importance. Nevertheless, anyone who believes that the untamed natural world is a place of simple harmony and unspoiled beauty doesn't know much about nature. There is plenty of struggle for resources between and within species. There are violence and suffering. There are many circumstances in which the natural environment does not provide the ideal conditions for something to flourish.

Even in the absence of human intervention, many living things are able to adapt to make the most of their conditions and develop qualities that help them survive and improve their positive characteristics. But with a little domestication, they become much more suited to human needs. In domestic grapes, little, sour seeds have become a variety of sweet, juicy delights. *Domestic* comes from the Latin *domus*, which means "home." When any creature is brought into the home, or made suitable to be in the home, it is gathered into a special environment.

We are domesticated by the people who care about us.

Think about some of the training we receive in life. At first, we don't understand the value of it, but we know there is praise, punishment, or criticism connected to certain things we do. From an early age, people may make us aware of a certain tendency or bad habit. As our parents bring this habit to our attention, we make some effort to correct it but may not be too concerned about it. We may even occasionally do the irritating thing deliberately as an act of rebellion. The same happens when we go to school. Teachers bring up the same problem, and again we give it some attention.

Then, at some point we enter into a relationship with a close friend or a love interest. It is no surprise that eventually this person brings up the same troubling behavior. It may go something like: "I love you very much, and this is certainly not a deal breaker, but I really wish you wouldn't do that." Suddenly, correcting the behavior leaps to the top of the to-do list with an urgency and enthusiasm we've never felt before. This is the power of love to tame us and to make us want with all our hearts to be our best and most domesticated selves. We want to please the loved one. We want to make ourselves more attractive. We want to smooth the road to a deeper relationship. We want the other to be proud of us, appreciate our efforts, know how much he or she is loved.

Love and belonging are not for the lazy, the indifferent, or the unmotivated. Love is a lot of work, but a work that we take on willingly and even eagerly. It is a motivator surpassing any other, enabling us to be greater and happier than we ever imagined we could be.

Grapes need a just-right
mixture of light and heat.
At first, big leaves around
them are good, to protect
them from the sun.
Parts that don't produce
fruit still have an
important part to play.

When they begin to mature
and require more light,
some of the leaves have to go.

a balance of

shelter & light

HELPS FRUIT MATURE.

IN A VARIETY OF RELIGIOUS TRADITIONS, THE images of heat and light are significant. In the Gospel of John, Jesus is referred to as "Light from Light," and one of the invocations of the Buddha speaks of the Buddha as "immeasurable (or infinite) light." Even in our secular vocabulary one "feels the heat" or "sees the light." Experiencing heat and light is one of the most basic sensations. Since the divine power is often described as a great or all-permeating light, *enlightenment* is the word for the experience of being filled with the light of a power greater than ourselves. Light casts out darkness and exposes everything in its path. In the Catholic Easter vigil, everyone lights a small candle from a single large one, slowly transforming the space with the light. The chant refers to the flame's ability to be "divided but undimmed." Intense heat also has the power to melt, purify, and even ignite and consume.

Successful growth is not just a matter of collecting the necessary elements randomly. The amount of rainfall needed may be several inches, but it has to be spread throughout the growing season. Receiving several inches of rainfall on the same day can be fatal to a tiny seedling but have little negative impact on a larger, stronger plant.

In our lives, we would like to have fair weather all the time. Nature, however, dictates otherwise. As the plant requires light and darkness, rain and dryness, so do we need the cycle of all the essential elements.

Sometimes our efforts at personal growth can be compared to sunbathing on a summer day. In pursuit of the perfect tan, we are tempted to stay at it too long, thinking that the intensity will produce the desired result, only to have our skin end up burned and peeling. The more desperate roast themselves in a tanning bed so that they have no need to rely on the natural cycles of the sun. This can force a result that does the job but is too intense and ultimately unhealthy. The most desperate might even go the "spray-on" route; it's quick and painless but not very natural looking and only skin-deep.

We must be warmed gradually and carefully to receive light and enlightenment. We must have the moisture of tears. We need breezes that refresh and dry. The shielding or exposure we give ourselves, or are given by those who care for us, matures us in a way that is timely and balanced and brings sweet fruit.

The fruit grows from tiny little pellets into full grapes, from green to pale shades of whatever color their final form will take.

At first, without the Vinedresser, I didn't understand how to look at places of mature growth, and I cut many of them too soon.

Grapes look ready to pick before they really are.

"How do you know when they are ready?" I asked the Vinedresser.

She held the grapes up to the light. I turned to look at clusters more closely. "See, the less ripe grapes have a kind of opaque skin, and the ripe ones are more transparent."

Don't be fooled: the color comes before the juice.

BY THEIR FRUITS YOU WILL KNOW THEM," says the Bible. One of the great temptations in life is to be all talk and no action. Sometimes it's hard to judge at first whether or not there is good fruit in those we meet. Eventually, though, we get a sense of whether their words match their actions.

Think about people you have known whom you considered holy or emotionally healthy or at peace or whatever you want to call it. They certainly didn't tell you that they were; had they, the fact that they announced it would confirm that it was not true! The sense that these people are special is something that we feel and experience from our interactions with them. In most ways, they are just like the rest of us. That is not to say that they have never had anything bad happen to them. In fact, they may be people who have had more than their share of suffering. But even when they are suffering, their sadness seems to hold some kind of inner strength. They do not feel, or pretend to feel, that everything is cheery and the world is just fine. Neither are they constantly bewailing the evils of the world and punishing themselves for real or imagined sins.

They don't go around floating off the ground or raising the dead or walking in some ethereal glow. They don't talk about religion or world peace or the afterlife all day long. If you didn't know them personally, you might not be able to pick them out of a crowd. How did you come to see these people as admirable? It comes from what you have seen them do and say. In what is experienced in the visible world, you come to believe that there is something interior, something not just at the level of action, that enables them to do what they do. There is clearly something greater at work in them.

Like the ripe grape, they have become clear. The sweet juice of their growth expands from the inside and develops a kind of transparency that shows the maturity of what is inside. They have come to an inner tranquility that gives them what the Greek philosophers called "equilibrium." The Stoics taught that every life is full of events that do not, of themselves, make us good or bad. For example, everyone is hungry sometimes. If we just accept our hunger as a fact, we remain undisturbed. If, however, we choose in our hunger to lash out at others or steal or are resentful of what others have or stuff ourselves uncontrollably the next time we see food, then we have become disturbed by what they called the "passions." These passions were believed to be the source of all evil and self-induced misery. When Christianity picked up this list of passions, they became the seven deadly sins.

Truly balanced people know that whatever happens to them in the external world cannot ultimately destroy what has come to fruition on the inside. Only their skin comes between them and the eternal truth and beauty of being. Those who encounter them can see in, and what they have can shine out.

Finally, if you've
worked masterfully
and diligently and the
weather has cooperated,
the harvest comes.

There are times when
you think you've picked
all the grapes, only
to crawl underneath
or push the leaves
a different way
and realize you've
missed quite a few.

You have to look VERY Hard AND FREQUENTLY CHANGE YOUR PoinT oF VIEW to Find All THE FRUIT.

WE CAN NEVER BE SURE OF WHAT THE harvest will be until it has happened. Sometimes the greatest gifts or the most powerful lessons aren't the ones we initially thought they would be. Most of us have had a difficult experience that we later realize taught us something very valuable. Most of us have performed a task that, though it seemed boring or irrelevant at the time, ultimately gave us a skill that was significant at some later time in another circumstance. Life is full of unexpected surprises. Many have had that experience of a family vacation to see some spectacular sight that everyone expected to be the highlight of the trip. Then something extraordinary happens and forever after, nobody talks about the Grand Canyon but about the funny thing that happened in the motel. This moment becomes the real bond because it is unusual and unforeseen; it gives the family a moment, a memory, and shared emotions that are uniquely theirs.

Every journey, and the whole journey of life, is filled with these unexpected twists and turns. No matter how many are the gifts we recognize, there are always more gifts being showered on us. No matter what we see and experience, we can find more in life about which to be excited. We come to appreciate that everything is a gift.

When I was a child, my aunt lived with us. I would often keep an eye toward the bus stop down the street to await her arrival from her exhausting factory job. I was especially attentive on Fridays. After cashing her paycheck, she would go to the dime store and buy us a small bag of candy or nuts. Almost every adult who has ever been greeted by a waiting child has heard the question I would ask: "What did you bring me?"

Unfortunately, I'm afraid I've never outgrown that question. I seem to keep asking it of my loved ones and of life and of God. I always seem to want more; everything always seems primarily about me and what I will gain from it. I realize now that the real answer to the question of what my aunt had brought me was not "a bag of cashews." What she brought me was far more valuable. I learned that I could trust in her love even on the days when she didn't bring me a treat. I learned that just seeing her approach and running into her arms was itself a treat. I believe she got delight from my delight when she handed me the bag, and I could feel that coming from her as well. I knew even then that I did not value her just for what she brought me, nor did I feel there was something wrong with me or that her love was withdrawn when she came empty-handed. This is knowledge I know I should transfer to the other relationships where I am still asking the question.

Even better than the Friday ritual are the unexpected treats of life. A gift for no particular occasion, a note of love or gratitude, an unexpected opportunity, can bring a very special joy. If we keep alert, we will see beautiful surprise packages left for us in so many places for no particular reason. Life can be like an endless harvest, where there is something around every corner and under every leaf if one looks hard enough to see it where others went hastily by. A life of gratitude provides an unending source of joy.

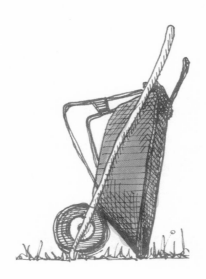

A note of warning though.

Even when you think you're doing everything right, things can still go wrong.

Beautiful grapes can get
some disease and fall off.

If conditions aren't just right,

You might have a
season with no grapes
at all.

Sometimes all you can do is
accept the ways of nature,
grieve, and go on.

EVEN THE BEST VINEDRESSER IN THE world will have a year with a poor harvest. There have been years when the vines were filled with tiny clusters of buds, but the lack of moisture prevented them from growing and they dried up. Even after the grapes have formed, they can shrivel up from drought or get a blight that has been carried through the air or by insects.

There are no magic formulas in life. Nothing comes with a guarantee. Bad things will inevitably happen to good people and vice versa. A good amount of it makes no sense. It is impossible to try to work out an explanation; it's cruel to try to assign blame in most cases. God gets blamed for all manner of things as if a loving God sometimes decides to pick random forms of suffering and visit them on random persons or enjoys creating crisis just to see how we'll do on this "pop quiz." Sadder still is when the need to blame turns into an agonizing self-examination as to what act of our own has brought down such misery as a "punishment," or when others imply that the person—the victim—had it coming.

Human beings are rarely comfortable with the thought that nature has its downs as well as its ups. There are simply things that are out of our control. No amount of designing or cajoling or avoiding can shield us. This is not to say that we should not make every conscious effort to plan or to take care of what we can control. Inevitably, however, there will be times of tragedy or trial.

I learned this lesson early on in the vineyard. I've seen bugs and choking weeds and heat and hail. Every time, though, it is hard to accept. I find I have to keep letting go in the face of this hard reality of life. It's a delicate balance between thinking nothing can ever go wrong as I try to solve my own problems and feeling the kind of helpless despair or fear that says, "Why bother?"

Because a bad thing, real or imagined, can be such a frightening prospect, I often meet it with the persistent thought that I, or someone, should have been able to do something to stop it. Especially when we lose a loved one, we may be tormented by thoughts that we should have done something to keep it from happening or should have done more for that person. On a larger scale we see this when acts of violence are met with revenge, or acts of terrorism with lashing out against whole cultural groups. I may not physically arm myself, but I certainly can obsess with trying to prepare for any imagined threat.

Nevertheless, there are times when I can't help the situation. Grief, as long as it does not become permanently debilitating, is a good and necessary thing. We have to let death be a real part of life. Children who are shielded from the realities of this process are less prepared to face it when they do finally have a close encounter with it. They may not know that their feelings of grief are normal and beneficial if they have not been permitted to see adults grieve.

The truth is that human life is like the life of every other living thing. Although we are more capable of conscious precautions, losses come. We are presumably more capable than other species of knowing we have experienced a deep loss and grieving that loss. So also are we more capable of processing that grief into something that can also be a gift. There may be grateful memories of persons we have lost and what they have done to make us who we are now. Failure may turn into determination to change what didn't work and to gain important life lessons. Tragedy may make us more compassionate to others or more appreciative of what we have. Sorrow and grief must be passed through but are never meant to be a permanent state.

The fruit may be gone, but the vine isn't.

Good harvest or bad, life waits in the trunk to burst forth again each spring.

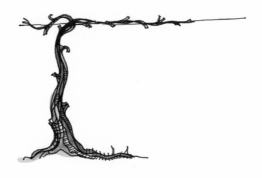

Sometimes vines die.
Slowly, at first, their fruit gets smaller and diminishes.
It can take years to really notice the change.

When you realize you don't have the vine you thought
you did, all you can do is chop it down.

THE WONDERFUL THING ABOUT grapevines and other such perennial plants is that there's always next year. When the days get shorter and plants lose their fruit and leaves, they draw back into themselves and hunker down for the winter. The sap that was feeding them by moving the essential nutrients around returns to the roots. Then the bare plant stalk appears to be dead. Experience of the cycles of many years and a knowledge of biology, however, have built in us a hope that looks are deceiving. We have every reason to believe that the plant will bounce back again in the spring.

We, too, have periods when we lose strength, especially after losses. It is necessary to return to our reserves of strength, just as the dormant plant regroups through its winter rest. What is beneath the surface will survive. In one of our chapel windows, as in many monasteries, is the coat of arms of an ancient Benedictine monastery. I paraphrased its Latin words in one of the sketches in this book: "Pared down it will grow new life." With the words, there is a picture of a large, old tree stump. It is completely lopped off across the top, showing its numerous growth rings and a flat, dead scar of a surface. From one place along the side, however, there is a little shoot with a couple of tiny green leaves popping out. It represents the experience and the optimism of a community that was repeatedly driven out by war, deprivation, and animosity. Sometimes in the midst of loss we can feel as if we will never recover. We can wonder if we even have anything in our core that will nourish us. The leaves fall; the cold winds blow; the sky is dark.

The plants teach us that nature is stronger and more resilient than that. Plants have an amazing sense of the cycles of life. They simply live quietly and patiently through each day. Eventually the days get a little longer and brighter by just a few minutes each day. What is deep in the plants' core can sense this. Miraculously, the lengthening day triggers a response. Plants "know" that the days of winter have passed, and a surge of energy begins. All the nutrients that were there, all the life that was waiting, start to push upward. They will find their way into the waiting branches and push out new buds that will turn into new canes. The color returns; the leaves emerge.

Last year and all the years before have not disappeared or been forgotten. The plant has simply turned all of its past into another present. The essential elements of its life return from the roots deep underground to the same old trunk, and the trunk produces new shoots in new places.

In our dormant periods we become more aware of what really matters. We explore our inner resources and search for what gives us comfort. Going deep into ourselves in our loss should give us a desire to emerge into new hope. There is no loss in this life that should be able to prevent us from growing again as long as our roots are strong.

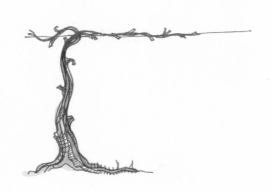

Basically, all I've learned from the Vinedresser comes down to this:

In early spring,

plant new vines and trim old ones down to a few canes.

In later spring,

clear the weeds and guide the branches.
Hope for sun and rain in right measure.

In summer,

watch the fruit develop.
Keep checking and trimming.

In fall,

enjoy the harvest but prepare for winter.
Remember that in every cycle, almost everything needs
to be cut but the trunk and the roots.

F**OR EVERYTHING THERE IS A SEASON,"** says the biblical book of Ecclesiastes (called Qoheleth in the Hebrew). The year definitely has its seasons. We cannot expect fruit before blossom, growth in a frozen earth, blossoms on a dead branch. Each life has its seasons as well. We must grow and learn from each day and each season.

In early life we are dependent on others for our well-being. How successfully that happens will affect us in countless ways throughout life. Contrary to what most teenagers think, there is a wisdom that comes with experience. On the other hand, if we were not propelled by the energy and idealism of youth, few would have the courage to take such giant leaps as marriage and childbirth. We continue to make a series of choices and "prunings" throughout our adult lives. In midlife, it becomes necessary not only to strive to achieve what we can, based on the wisdom of experience and the blessings of love, but also to make peace with what we had dreamed about but may never accomplish. There may be periods when we have to readjust our expectations. Perhaps we become aware that all the energy was going into a career to the detriment of relationships with loved ones. Perhaps a health crisis requires that we make major changes in lifestyle.

The midlife crisis is a well-known concept in our culture. As we sense the shifting of seasons in our lives, we feel the need to prepare for the next one just as animals and plants do. We hear mostly about the extreme acts, the person who gives up all of his or her comforts for a cause or a drastic career change. Unfortunately, we also hear about that stereotypical midlifer who runs off with a flashy car and a much younger companion. These are all responses to the same realization. Time is passing; this season will not come again; I must take action now to be who I really want to be before it is too late. First, though, we have to be very honest and intentional in understanding who we really want to be or ought to be. In our later years, we come to an increasing consciousness of the limited time we have left. It is a period of knowing that it is time to let go of many things and to focus on that which is still possible, beneficial, and meaningful. It is not a time to go limp and wait passively for death.

Many psychological theorists see life as a series of stages through which we pass. Successful negotiation with each enables us to move to the next with the skills we need.

Each stage asks something different from us, but there is a continuity in them as well. Many of us face transitions to a job change or retirement with the same personality traits that we exhibited when we walked into high school or into kindergarten. Perhaps this is like the yearly cycle of tasks in the vineyard. I face basically the same challenges time and time again. I do not conquer them once and for all. I hope, however, I learn a little more each time. I've seen certain new things as well as many of the same old things. I have more practice and have learned how to work more efficiently. In spring, I know that surely summer will come and I can prepare for it. There are times of rest between great flurries of activity.

This is how nature functions. In our material lives, we may have air-conditioning to cool the summer and heat to warm the winter, lights to turn night to day and shades to keep out the light. In our human nature, the natural rhythms of life are always there. Ultimately they will not yield to a climate-controlled environment so we must live them as they come.

Tending the vineyard takes the entire year.
Even winters are productive, with more cutting to do.
The canes get very brown and stiff and wrap very tight.

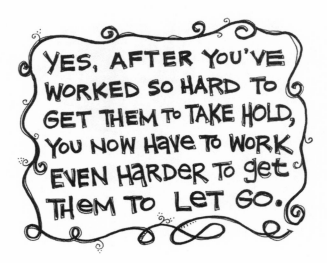

YES, AFTER YOU'VE WORKED SO HARD TO GET THEM TO TAKE HOLD, YOU NOW HAVE TO WORK EVEN HARDER TO get THEM TO LET GO.

You have to wrestle winter canes off the frame.
Sometimes as you work, a cane comes loose with such
backlash that you get whipped or scraped.
Vinedressers have the scars to prove it.
Expect scars.

MY ABSOLUTE LEAST FAVORITE TIME OF year in the vineyard is the winter pruning. It reminds me that the harvest is over. The leaves fall off the vines and the temperatures begin to drop. The days get shorter and the light diminishes. Meanwhile, I have to go out and do the hardest manual labor of the year. Once tendrils curl, they will never uncurl. That means that the vines I've worked so hard to get trained to the wires are not about to let go without a fight. The wire and the branch are often so tightly wound against each other that I can't get the shears between them to cut the end of the tendril and release the vine. The only hope for ending that relationship is to pull with all my might until the tendril breaks from its branch.

It's not easy and it's not pretty. The bond may break abruptly, and I land on the ground on my backside. One end can whip around as it lets go and whack me across the arms or face. We have a particularly annoying weed that loves to grow amid the grapes. Because it has a very spiny stalk, I've had close encounters with it that look and feel like rope burns.

Whatever we are deeply connected to, whether it is good or bad, is hard to disengage from. Inevitably, marks will be left upon us like scars. A scar means that something has pierced through our protective layer. We have been able to recover and cover the hole, but the skin there will never be the same as before. In our bodies, a scar might be a reminder of a bad thing, such as an injury, or an ultimately good thing, like a life-saving surgery.

Sometimes as I fight a particularly difficult vine, I think about how I have wrestled with habits and attitudes that I want to dislodge. They grasp my soul as vigorously as the vine, and when I struggle against them, they fight back. There is backlash as they come at me from another direction or punish me in some way for my efforts. They have often attached themselves to others so that I have to grab a whole cluster of them at once in order to make any progress. The battle in my soul will leave its mark, but it will be covered with a protective layer of new resolve and stronger character.

It's hard, too, to let go of good things in this life. Inevitably there will be losses and I do not want to release my hold. Life itself wrestles us and will succeed in breaking our grasp. Again, we have been wounded and will bear a scar, but although we do not have what was removed, we can grow a protective layer that is a mark of healing and a permanent reminder of something that has brought us new life.

I'm rather comfortable with my scars. Fortunately, none have permanently disfigured me. They are a symbol of my intense interaction with life. I did not sit by and try to preserve my baby-soft skin. I did my part and I fought hard. According to Scripture, when Jesus rose from the dead, he did not have a fresh postresurrection coat of skin. He proudly showed the holes in his hands and feet and invited doubting Thomas to probe them. He declared with his body that the scars are an essential part of the victory.

"This is an awful lot of work," I told my Guide.
"You have to do this all year round.
You have to keep changing tactics. You have to think
simultaneously in past, present, and future. You have
to be in the vineyard, pay attention, and care."

"Of course you do," she said softly.
"That's what it means to be a vinedresser."

ANYTHING WORTHWHILE INVOLVES A FAIR amount of work, and some really desirable things demand even more. It's not just the actual physical effort; it's all the work that goes on inside the worker too. First, there's patience. If there has to be work, that means I can forget about instant gratification. I have to let go of "I want it now" and focus instead on "I want the patience to accept that it won't happen right now." In fact, it won't happen at all if I don't do what I need to do with great care and attention. Sometimes it's hard to keep having the trust and hope that it will ever happen, but these virtues are what will sustain me in continuing to do the work when I would rather not do it.

The dream of fresh produce and beautiful plants is delightful, but actually tending a large plot of land through all the seasons of the year is not. There is a lot of sweat and weariness and discouragement. It's real work.

People who love the work they are doing often say they don't feel like they are working. In other words, we define work as a negative thing, a time of drudgery, exertion, and unpleasantness. These are not qualities to which one is normally attracted. Yet we also know that work is necessary and, in the end, can bring real satisfaction and a sense of achievement in addition to the tangible rewards we earn. As Freud famously said, love and work are the corners of our humanness. Of course, we like love much more than we like hard work.

Nevertheless, we know that we must almost always work hard to achieve a good end. Another story from the early Christian desert tells of a man who comes seeking enlightenment and tells the *abba* that he wants to live like the angels. He is shown to a cave, where he remains for a couple of days. When he sees a man go by, he stops him and asks if the brothers have eaten that day. "Yes," he is told, "we ate about an hour ago." He then asks about the day before and is assured that there were meals that day as well. "Why was I not called?" he inquires. To which he receives the reply, "*Abba* said not to disturb you because you wanted to live like an angel."

Obviously, we are not angels and thus must do what is required for human life. Even a plant has to eat to live, and in a sense, it has to do its own work. However, its work is spontaneous and provided by nature. If we are to receive the gifts of that plant for food and shelter, we have to put in some conscious effort, unless we expect to live under a sheltering tree and let ripe fruit drop into our laps.

We are all called upon to work—not just physical work but the work of tending our souls. The truths and happiness of life will rarely just fall into our laps either. Each of us must tend our vines, and for those who read the Old and New Testaments, there is a recurrent image of another vinedresser who guides and nurtures all of the vines in the universal vineyard that is creation. It is a powerful image of a great and unending work.

Now I tend vineyards and teach others about
the canes, shoots, and seasons. That's what I do.
Once you get the rhythm, it's not so bad.
The vineyard is my responsibility. I have to do it.

The vines were already here when I came.
I couldn't just ignore them.
And hopefully, if I've done my best,
and the seasons and years are agreeable,
those vines will still be there when I'm gone.

VINEYARDS AND ORCHARDS ARE VERY different from fields of corn or wheat. They have a sustained life that does not require a fresh start every year. Consequently, they must be regarded through the perspective of extended history. Well tended and barring certain tragedies, they can easily outlive a human caretaker. They maintain a continuity and thus may be accompanied by a succession of people.

The word *stewardship* has become very popular in recent years. It shows up in the world of environmentalism and business as well as in religious institutions: we are told to steward the earth, and be good stewards of our talents and skills, and to steward our money (by which the speaker often means donate the money to a good cause!). *Stewardship* is used to remind us that we are not the owners of anything in this world. Nothing we have or use ultimately belongs to us because, as an old proverb says, "a shroud has no pockets." That should inspire us to handle the earth and our treasures and even ourselves with care. Instead, it can lead to a feeling that we need to take as much as we can while we have a chance. It can lead to denial, preventing fear from taking hold by convincing ourselves that it really isn't that bad and that the reports are greatly exaggerated. Another form of denial is the kind of optimism that says we don't need to do anything because science and technology will always invent a way out.

For those who are concerned about the big picture and about the world they will leave to the next generation, they may have the feeling that their lives are too small to matter. Nobel Peace Prize winner Wangari Maathai was just an ordinary Kenyan girl when she came to our college in Kansas as a Kennedy Scholar in the 1960s with one suitcase and a big heart. As the world opened up for her, she was attentive to small practical things she could do, such as encouraging one woman to plant one tree, and Maathai's work came to be recognized by the whole world.

She was fond of telling the folktale of a hummingbird that flew back and forth dropping tiny droplets of water from its beak onto a raging fire. It was mocked and scorned by the other larger animals who were standing by in presumed helplessness. When asked why it continued to do something so small and obviously futile, the hummingbird's response was, "I am doing what I can." To see a need and stand by because we think we have nothing to offer is to deny that we are stewards, that we are all in this together, that we have been gifted in some way, no matter how small. What a different world this would be if we were more mindful of the world around us and attentive to other people, and just decided to do what we could.

Some vines die, and I'm disappointed.
Others surprise and delight me
with unexpected fullness.
Either way, disappointment or surprise,
I'm called to do what I can.

I leave some grapes for the bees and am careful not to disturb the bird nests.

**When I'm weary, I sit in the arbor shade.
The seasons come and go.**

IT'S HARD TO MAKE PEACE SOMETIMES with "doing what I can." Perfectionism is a dangerous trap. It is good to try to do the best of which we are capable, but sometimes the best comes up short. At other times, the best is quite acceptable, but we continue to criticize and downplay it and remain dissatisfied with our accomplishment. I've known people who were involved in some kind of serious competition, such as sports or musical performance, from an early age, and many struggle for the rest of their lives with acceptance of imperfection. They say that they always felt that they were only as good as their last performance and that they had to keep analyzing, fine-tuning, and pushing themselves to be ready to surpass it in the next one.

A false sense of our own badness or our own goodness is equally unhealthy. Evaluation by others is helpful in keeping us honest. So is love. If I feel that I am loved as I am, I will try to do my best but will know that I am acceptable even without being perfect. Sadly, I have met children who, when asked to describe themselves, can't think of a single good thing about themselves, even with repeated prompting. Their communication with elders is usually based on some correction. They are noticed only when something is not right. Perhaps this is why, when some people internalize the admonition that God is watching them, they think about being under constant inspection for some failing that will result in punishment. They see God as having a giant checklist.

There is, however, another way of approaching the all-seeing eye of God. Think about a child playing in the vicinity of a loved adult. There are shouts of "Watch me!" and "Look what I can do!" The child wants to be watched, wants to show achievements, wants undivided attention. Even when you're not quite sure what the child has just done, the automatic response is one of "Yes, I saw that, good job!" The child thrives on the praise. The child also expects to be protected from danger. As much as children do not like to be told to stop doing something or to be careful, they know that the adult is concerned about their welfare and has their best interests at heart. They also expect that the adult will come running if they are injured and may even suffer more dramatically once they know they have the adult's attention. Being watched is comforting and a bond of love. Isn't that a better way to think about God watching you?

I don't mind at all that God sees me sitting in the shade sometimes and not working every minute because the loving parent is always watching for our safety and happiness. I think God admires the bird nests along with me and is glad that I see the bees and birds as God's beloved children and my brothers and sisters, just as the watching parent wants to see the child play well with others. It is in these quiet moments that God and I watch together. Isn't that a better way to experience (and share) the eye of God?

My teacher died years ago.
But at harvesttime I still feel her there with me.

I look carefully at each cluster with her eyes and
harvest the vineyard when it's ready.

One of the things I like
about grapes is that they
come in bunches. They're
together but still separate.
I eat some right away and
let the sweetness fill me.
I don't keep them all separated,
though. Sometimes I put
whole bunches together.

THE MENTOR WHO BEGAN MY LIFE WITH the grapes is with me whenever I work because I could not have done it without her. This, I think, is part of what the notion of eternal life means—each of us keeps living in those things we have passed to others. Our DNA, our good deeds, the values we exhibit that inspire others are all ways in which our lives continue after we are physically gone.

Each of us is carrying genetic traits from centuries past that belonged to other human beings. The vine doesn't start new each year but comes from a deep place of origin. It will be the same type of grape every single time. While each individual grape is different, all of the grapes on that vine will have some basic inheritance. Each and every one will be purple and not green, seedless and not with big seeds, or whatever their breeding has established as their basic characteristics.

Those who have started religions or social institutions or dynasties have lived on in countless lives through the ripple effects of what they did. When we share DNA or a belief system or any other commonality with other humans, we are bound to them in a special way. If we think about all the commonalities that we may have, it becomes clear that each of us is in some way connected to every other one of us.

Although each of us is a separate entity, we are all part of the same cluster, dangling from the same vine. We grow at different rates; we have different tones and size and sweetness; we drop off at different times. But still, we are part of a bunch. We are nourished by the same things, have the same desires, feel the same emotions, share the same type of body and blood. Perhaps if we were to look at others with this filter rather than the filter of how we are different, we could change the world in ways both small and large.

Sometimes when I think I am fairly independent and successful, and have good control of the vineyard, I remember how many other circumstances and people are involved. I remember the helpers (some easier to work with than others!). I remember the sister from whom I learned all this. I am especially grateful for the friends who see that things get done if I'm not here when there's an immediate need. On any given day, I need to remember all the people who made my day possible: the people who built my house, grew my food, and made my clothes; who keep the lights on and the water running. That's not to mention all the people who made *me* possible: ancestors, educators, loved ones. Like the grapes, we have all grown together on a single vine. It's quite a bunch...not separate plants in different fields, but a bunch.

It's **OK** that not all the grapes are perfect.
Some are sweeter than others.
Some don't look appealing.
Some have damage.
Some aren't quite ripe.

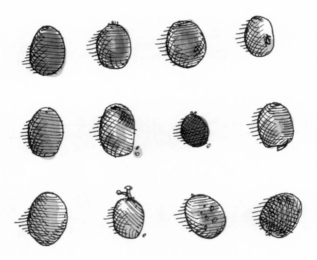

Each is a different color and size.
Together they balance out.
Together, when the grapes are turned
to juice, it doesn't look or taste like any
one of them would have alone.

When time comes to extract the juice, I feel the presence of everyone who has ever helped.

We dance the grapes to softness, squeeze them to sweet juice.

That could be the end of the story, but we take it one step further.

SOMETIMES AS I LEAVE A STADIUM OR auditorium or other assembly of thousands of people, I marvel at how different each of them is from all the others. As I look at them, I realize that few of them bear much of a resemblance to anyone else that I know either, and I have probably known hundreds of people in my lifetime. This is amazing and incomprehensible. If each of our bodies is so unique, even more so our interior lives must be because every one of us, even those raised in the same family, even identical twins, have an unduplicated life experience.

The beauty of community is many faceted. First of all, when we form communities with other people, whether the small community of a family or the larger ones of church, organization, or civil entity, we get support. We no longer have to do everything alone, and we no longer have to feel that our efforts are only for ourselves. We also feel safer and more protected. We count on these people to have our backs, and to provide strength and security. We compensate for one another's lacks and complement one another's abilities. No one has all the gifts and so no one has to bring all the gifts. Community is a potluck, where I bring something that can be shared and I get to share in everything else that others have brought.

Wine and bread are important symbols of the common banquet. In the Western world they have come to symbolize the staples of human nourishment. We don't generally talk about this in terms of wheat and grapes, but of their products, bread and wine. Perhaps this, too, is an important shift in the image. Wheat and grapes are edible as they are; they comprise very small singular units that grow together in groups where each grain or fruit is individuated. But bread and wine are not available in nature. You can't go out and pick bread or wine off a plant. They have to be gathered and processed. They can only exist when they are created by conscious human action.

The action itself is symbolic. A large number of individual units is required, of which none is singled out as most important, and there is no attempt to select only the perfect. They are crushed and refined by their maker. The final product of this crushing means that the juice will not have the exact flavor of any one grape. The sourest ones will modify the flavor of the sweetest ones. The ones that didn't ripen will still contribute to the mix.

The color will be neither as rich as the brightest nor as dull as the palest. Size and shape will become irrelevant.

This process of blending is irreversible. The grape is no longer a separate individual. It is no longer like something in a fruit salad where you can take out the item you don't like the taste of or the one that doesn't digest as well. It is what it is, with all its components. It has become part of something that has been transformed to be an entity different from its components. It has undergone the transformation that is community—a whole much greater than the sum of its parts.

We put the sweet juice together
in their bottles to ferment.

We leave a way for the air
to get out but not in.

Then we wait
. . . and wait.

Waiting isn't easy
but interrupting
the process
will spoil the wine.

Finally
We open the bottle . . . Pour it . . .
Gaze at it . . . Savor the aroma . . .
and then drink deeply our wine.

The long hours, the learning, the pruning, the harvesting, the juicing, and the waiting have been worth it.

And now, as you tend your own vineyard, may you have sun and rain as needed, hours of good labor, lessons learned, and sweet fruit in abundance.

NOT ONLY ARE BREAD AND WINE BOTH blended, they share another feature. They become their savory selves by being acted upon by other agents. It takes time and the working of a chemical agent, a yeast. The air bubbles form within them and create a physical reaction.

Each of us is transformed by the people with whom we form communities and who form us. A healthy community is one that is always bubbling—not roiling with dissent or dissatisfaction but getting bigger and better by an internal spirit of transformation and growth.

Most of life is not made up of big events. If it were, it would be exhausting. Few are called to lead peoples or go on constant performance tours or engage in years of regular competitions. Rather, we are mostly living ordinary moments that gradually lead to milestones or insights or achievements. It would be a mistake to think that nothing is going on in the downtime. We are always living the one more day that leads to the milestone or having the series of thoughts that leads to the insight or accomplishing the one small task or experiment that leads to the achievement.

We are growing and changing, sometimes in spurts, sometimes imperceptibly. I can't see the grapevines grow from day to day, but when I cut them back to almost nothing and then see a leafy and fruitful vine within a few months, it is obvious that something has been taking place.

There is a story in the early Christian literature of the Egyptian desert people that tells of a young man who was having trouble keeping focused on his spiritual reading and didn't feel as if he was getting anywhere. The *abba* instructs him to put a basket outside his door and fill it with sand. Each day as he finishes his reading, he is to pour a cup of water into the basket. The disciple goes home baffled but obedient and returns some time later. When asked how it is going, he reports that he still doesn't feel like anything is changing or improving in his meditation. Then the *abba* asks him about the basket of sand. Still puzzled, he reports that it is now empty, the water having pushed the sand out through the woven exterior. Just so, says his wise guide, are the mind and the soul. The steady practice of meditation may not show quick and discernible results. Gradually, though, the other thoughts and desires are seeping out as they are replaced by the grace and wisdom of the holy reading.

Without fermentation, the grapes will just be grapes. With it, they are infused and energized into something richer and more potent. The spiritual yeast we ferment through our faith and spiritual practice is bubbling and transforming us all the time. It will take some time, but don't interrupt the process.

Epilogue

JUST WHEN I THOUGHT I HAD SHARED EVERYTHING I knew, I had two new insights in the very week that the text for the sketches in this book was finalized. That is as it should be in lifelong learning. The first was one of the hard lessons. I went to check on a vine that is the only one of its variety in our vineyard, and which has a sweet grape that I particularly like. The grapes were perfectly ripened, but the evening was hot and I was tired, so I decided to wait until morning to pick them. When I came at dawn, all I found were a few grapes scattered on the ground and a large heap of deer droppings.

This is a lesson most of us experience often in life: sometimes we're all set for grapes and all we get is... well, there's no polite way to say it or draw it (although deer scat does have a fair resemblance to grapes, and there could probably be another lesson to write about).

The second lesson is a much more optimistic one. We recently began raising bees. Bees can be opportunists and will find anything sweet that is nearby. If damage from nature or another creature opens the skin of grapes, bees will take advantage of the opening to extract the sweet juice from inside. A recent batch of honey had an unusual hint of some other flavor that we knew was different but couldn't quite identify. By recalling the bees' activity, the beekeepers eventually concluded the extra ingredient to be the flavor of grapes.

This is another confirmation of the principle that we are what we eat. Everything we choose to put into ourselves flavors us. One of the major figures of early monasticism was a hermit named Antony. He was described by his biographer as being like a wise bee. When he was a young man, he would seek those people who had a reputation for a particular virtue and try to learn it from them. He took only the positive, as a bee selects what is needed from a flower. He is said to have chosen not to limit himself to imitating a single mentor, but to learn how each virtuous person excelled in a distinctive virtue, and not to be concerned with any flaw that person might have in other areas. Thus he was able to concentrate more fully on attending to the important lessons of life. Antony collected all of the best that he could learn and then was able to distill wisdom for himself.

The best lesson I can leave you with is this: keep cultivating and pruning and growing. You will never know how many times something you did will have added that distinct, never-repeated, mysteriously unidentifiable sweetness somewhere.